GOLBORNE

To Dave

Best wishes

13/8/11

Britain in Old Photographs

Golborne

Robert D. Hughes

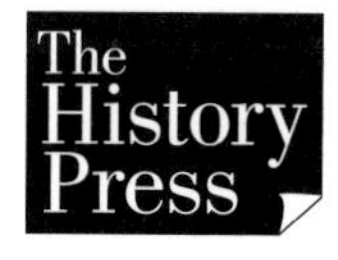

This book is dedicated to the memory of Reg Thompson, founding member of Golborne History Society and my grandfather-in-law. Although he is no longer with us, his work lives on through the discoveries and documents that he and the society recorded over the years. It was this legacy that eventually influenced me to write this book. For that, I am very grateful. I hope I can continue to unearth the rich pool of undiscovered past as Reg did many years ago and make it available to everyone to discover.

First published 2011

The History Press
The Mill, Brimscombe Port
Stroud, Gloucestershire, GL5 2QG
www.thehistorypress.co.uk

British Library Cataloguing in Publication Data.
A catalogue record for this book is available from the British Library.

ISBN 978 0 7524 6081 9
Typesetting and origination by The History Press
Printed in Great Britain

CONTENTS

ACKNOWLEDGEMENTS

I would like to send out a massive thank you to all the kind people who have given permission for their photos to be used in this book. Without your support, this book would not have been possible. In no particular order you are: Paul Maconie, Geoffery Sutton, Beryl and Bernard Cocoran, Gladys Franzen and Golborne Library, Jeanette and Martin Harrington, Kath Else, Len Russel, Lewis Knight, Sid Sutton, Anthony Richardson, Sheila Lyon, Margaret Mulcrow, Gaynor and Brian Thilwind, Peter Marsh, Ken Dunn, Steven Flynn, Evelyn Swannick, John Tully and Jennifer Appleton.

INTRODUCTION

The origins of this book came to life on the internet, through the creation of a group on the popular social networking site Facebook, called 'Ye Olde Golborne'. I thought it would be a good idea to create a group, as I had permission to use some old photographs of Golborne that I had collected over the past few years to use on the web. This began in November 2009 and, within a couple of weeks of the group being formed, hundreds of Golborners were visiting the site and uploading their own old photographs. The group has become a local legend, and has even seen many of the members reuniting with old friends.

Some of these photographs are familiar to Golborners as they have been seen before in previous publications and on the internet over the years. The majority, though, have been collected from private and personal collections and, with permission, have been included in this book. I call this memory liberation. I am very grateful to the people of Golborne for allowing their memories to be liberated from long-forgotten attics and photo albums. Many and varied people posed for photographs that feature on the walls of shops and schools of our village, ranging from professionals to schoolchildren.

So, as you thumb your way through over one hundred years of Golborne's pictorial history, you will see how the landscape, transport and various fashions have changed. Many of the buildings appear to have remained the same, but the businesses inside them have changed and developed considerably.

I hope that this book will influence and encourage today's inhabitants of Golborne to photograph and record the modern Golborner so that future generations can enjoy taking a glimpse into their past, as you hopefully will by reading this book.

Should you be interested in visiting the Golborne Facebook page, please type 'Ye Olde Golborne' into the search facility on the social networking site.

I hope that you will enjoy reading this book, and as a point of interest, see if you can recognise anyone you know!

Robert D. Hughes, 2011

1

STREET SCENES

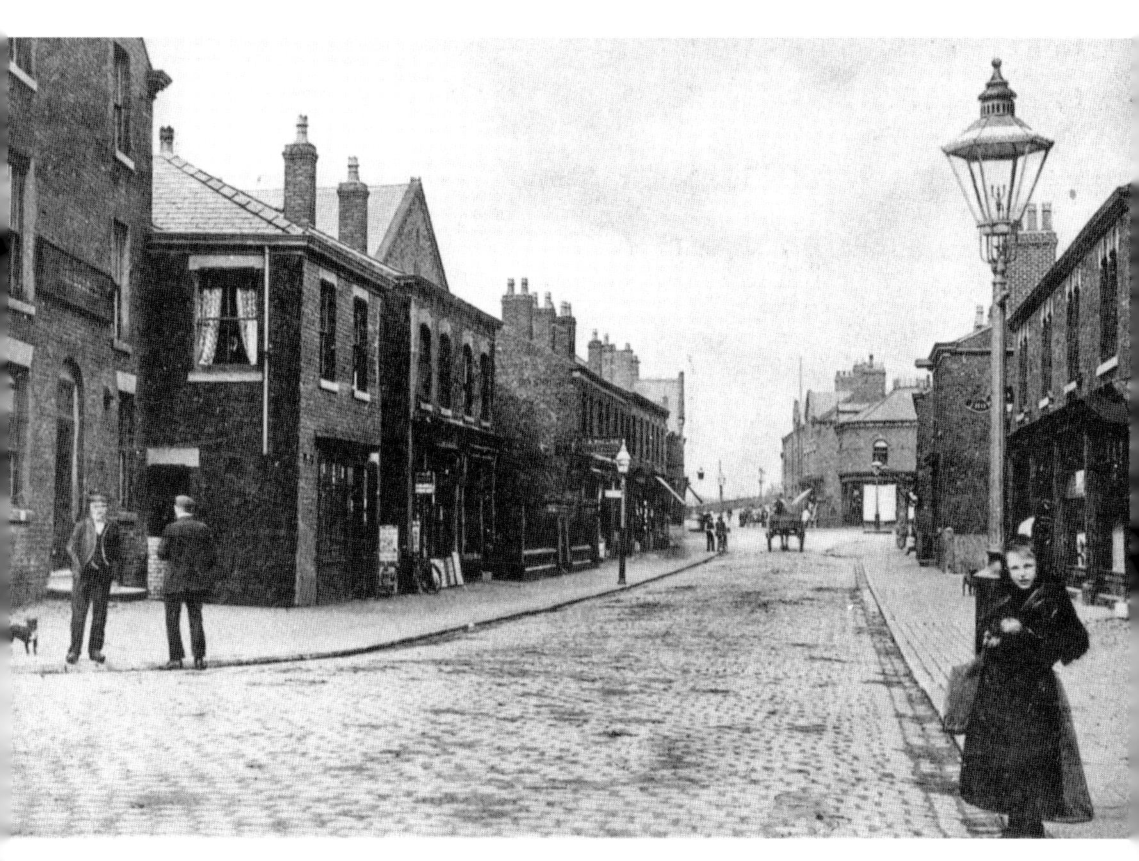

This is the oldest image of Golborne centre that the author has found. Taken in around 1900, the New Inn public house is situated where Peter Kane Square is now. This is a very interesting picture, showing the original cobbles in the road and a horse and cart travelling away towards the railway station in the background. We have found no clues as to who the people are in this picture, but the girl dressed in black in the foreground of the image completes the authentic Victorian look.

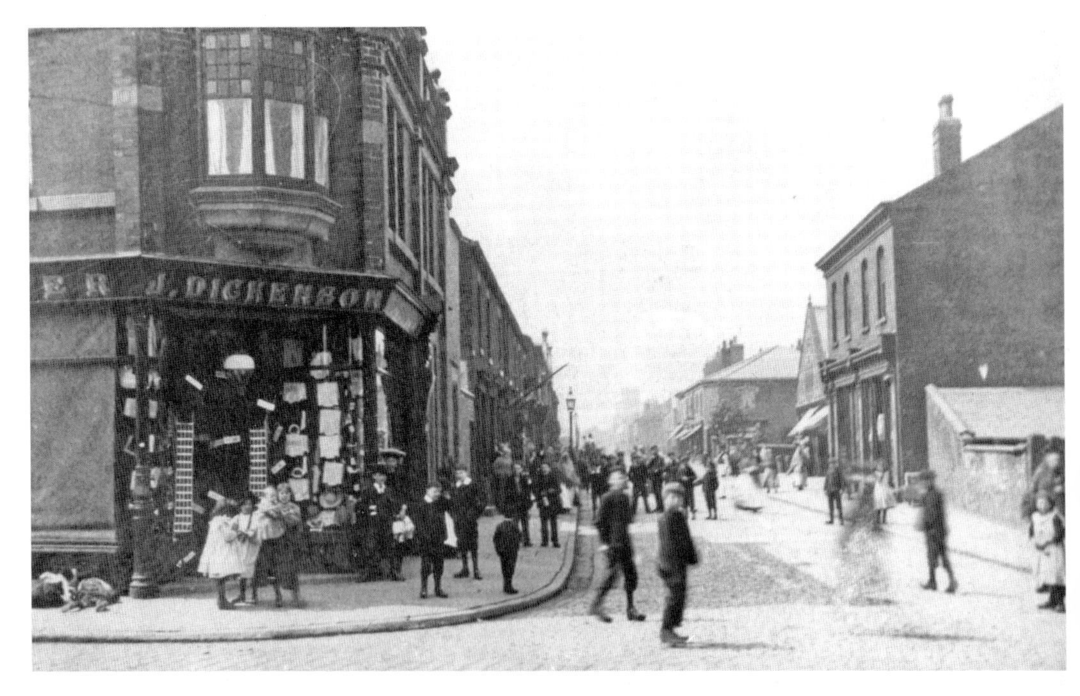

This view of Heath Street was taken from outside the Charles Napier public house in 1903. J. Dickenson Clothiers is where the Co-op Chemist is today. To the right of the picture you can see the side wall of the New Inn. In the distance are the various shops of Heath Street. Outside the shop two children appear to be searching for something – I wonder what it could be?

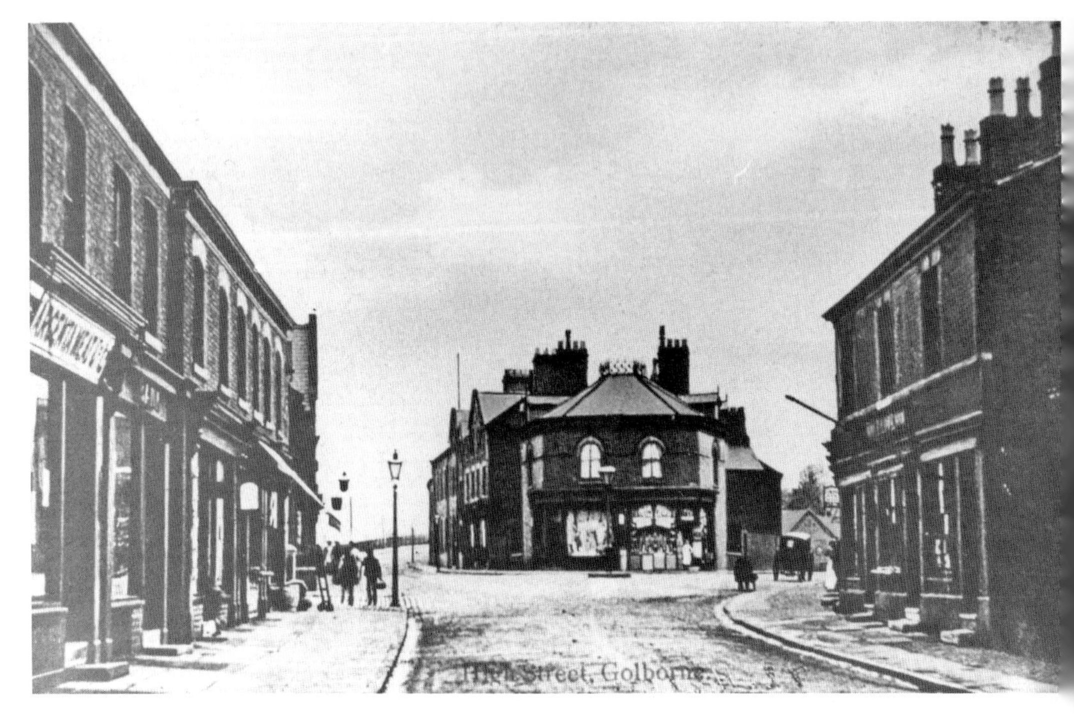

This photograph, taken in the 1900s, again shows the cobbled High Street in the centre of Golborne.

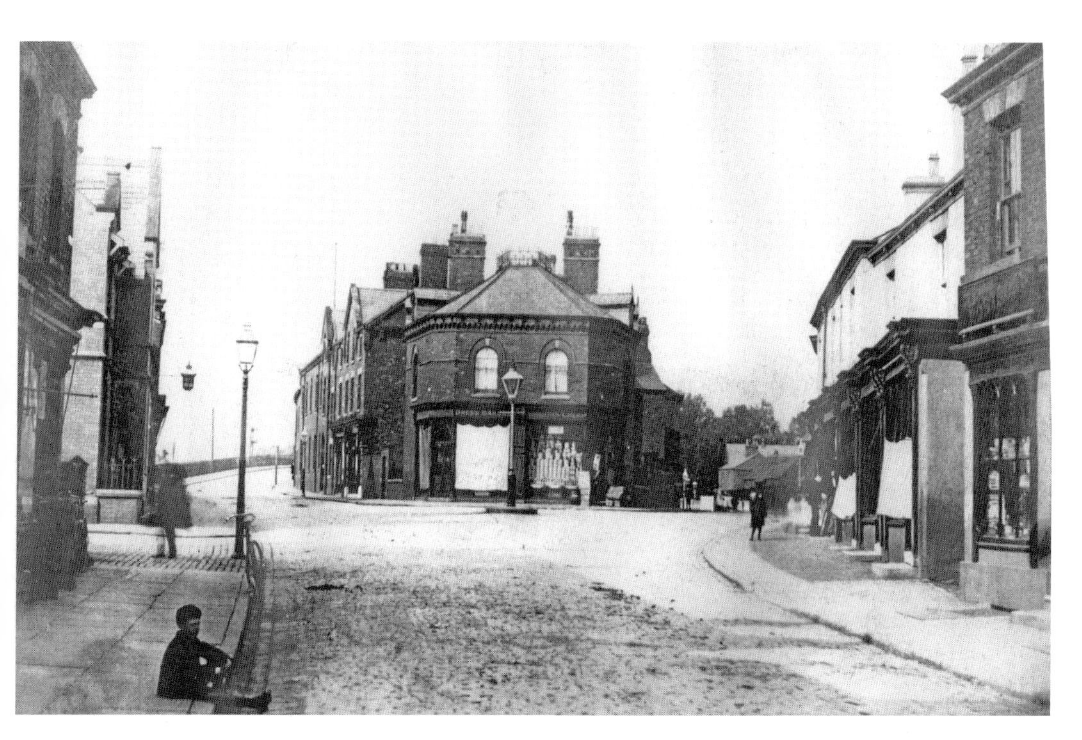

This photograph shows another view of the centre of Golborne, taken in 1904. You may notice how the bridge (to the left) does not appear as steep as it is today. The bridge was raised to accommodate the overhead cables when the railway became electric.

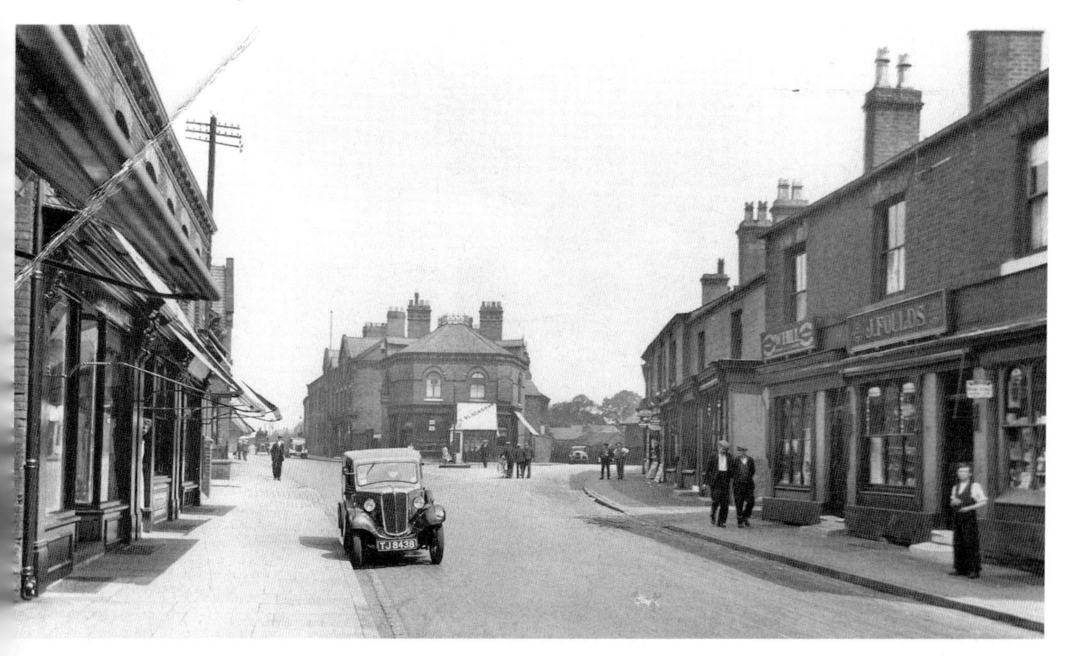

This picture shows a more detailed view of Golborne High Street, this time taken in the 1950s. You can see the Union Bank of Manchester Ltd, where a dentist is now situated, along with C. Blackshaws in the distance. To the right of the picture are W. Hills & Sons, decorators, and J. Foulds, butchers.

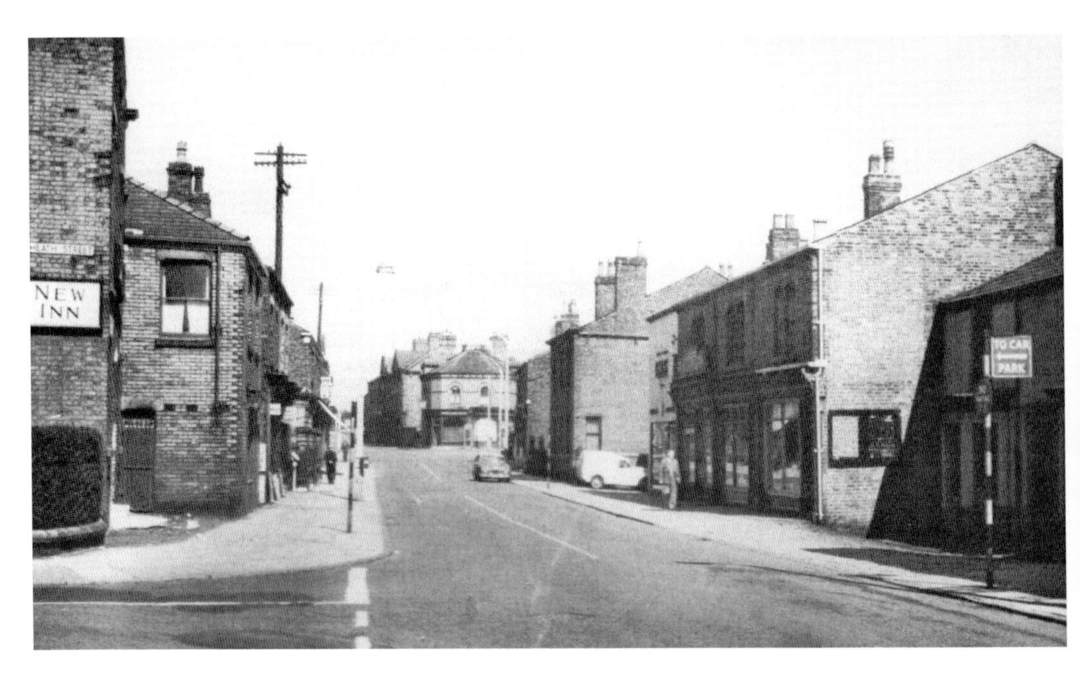

Moving forward a decade, this picture shows Golborne High Street in the 1960s. On the right of the picture, is the Prince of Wales public house, which has since been demolished, and facing it, on the left of the picture, is the corner of the New Inn public house. Notice how the street appears to be quiet, and how few cars there are on the road – a stark contrast to modern-day Golborne!

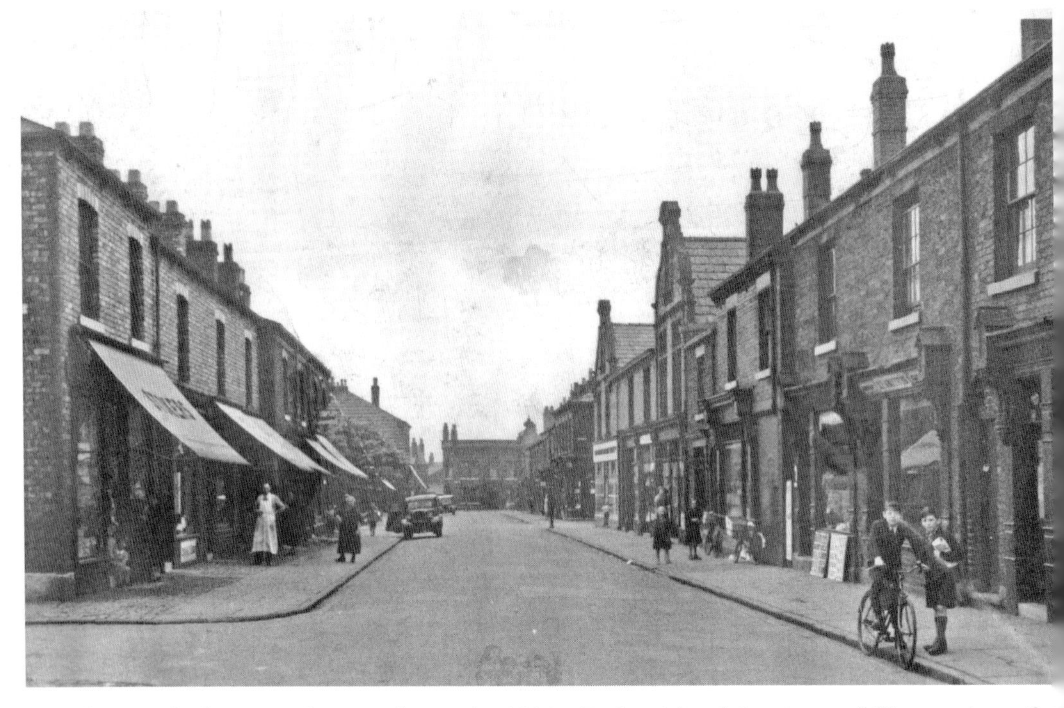

This photograph shows Heath Street during the 1930s. To the right of the picture children cycle on the street, and appear playfully curious of the photographer.

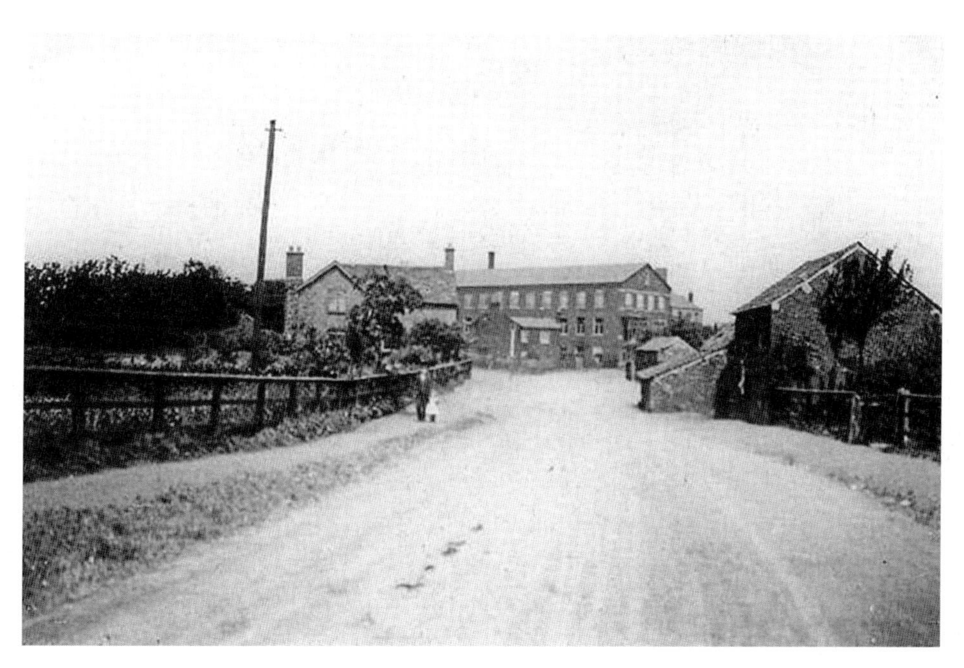

This picture, taken between 1903 and 1904, shows the dirt track entrance to Halliday & Constantine Mills on Barn Lane.

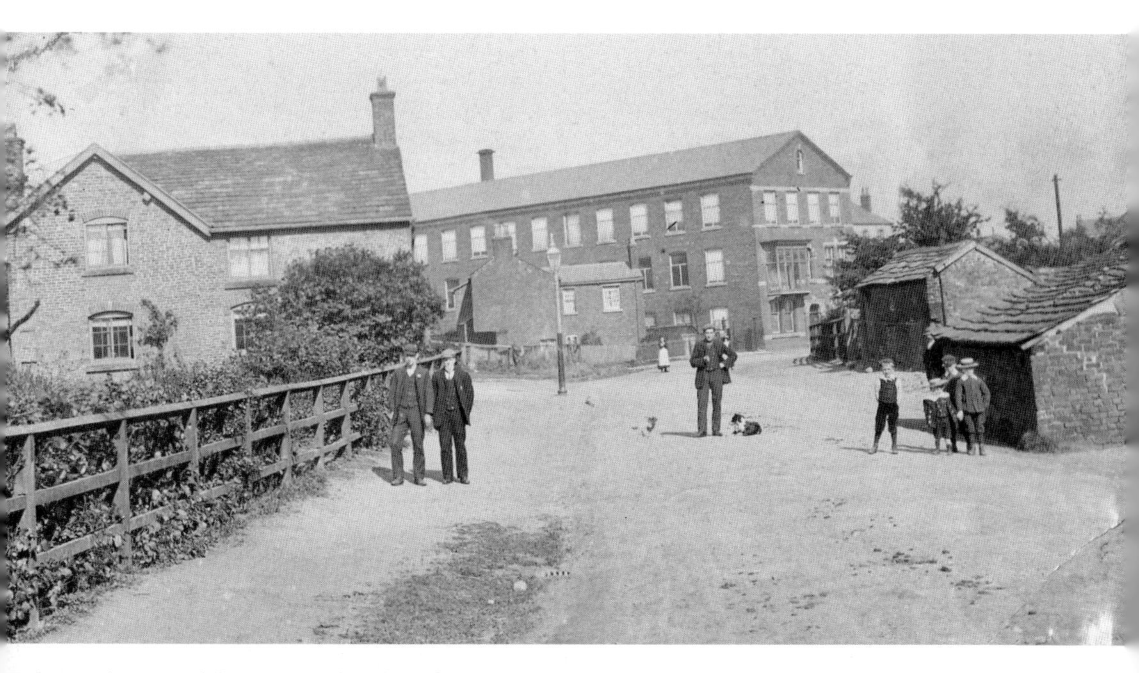

Taken at the turn of the century, this photograph shows an alternate view of Barn Lane. The building in the distance is Upper Mill, also known as the Blacking Mill. When this particular picture was taken, the mill was manufacturing cotton. When cotton manufacturing declined, the building then housed Harrison's Chair Works, which made seating for cinemas, and a second-hand car sales room.

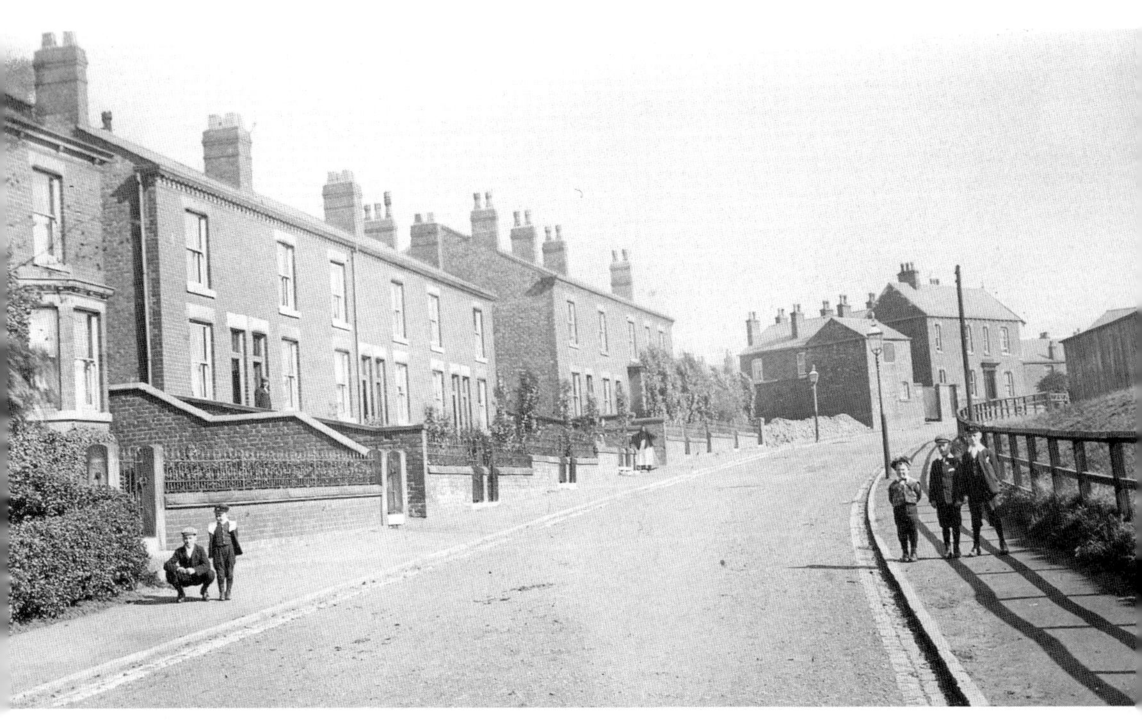

Another view of Barn Lane, taken a little later than the previous picture. This photograph shows a residential area. The young boys are obviously curious about the photographer.

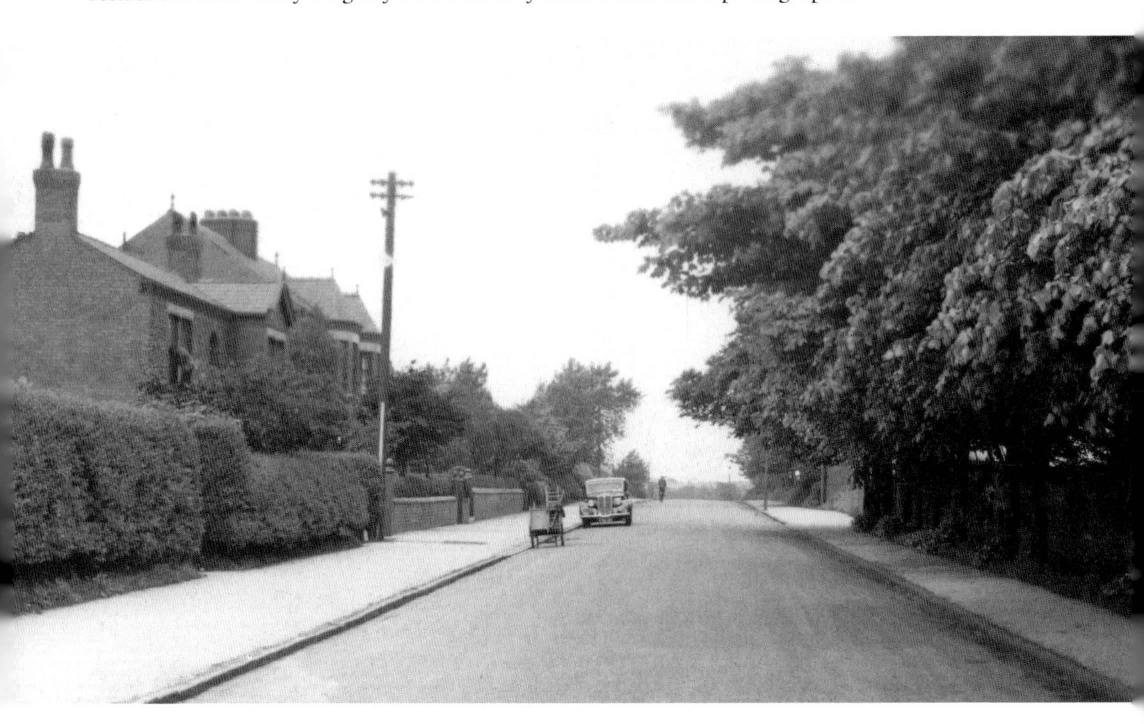

Taken around the end of the 1950s, this photograph shows Barn Lane from the Park Road end – quite a deserted street as you can see!

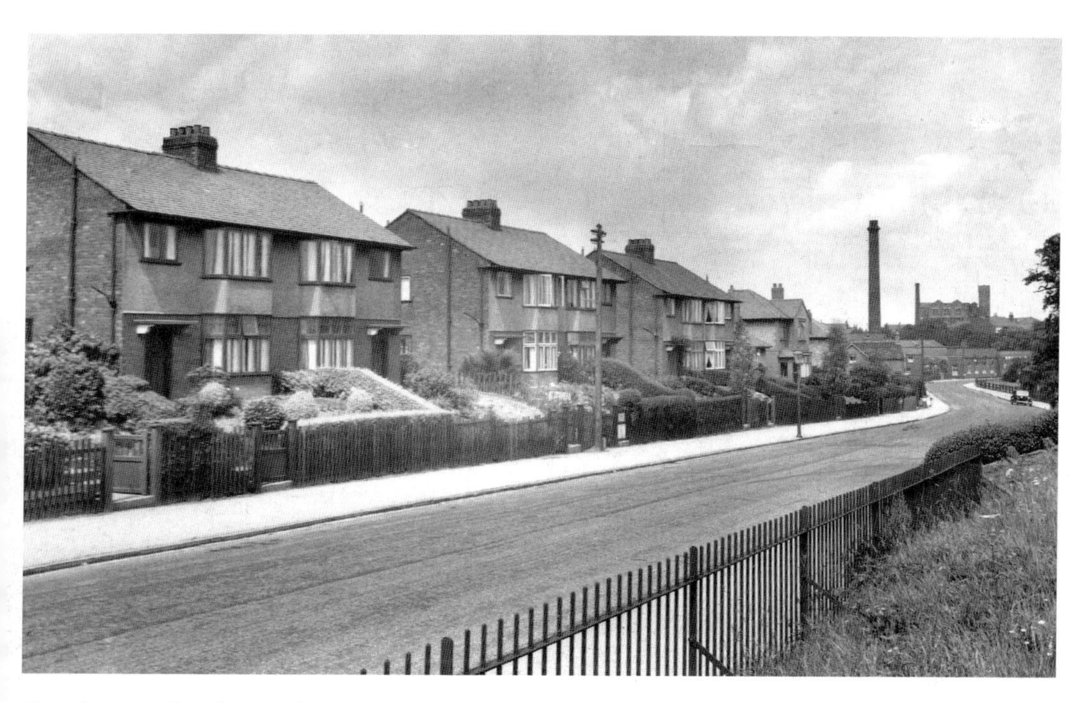

This photograph, taken in the mid-1900s, is also of Barn Lane. To the right of the picture is the sports ground, or the cricket field, as it was once known to the locals. In the background, to the right, is Rothwell's Chocolate Works.

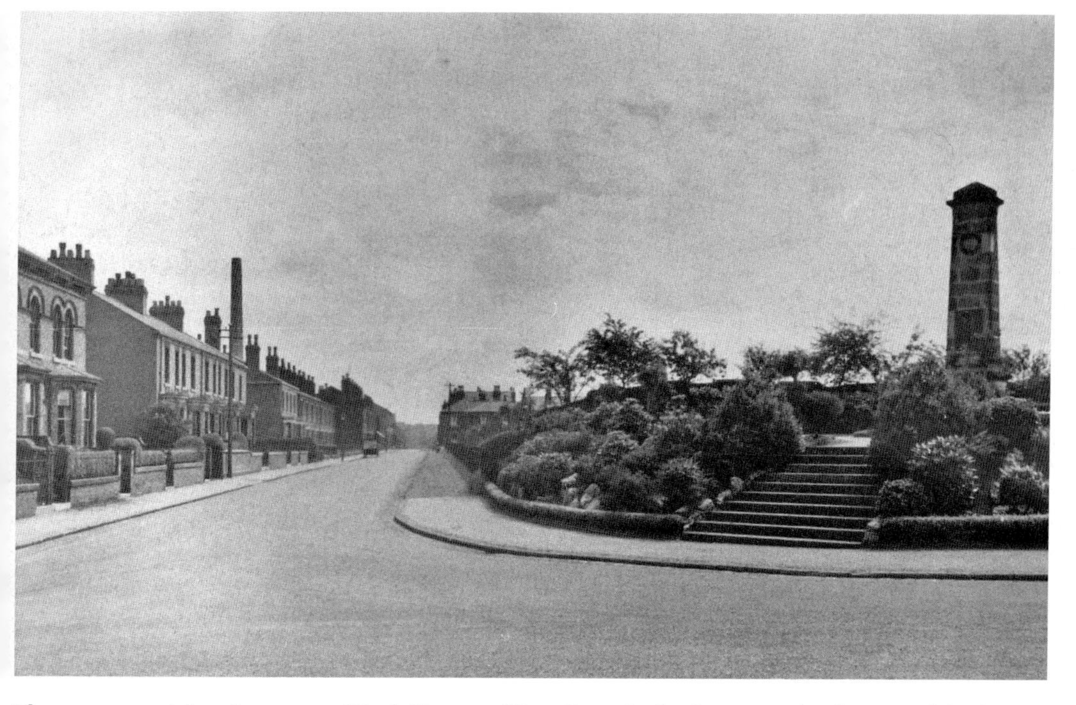

The war memorial on the corner of Legh Street and Barn Lane. In the distance is the chimney of the factory, which was Sunpat at the time.

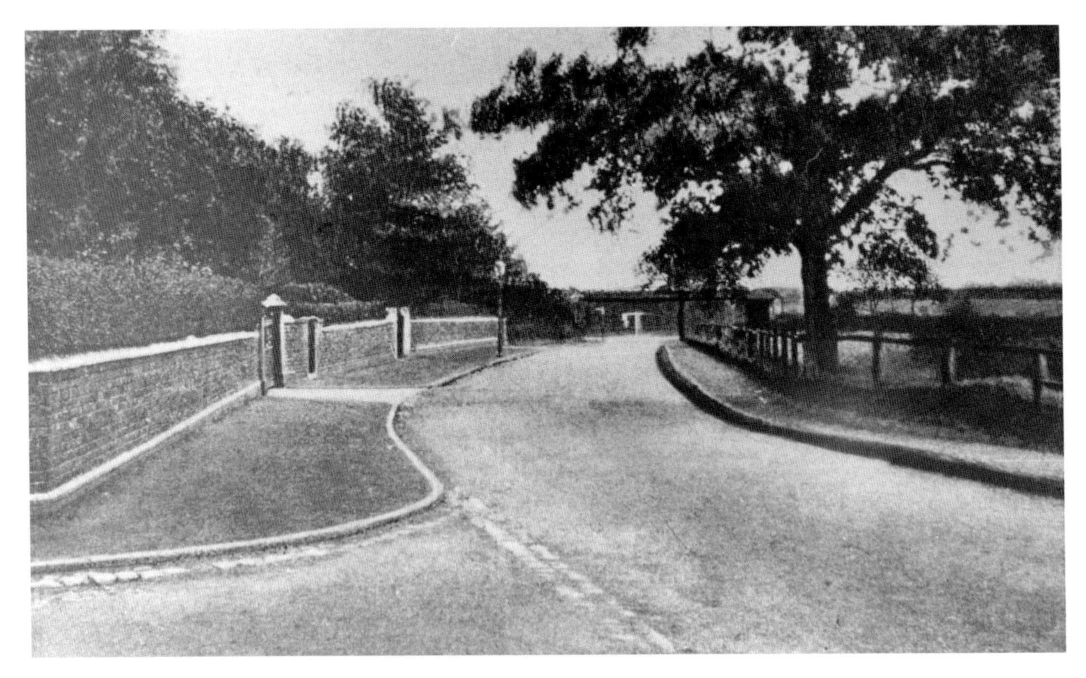

This photograph shows Park Road, looking towards Bridge Street from the Barn Lane junction.

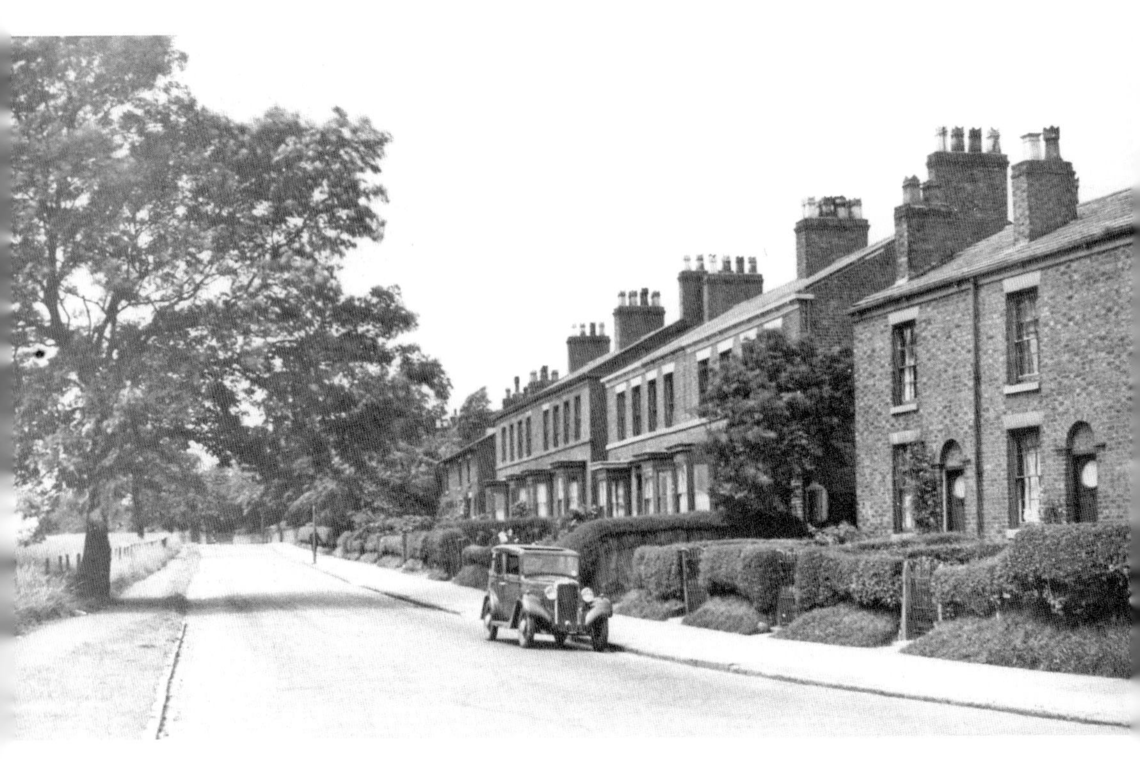

Probably taken in the 1950s, this picture shows the opposite end of Park Road, looking towards Keepers Lane. The car that appears in some of these photographs may perhaps belong to the photographer.

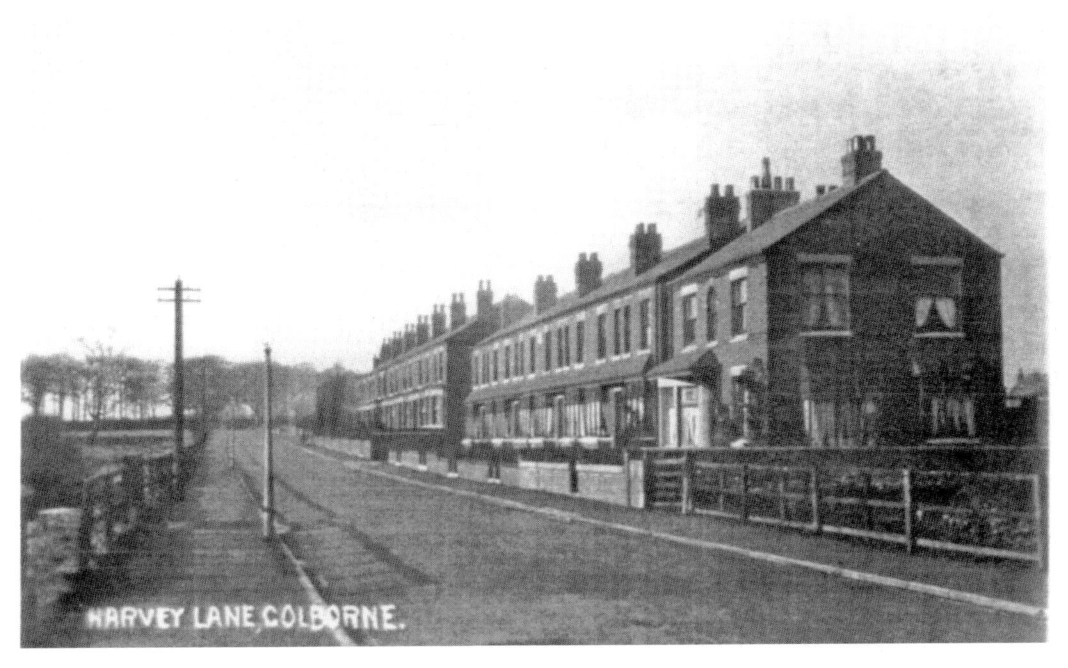

Taken in around 1910, this photograph of Harvey Lane makes clear the absence of all the houses we know so well today.

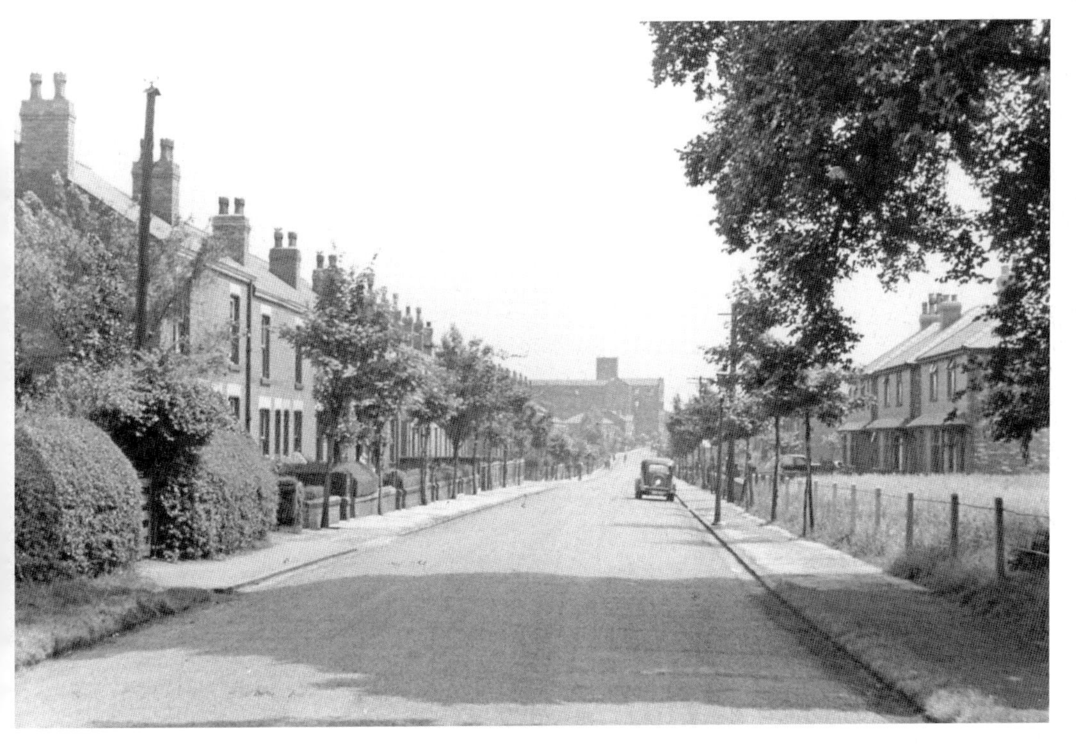

Taken in the early 1950s, this photograph shows Harvey Lane from Keepers Lane, looking towards Heath Street. Rothwell's Chocolate Works can again be seen in the distance.

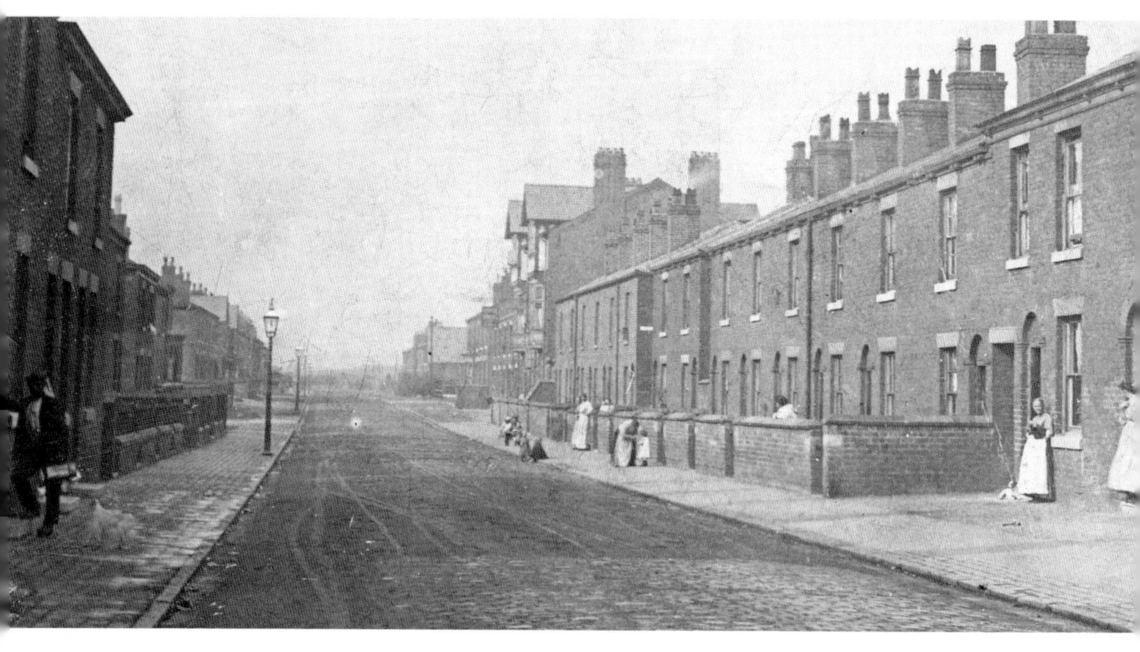

This picture is one of the most interesting in this collection. Taken in the early 1900s, it shows a typical day in Bank Street; cobbles, cart tracks on the dusty road, housewives, children playing in the street, a man seemingly just returning home from work carrying his 'snap' (an old Northern term for packed lunch) – there are even chickens roaming free on the right-hand side! Also visible in the distance are the Royal Hotel and the Welsh chapel.

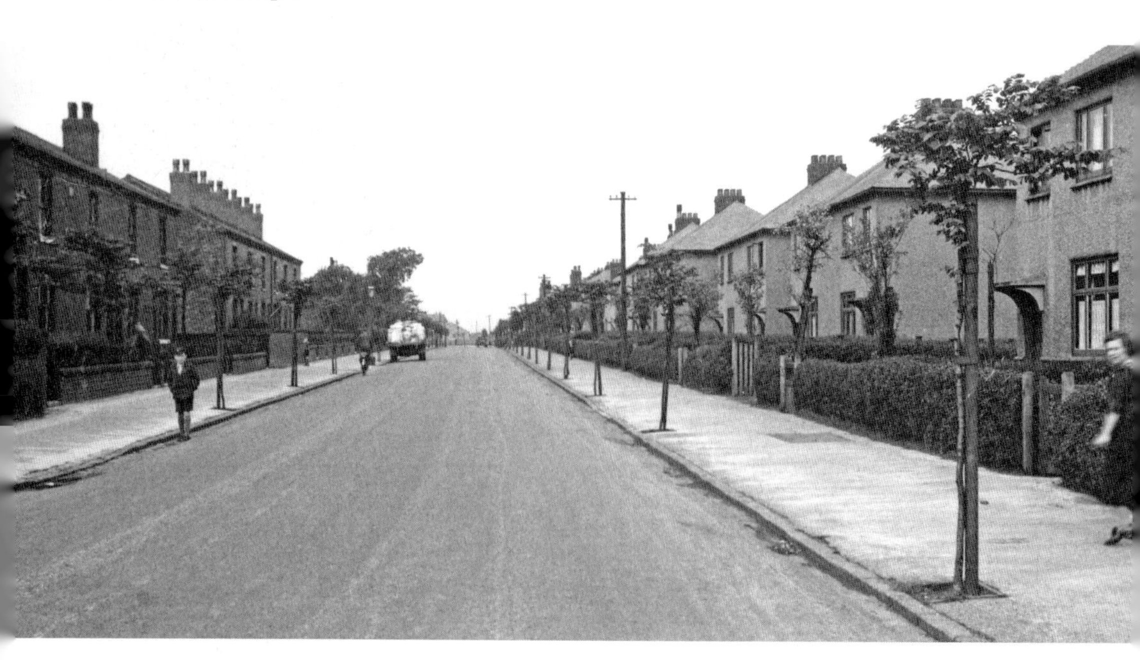

Taken between 1944 and 1945, this photograph shows a quiet Edge Green Lane. The cart on the left of this picture, further down the street, is where ASDA supermarket is situated today. The photographer appears to be attracting curious looks from the woman on the right of the picture and child on the left-hand side.

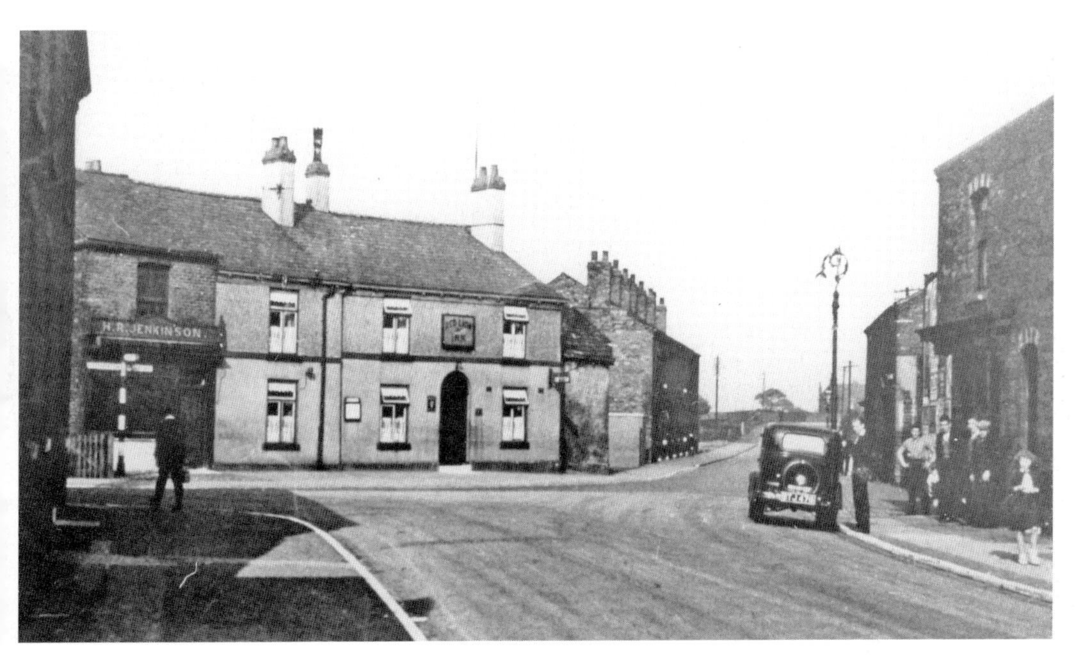

This photograph was taken on Lowton Road (formally Factory Lane). The road leading off between the houses on the right-hand side of the picture was Winnnard Street. Henry Peers' toffee shop was opposite in the row of houses and Bill and Bet Reid's chip shop was opposite the Red Lion Inn, the second building from the left in the picture.

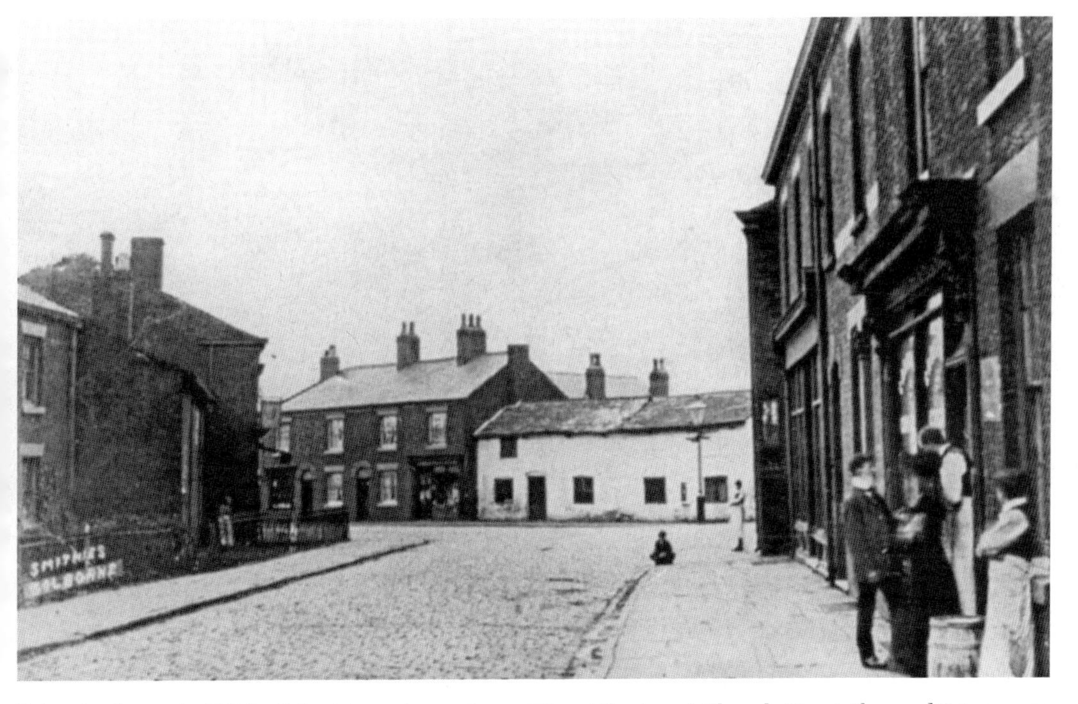

Taken in the early 1900s, this picture shows the smithy at the top of Church Street, the road it is on was thereby called Smithy Lane.

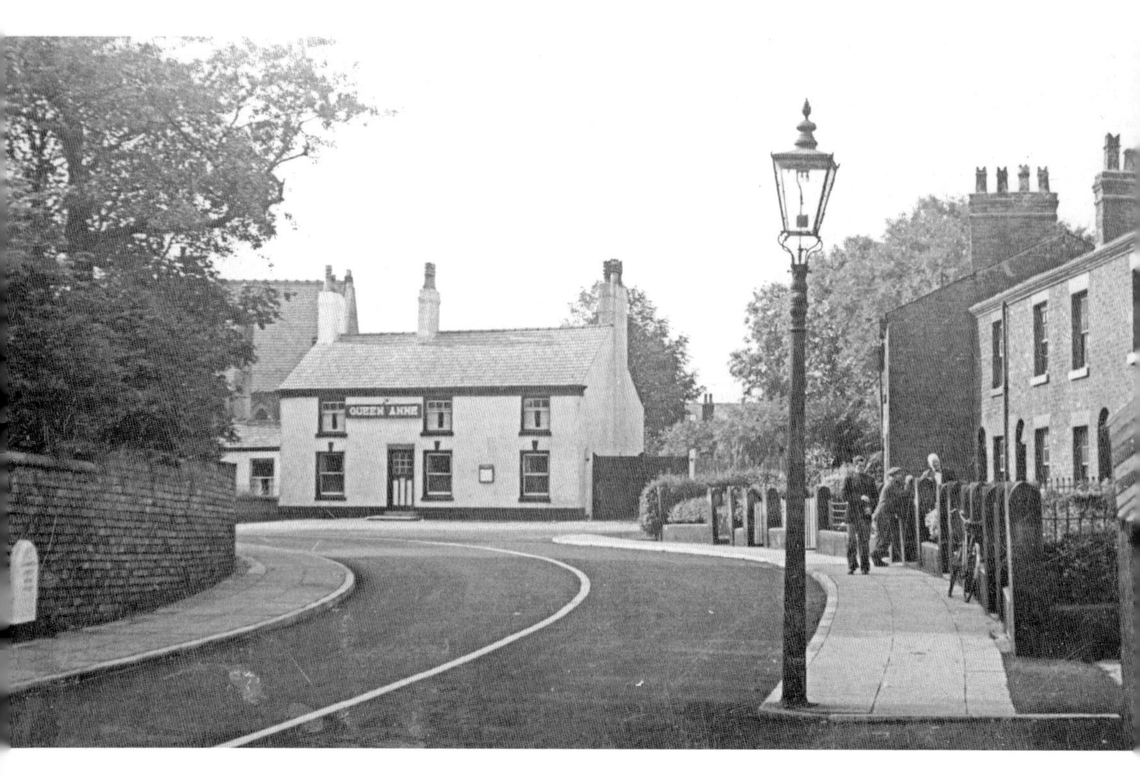

This photograph, taken on Bridge Street, shows the Queen Anne public house on the corner of the road.

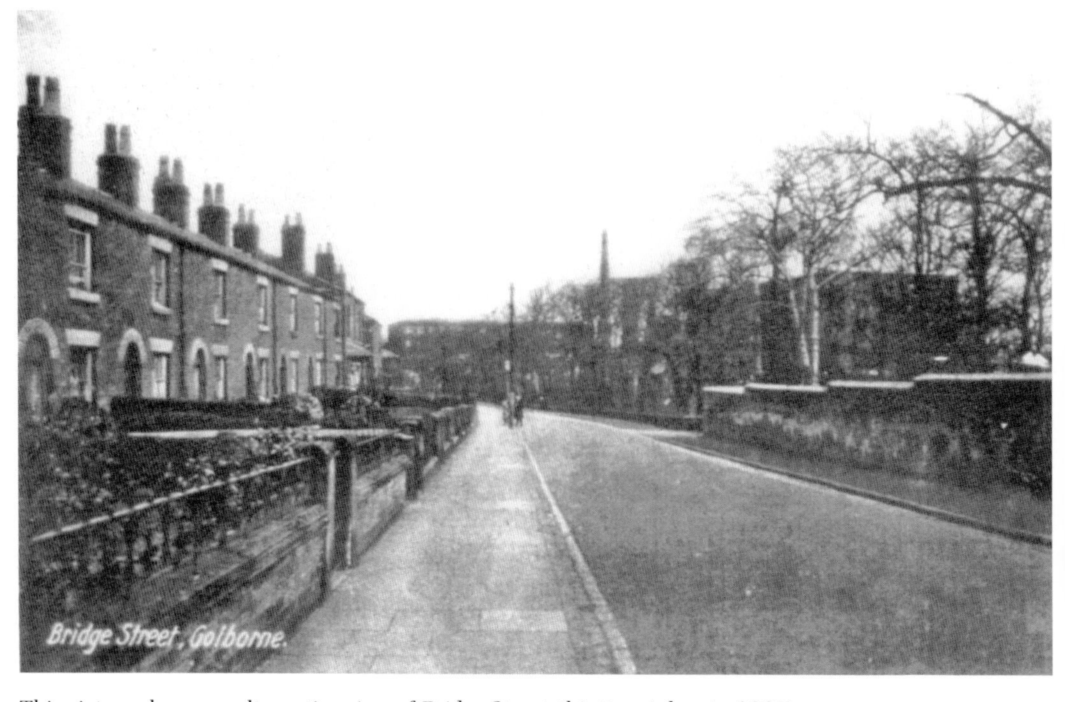

This picture shows an alternative view of Bridge Street, this time taken in 1937.

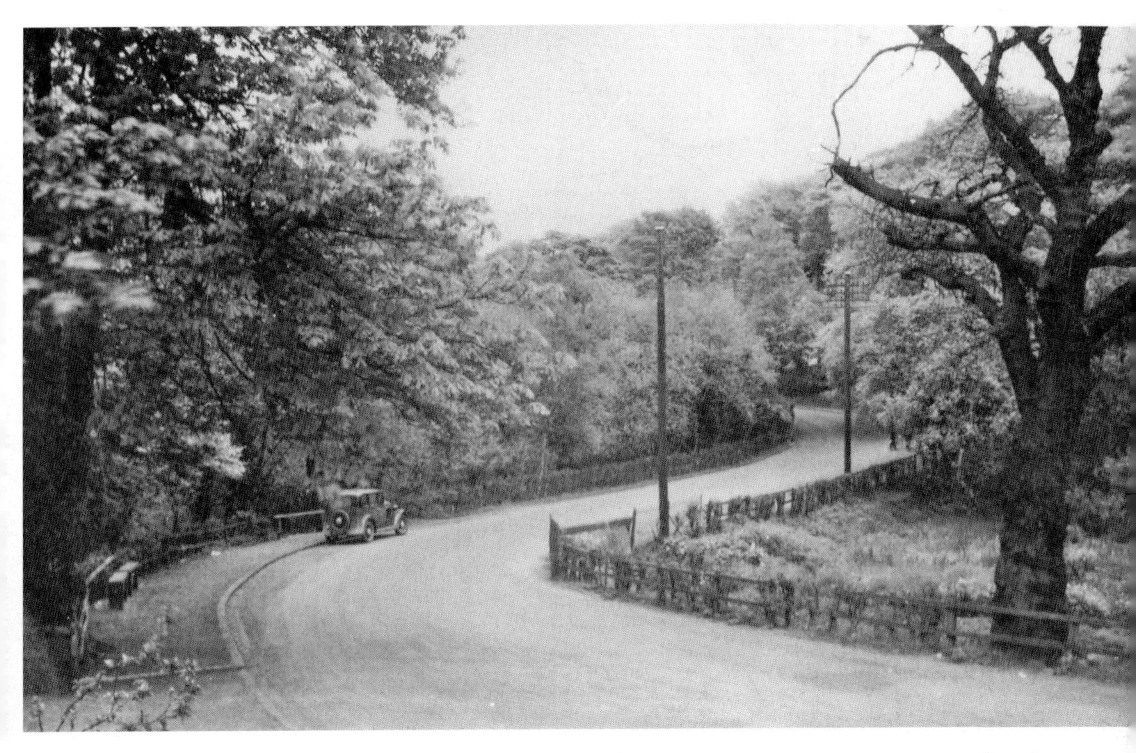

Taken in the 1950s from a postcard, this picture shows Golborne Hollows. It is interesting to note that the exact same image is used on a Newton postcard entitled 'The Hollows, Newton-Le-Willows'.

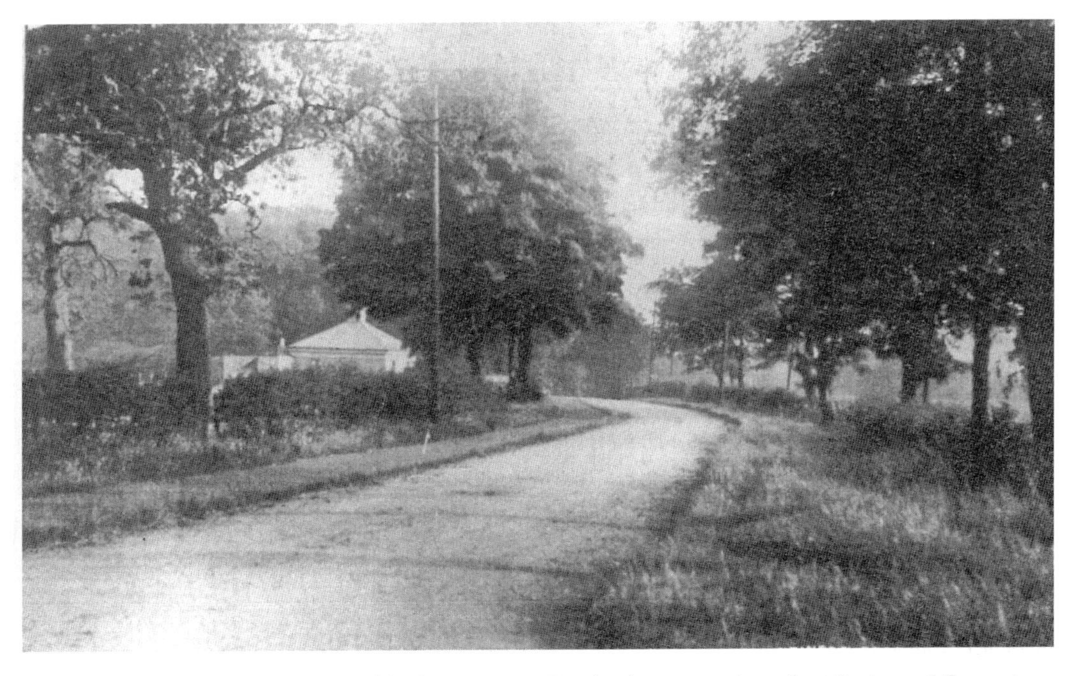

This photograph shows a rather rural-looking Newton Road, taken approximately at the turn of the century.

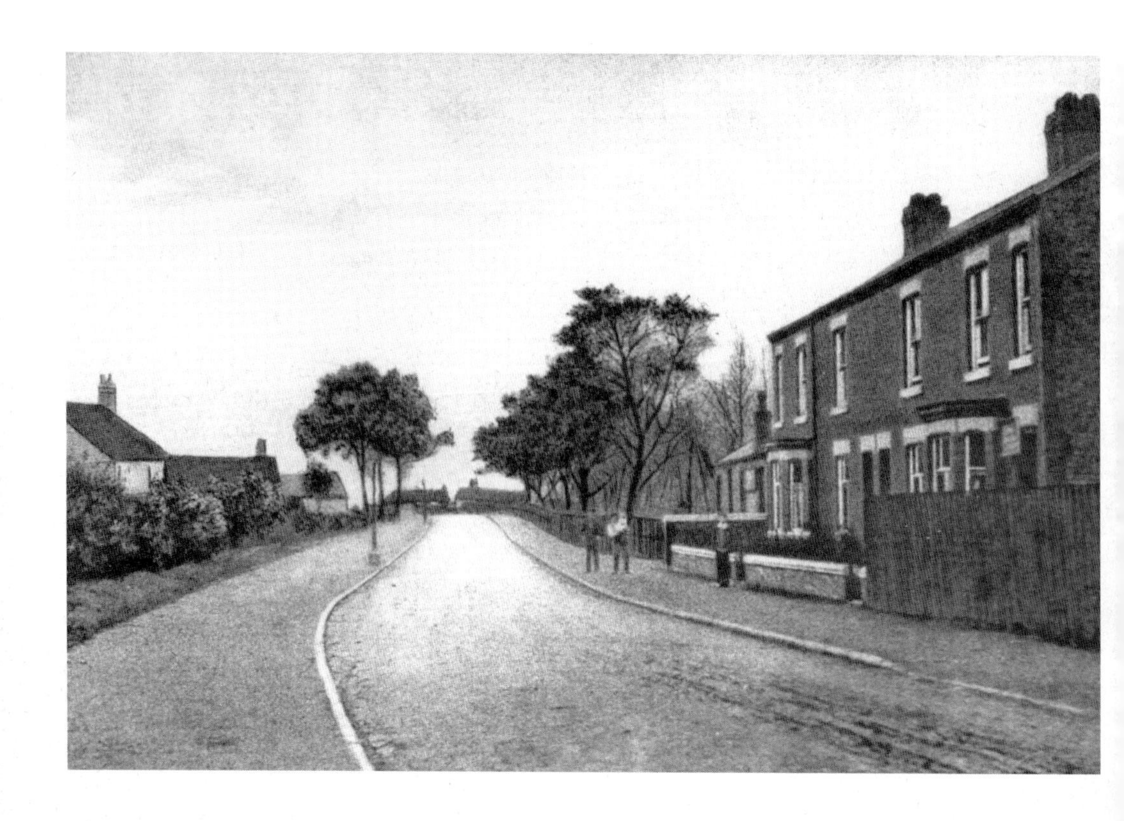

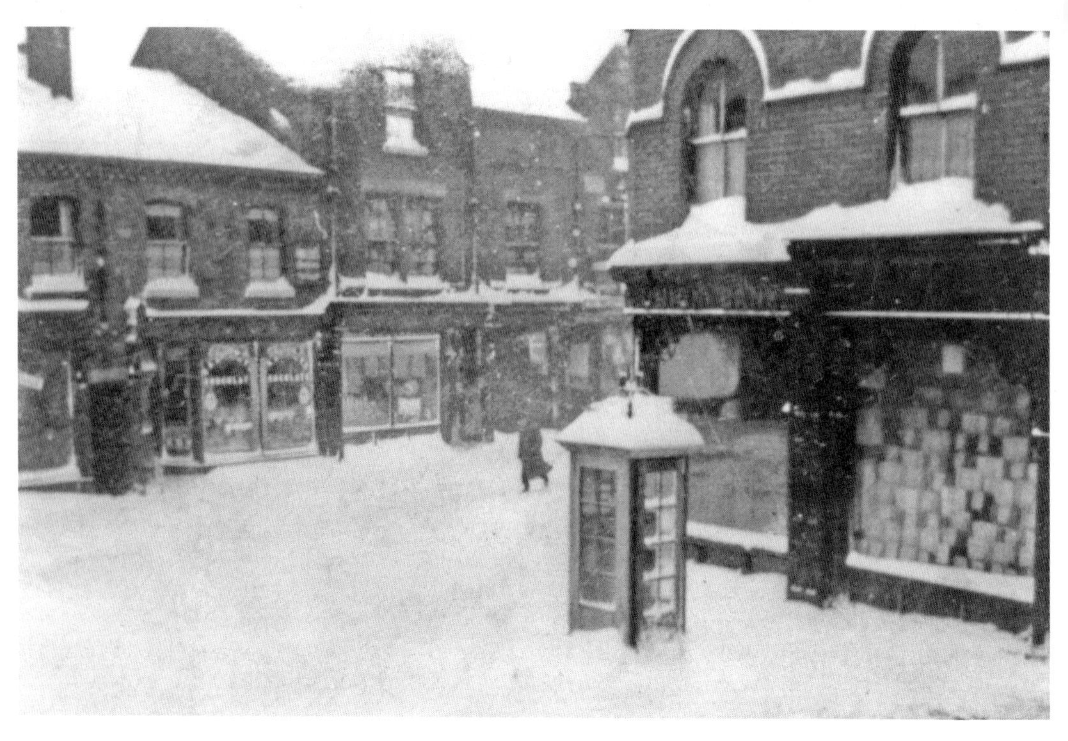

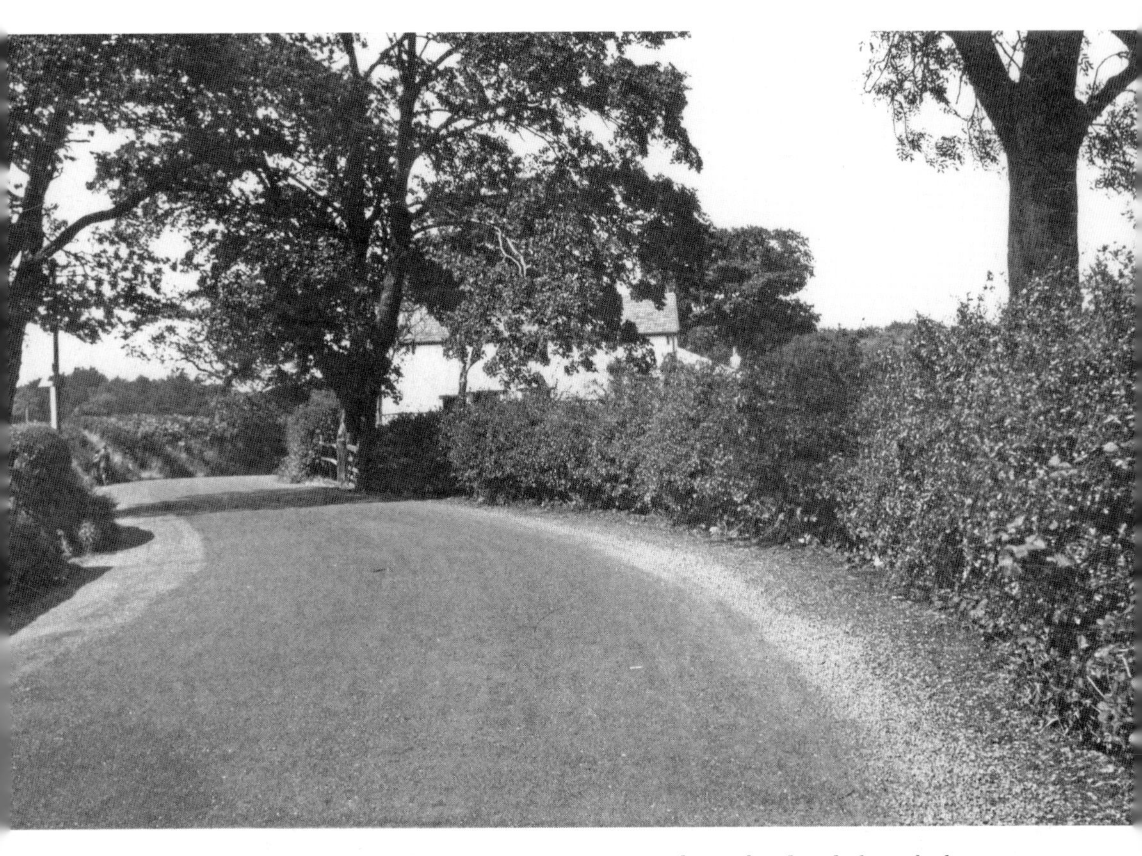

This photograph shows the very pretty Keepers Lane, somewhat isolated aside from the house concealed by trees. Sadly, the year is unknown.

Opposite above: This early photograph shows Lowton Road in Golborne. The road appears deserted aside from two children walking along together on the right hand-side of the picture.

Opposite below: Golborne centre in the winter of 1947. Golborne, along with the rest of the British Isles, experienced record low temperatures and persistent snow, which formed a constant cover over the village. This epic winter has only been matched by the winter of 1962/63.

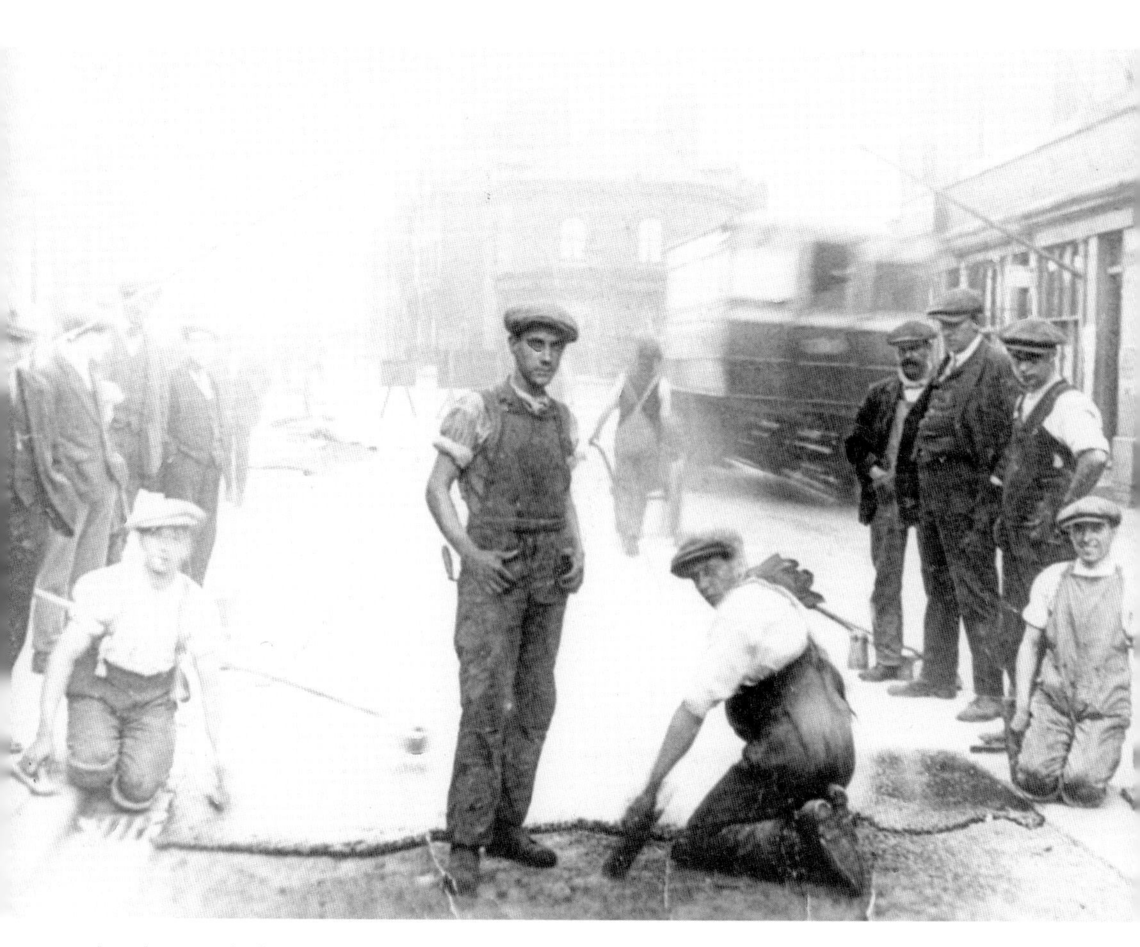

This photograph shows men tarmacking the High Street. Sadly, the year is unknown.

2

CHURCHES

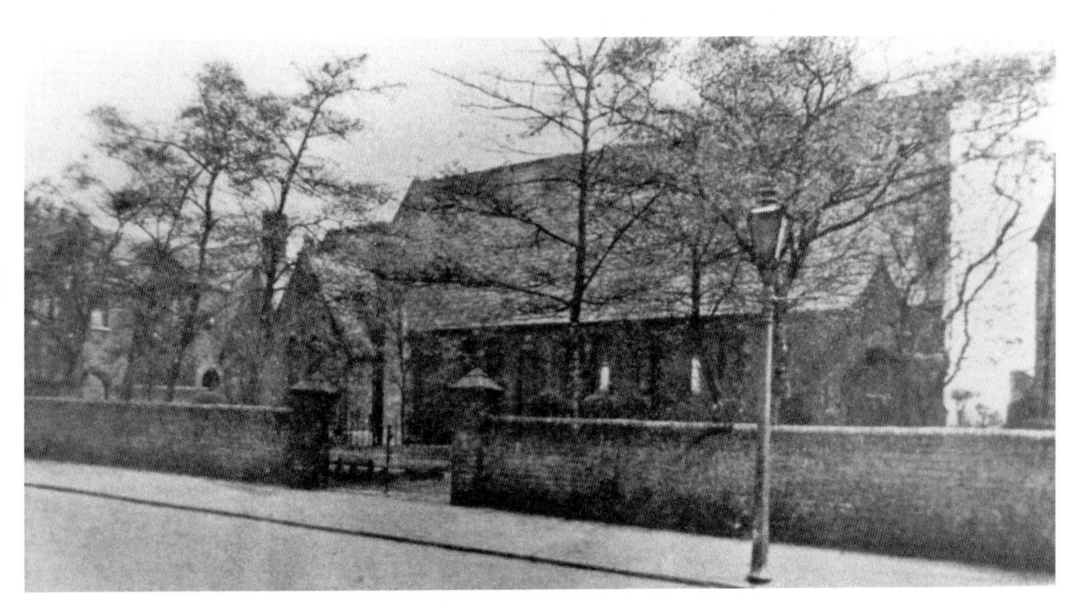

Taken in around 1863, this photograph shows the first All Saints' Roman Catholic Church, which was in Church Street, where houses now stand opposite Church Street chippy. Before this, St Oswalds in Ashton was used for worship. As early as 1913, mining subsidence had rendered the building unusable, so a new, more suitable location to build a church had to be found, and High Street was chosen.

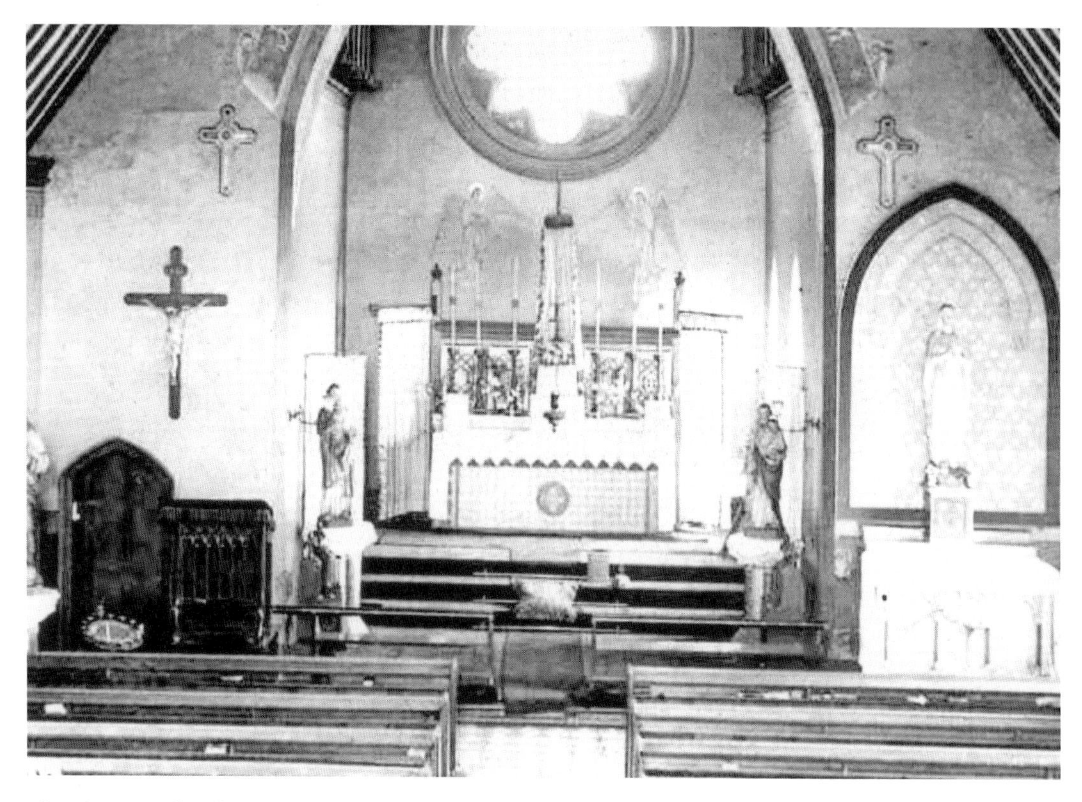

This photograph, taken some time before 1927, shows the interior of the rather ornately decorated First All Saints' Roman Catholic Church.

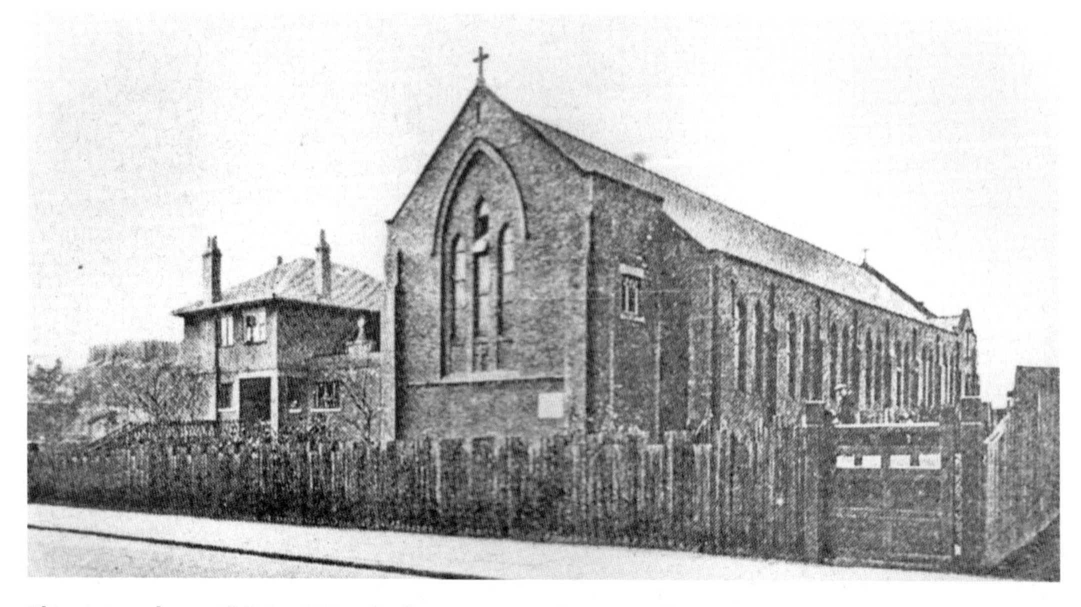

This picture shows All Saints' Church after it was moved to its new location on High Street. The funds raised for the building of this church were due to the efforts of Father Kelly in 1926, and the first sods were cut by some of the older members of the parish in 1927.

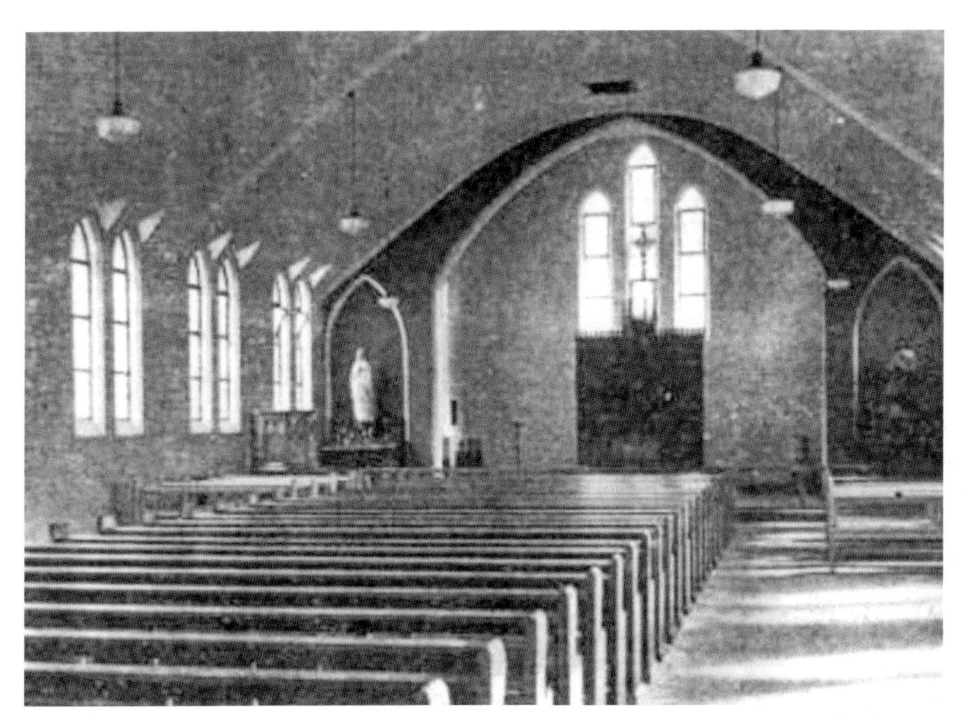

The interior of All Saints' Church on High Street; evidently a larger venue than its predecessor.

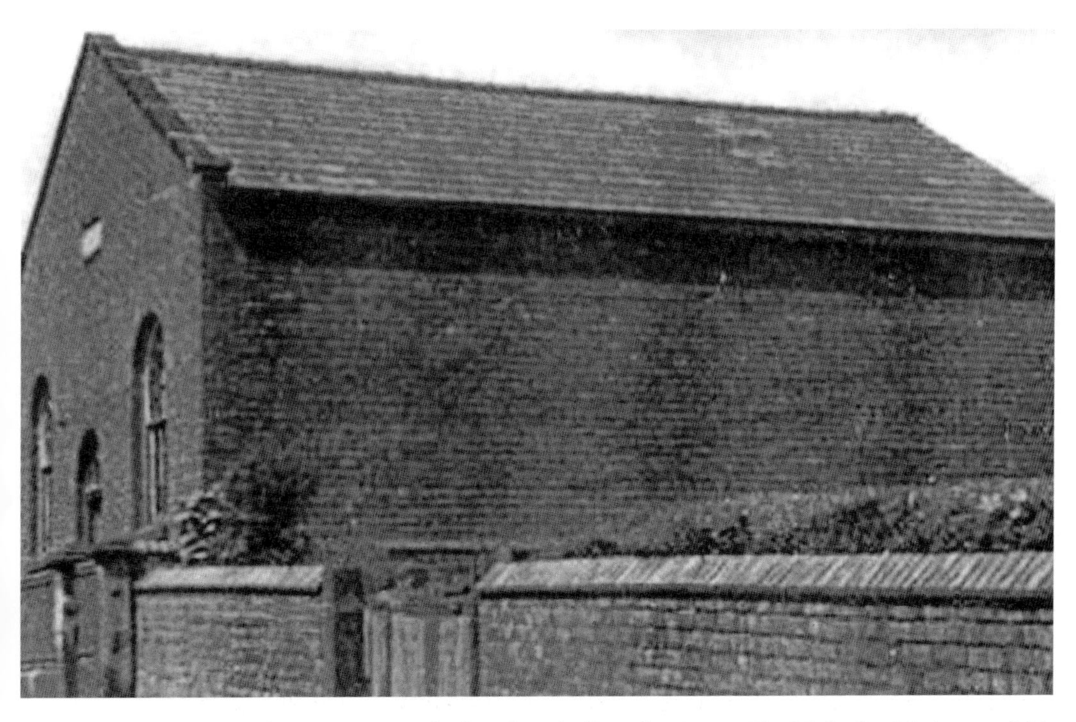

This photograph shows the Primitive Methodist chapel off Bridge Street. The Methodist Minister and his family continued to live here after the church closed.

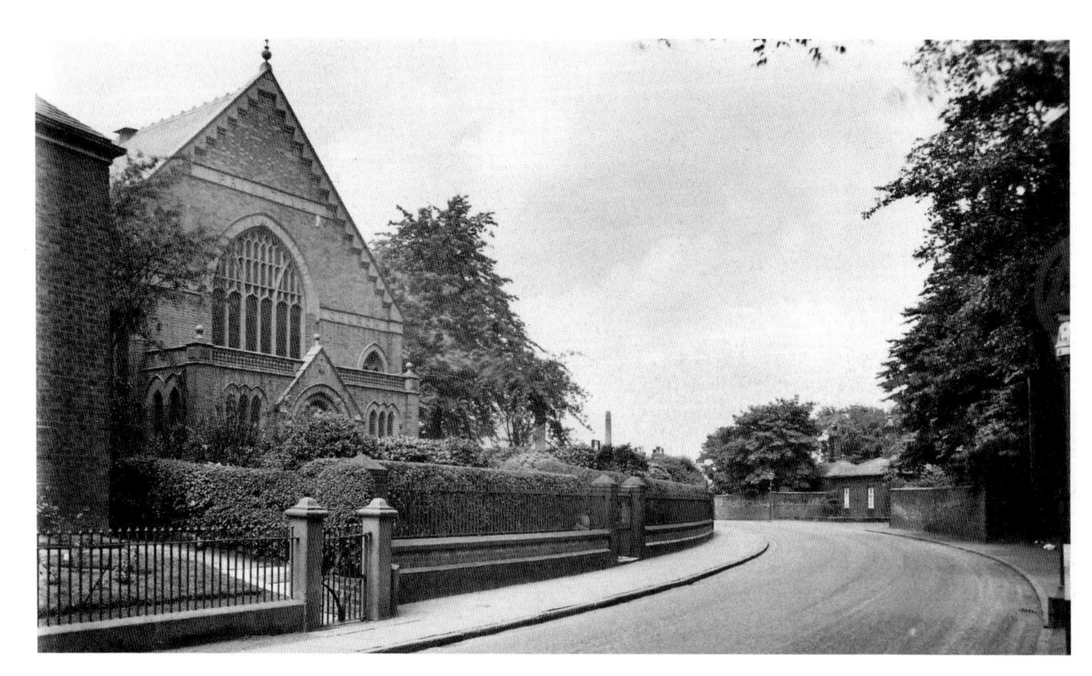

This photograph is taken from a 1950s postcard and showsTrinity Primitive Methodist Church, located on Bridge Street. It opened in 1847 and had its closing service nearly 140 years later on 31 August 1986 – it has since been demolished.

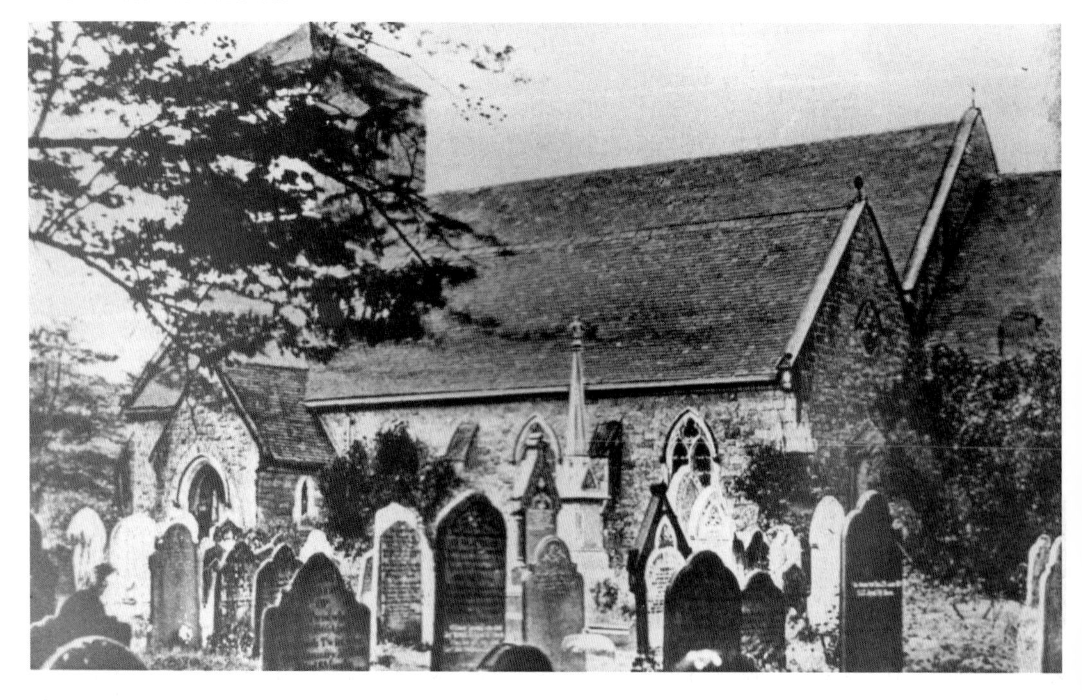

This picture shows the parish church, which was consecrated on 31 October 1849. The stone used for the building was quarried a few miles away from what is known as Billinge Delph, and was delivered by horse and cart direct from the quarry. Additionally, the stone pillars arrived by canal to Dover Lock and was carried for the rest of the journey to Golborne by horse and cart.

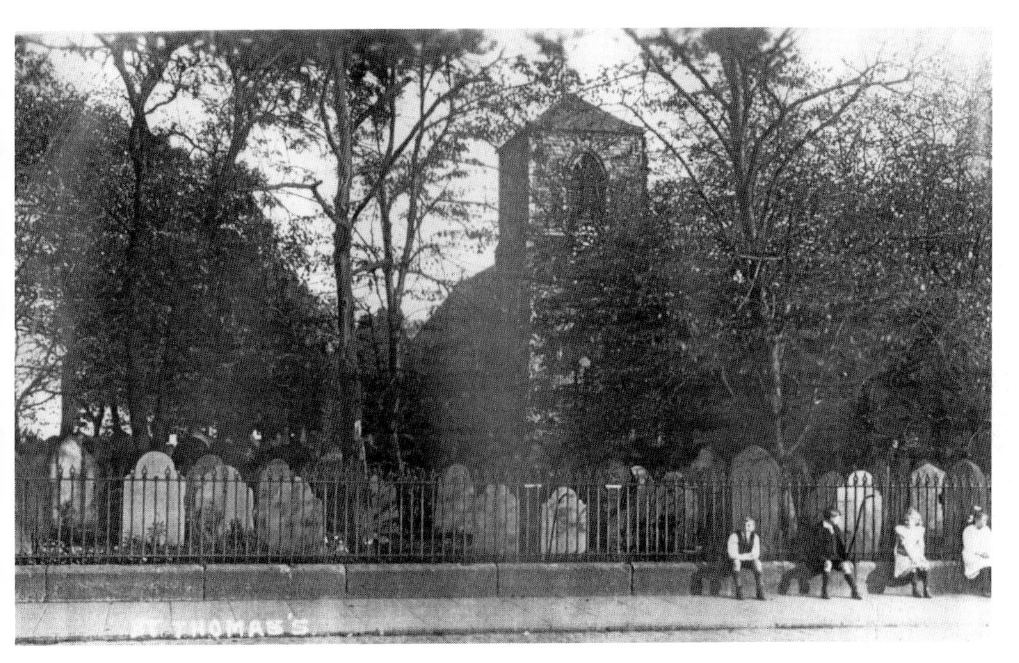

This photograph again shows the parish church, taken in around 1919. Are the boys and girls sitting on the right-hand side of the picture waiting for the ice cream man? Are they waiting for the church to open? Is it the start of a romance perhaps? Or are they watching the world go by? I guess we'll never know!

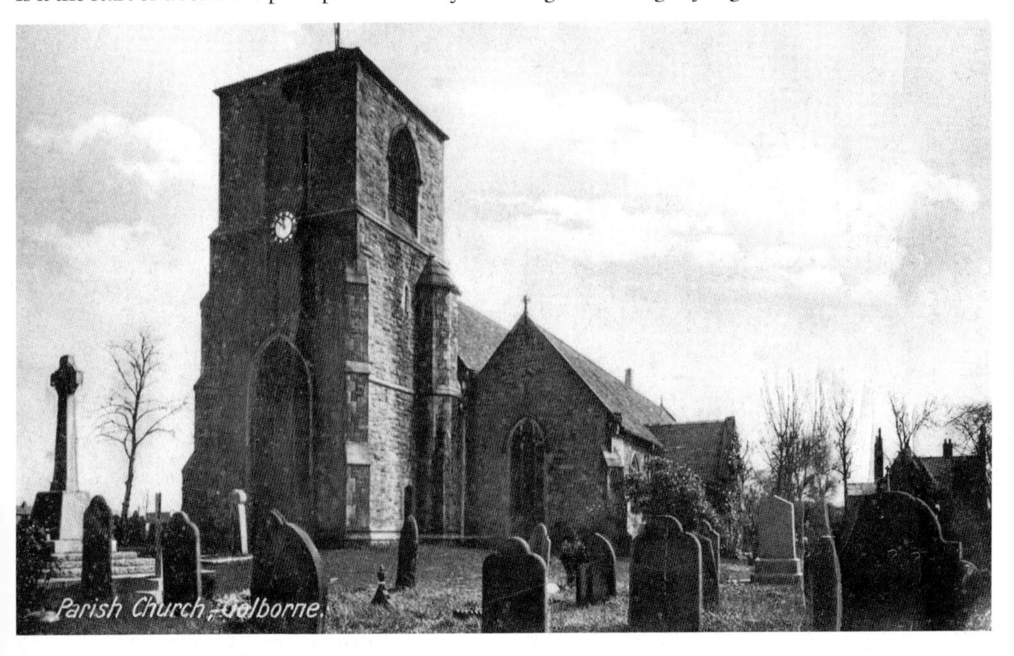

Another view of the parish church. The first baptism was carried out at here on 25 November 1849. Being baptised was Sarah Barker, daughter of George and Ann Barker of Golborne. Additionally, the first marriage was on 25 December 1849 between William Nicholson (thirty-two) and Esther Edwardson (thirty-six). The first burial was William Shiner (forty-nine) on 13 January, 1850. All ceremonies were performed by Revd Alan Greenwell.

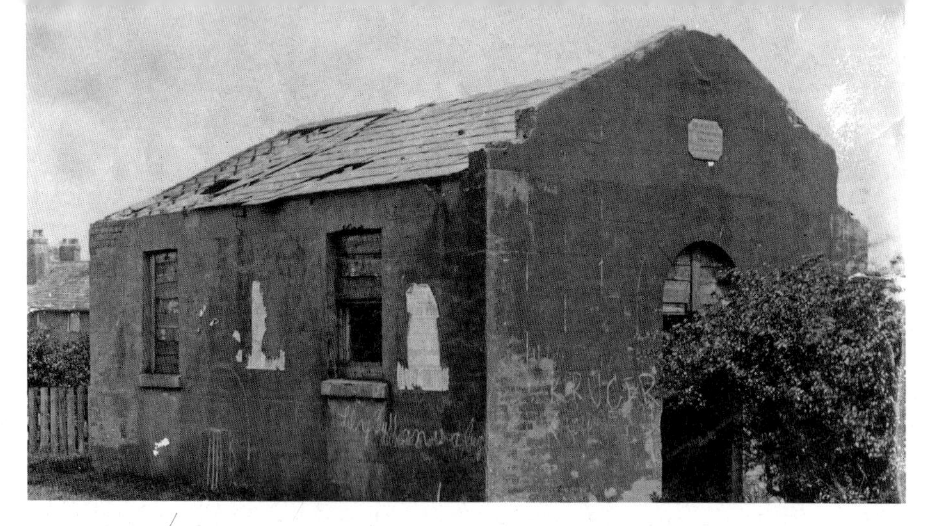

This photograph shows the first Edge Green Primitive Methodist Church. Situated on Dam Lane, which was then known as Cale Lane, the church was located at the end of a row of cottages named 'Glory Row'. It took fourteen days to build and was opened on Sunday, 12 June 1846. It served for twenty-one years before it was decided to build a new church on Edge Green Lane. Later the building was used as a day school. The organ and the stone over the door, which had the inscription 'Hitherto hath the Lord helped us', were transferred to the new chapel. This chapel was demolished during the time of the Boer War.

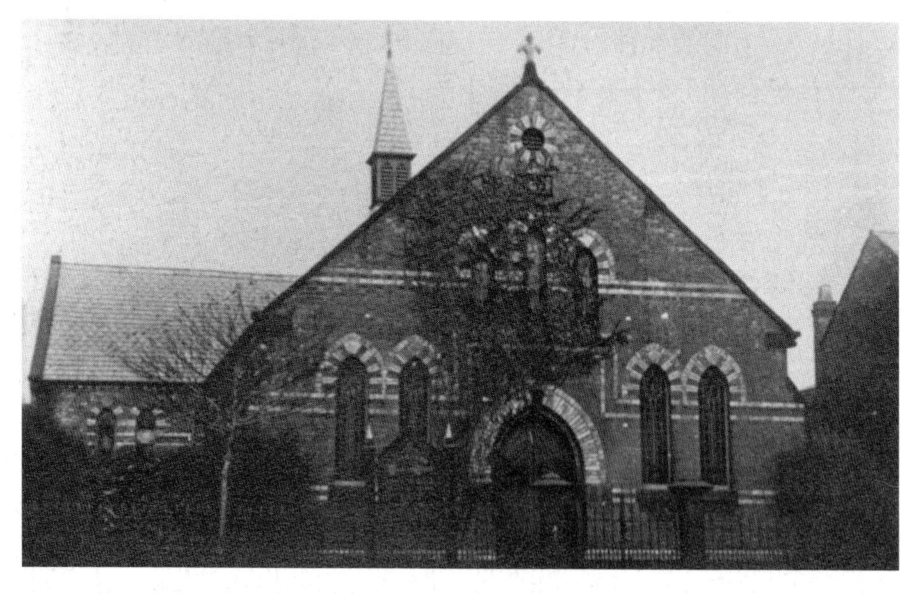

Taken in 1922, this picture shows Heath Street Methodist Church, which was built in 1871. Mr Constantine, an owner of Halliday and Constantine Mill on Barn Lane, was an early member of the church. The church began in a cottage beside the brook on Harvey Lane, which belonged to a Mr Bate. As the congregation grew, the cottage became too small so Mr Howard, owner of the Spinning Mill in Harvey Lane, gave permission for one of his rooms to be used as a meeting room, thus becoming one of the founding members of the church. Again, the numbers grew and the meeting room also became too small, so it was decided a new chapel was to be built in Heath Street. When it was built, bottles with coins in them were placed in the church foundations and the Sunday school children brought bricks for the foundations.

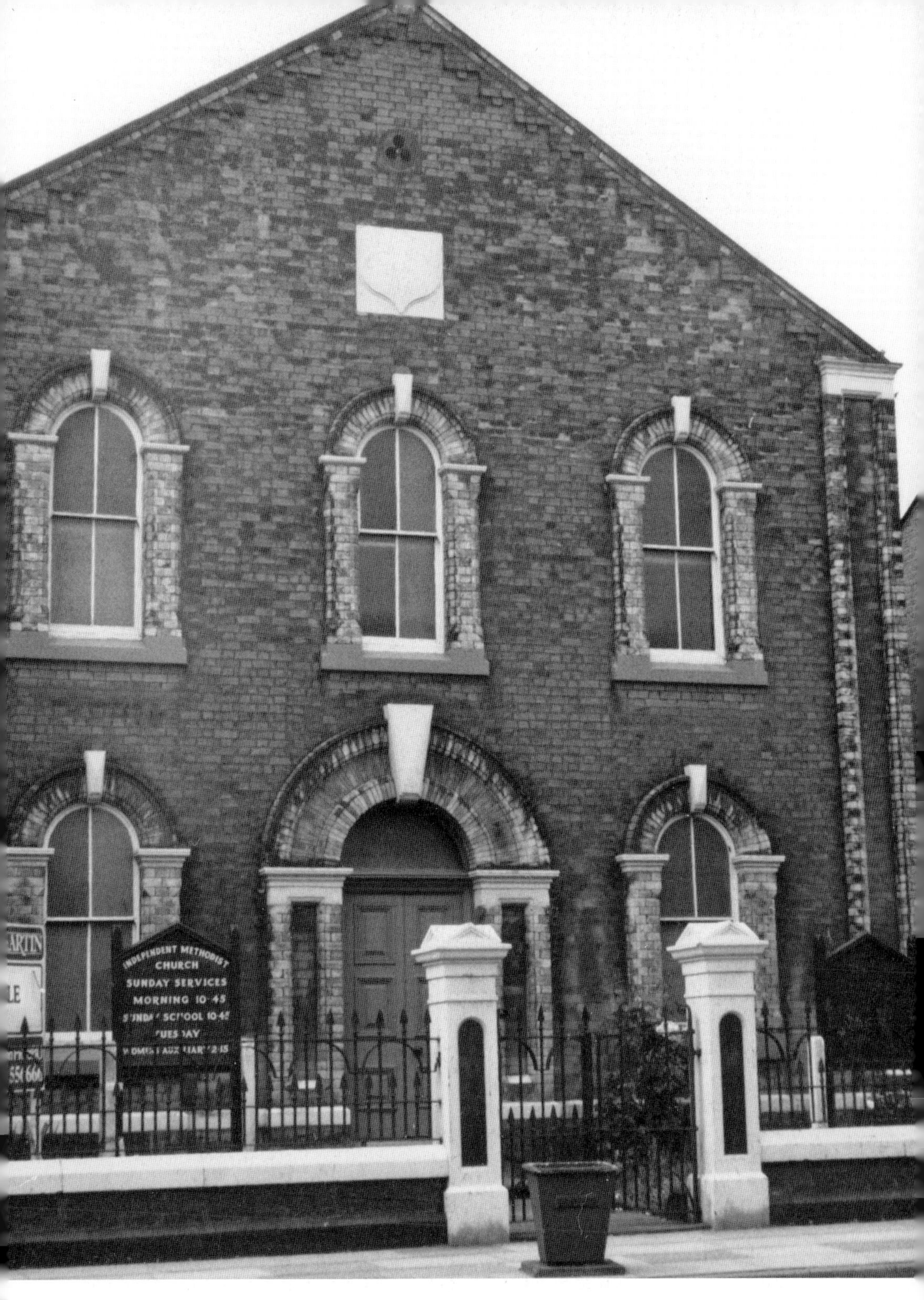

This picture shows the Independent Methodist Church on High Street, which was built in 1871 and closed in 1987. Keith Lightfoot, the joiners, took the property over after the chapel's closure.

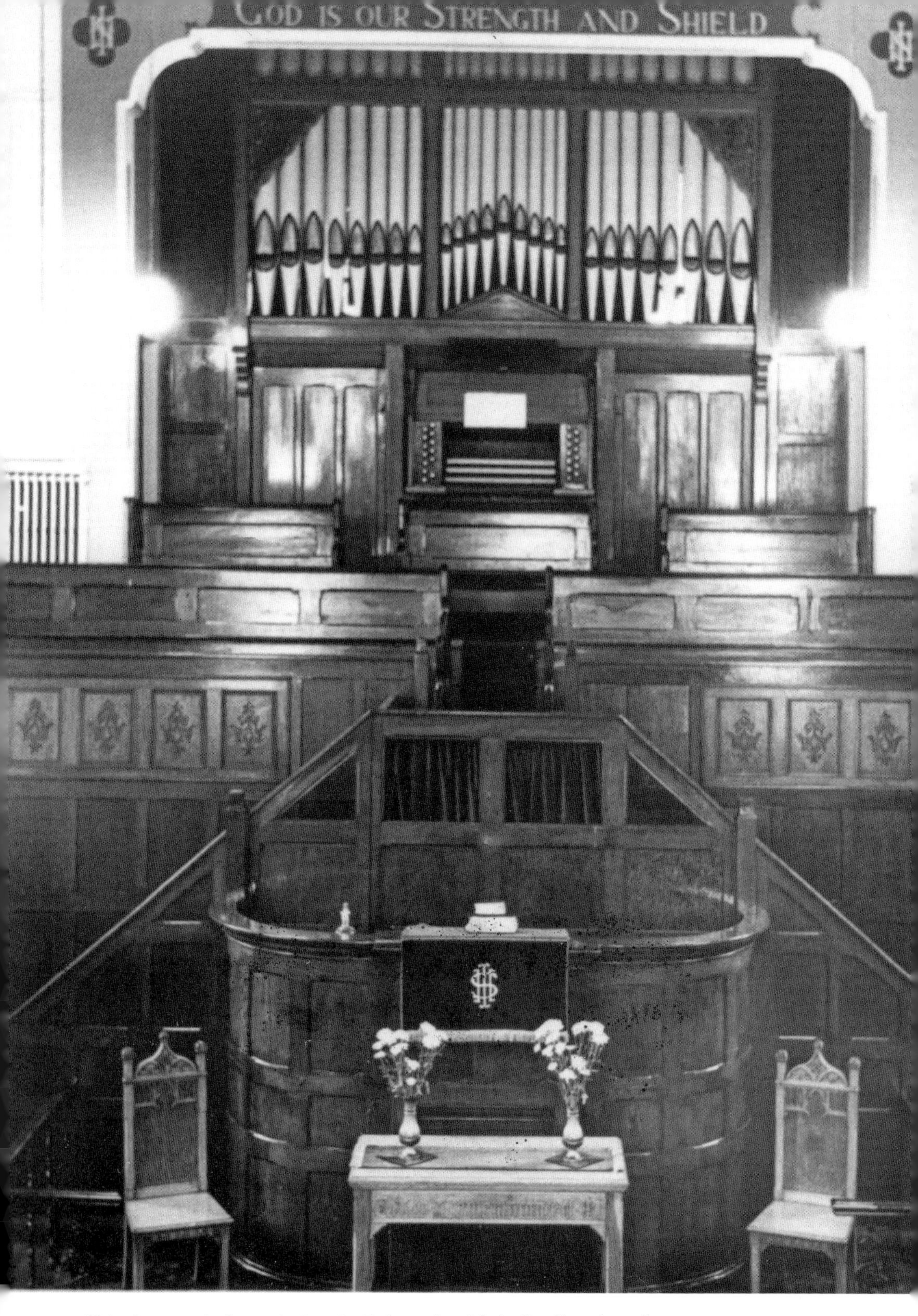

This photograph shows the interior Independent Methodist Church, and its impressive organ.

3

PEOPLE AND GROUPS

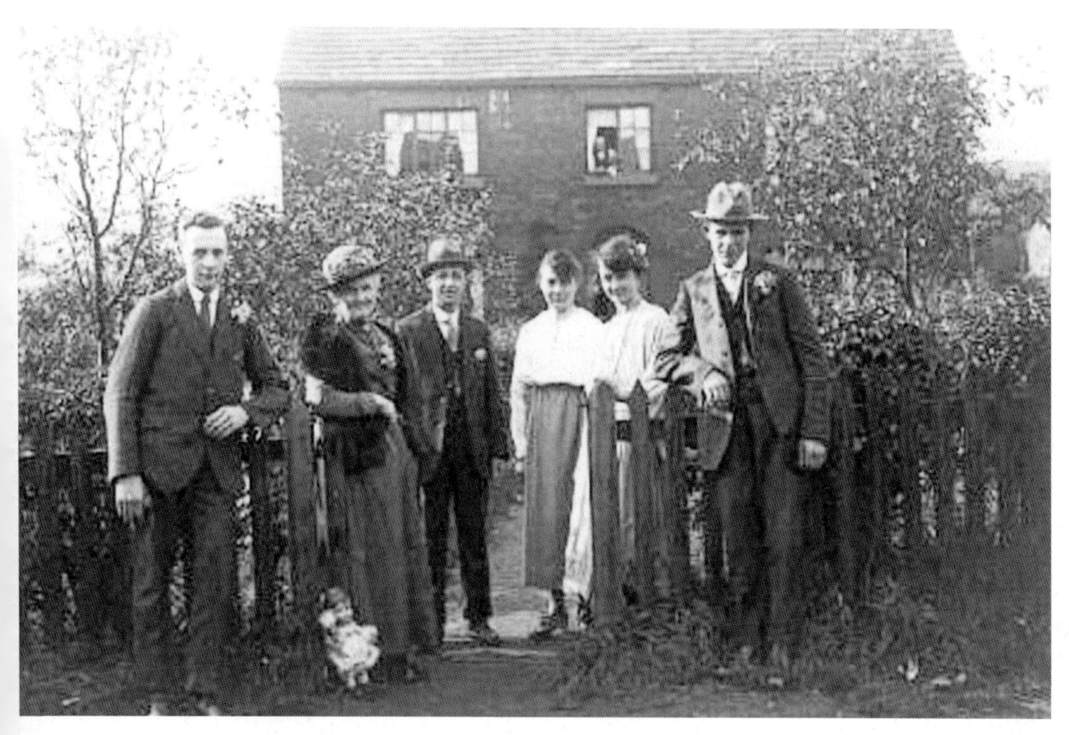

Shown here is James 'Charles' Jenkinson and his family outside Bank Heath House. The house used to be across from where the Labour Club is now and the surrounding farm land belonging to him, Bank Heath Farm, is where the new estate is now down Beech Road. An interesting fact about James Jenkinson is that Charles Street was named after him. He always stood at the end of Beech Road near the Baptist Chapel, watching the world go by. Locally known as 'Charlie Chuck', the children of the time used to sing a lovely little verse about him:

> Charlie Charlie chuck chuck chuck,
> Went to bed with two white ducks,
> One died the other cried,
> Charlie Charlie chuck chick chuck.

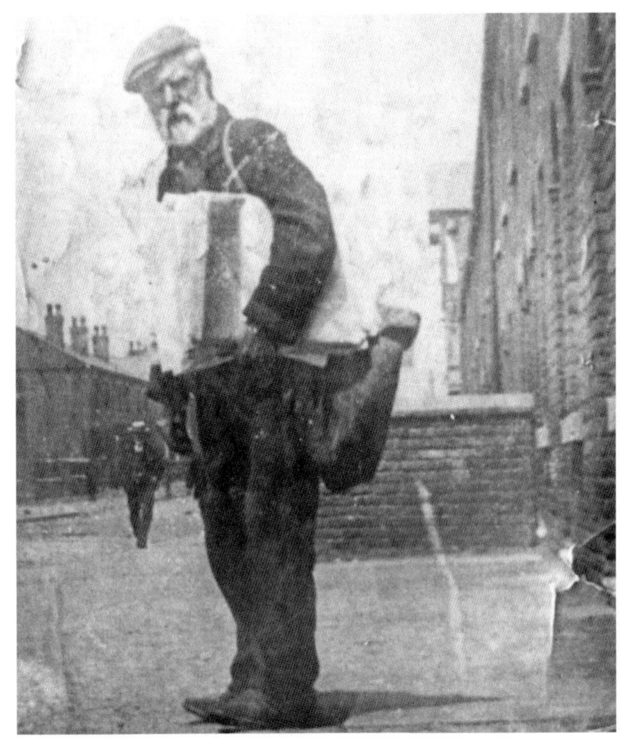

This picture of Tommy Lowe was taken at the top of Bank Street in around 1905. Tommy was the agent for the *Umpire*, *Reynolds News* and *The Sunday Chronicle*, which were the only Sunday newspapers at the time. He was a cobbler at No. 9 Legh Street and he died in 1910.

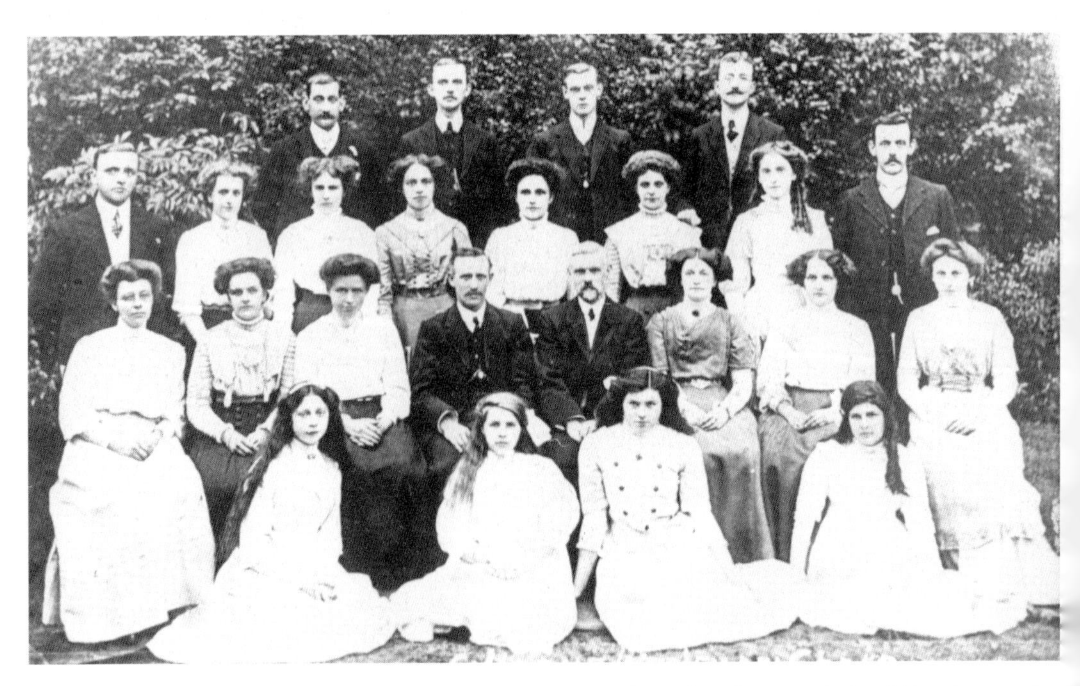

Shown here is the Golborne Wesleyan High Street Methodists Choir. This photograph should be of particular interest to locals as the founder of Mather's Jam, Mr W.T. Mather, is in the centre of the picture, sporting a rather wonderful and gracious beard. He was the choirmaster for a length of forty years. Also in this picture is Mr Clayton, the owner of Northants Shoe Shop, which is now Middleton and Wood Funeral Directors.

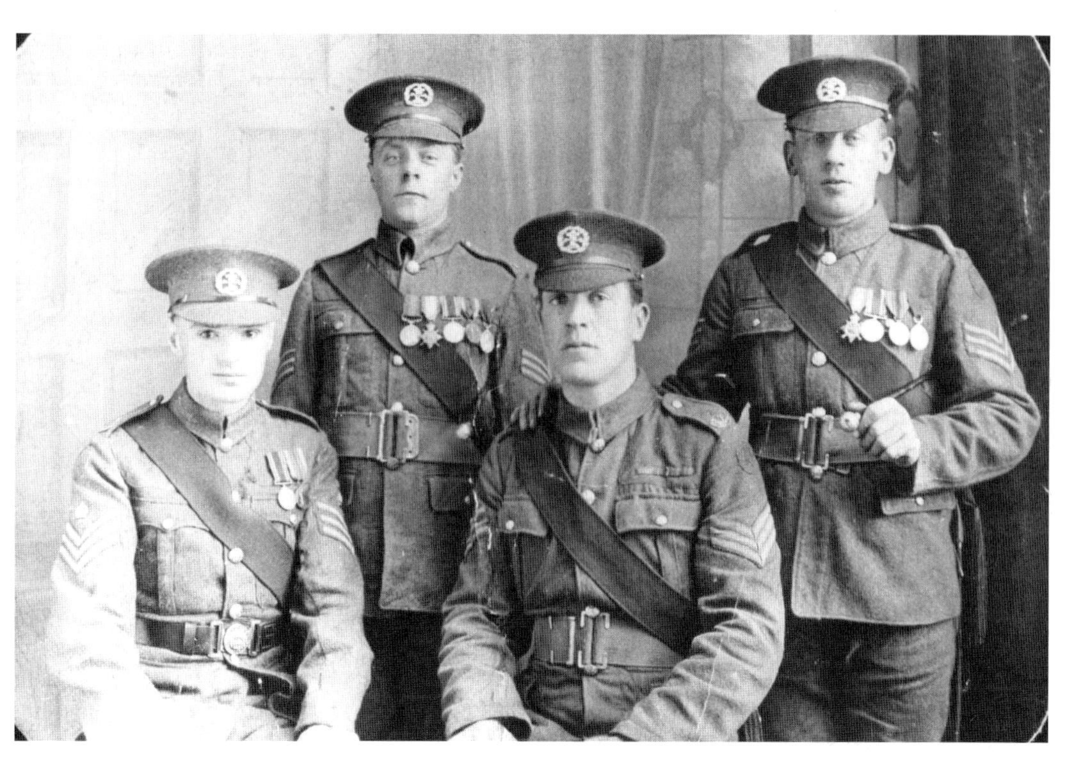

Taken in 1921, this photograph shows, from left to right: Robert Ratcliffe from the High Street, Mr Ness from Padgate, Thomas Charles from Church Street, and Harry Heath, also from Church Street.

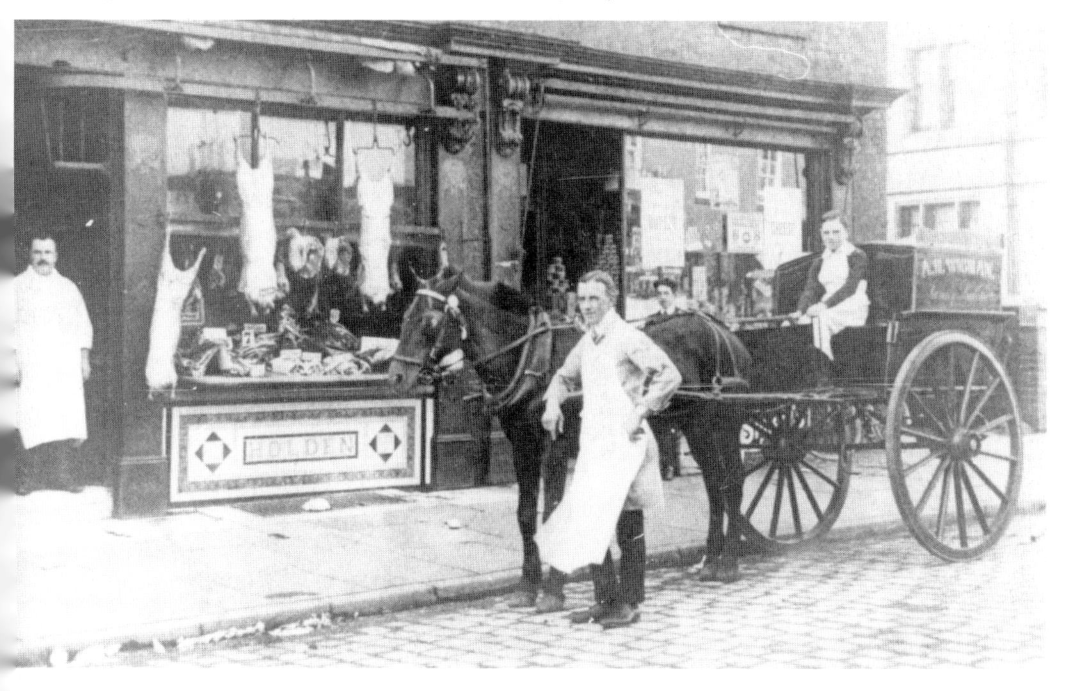

This picture features three generations of the Wigman Family Butchers from the High Street going about their everyday business. The photograph was taken during the early part of the 1900s, hence the horse and carriage.

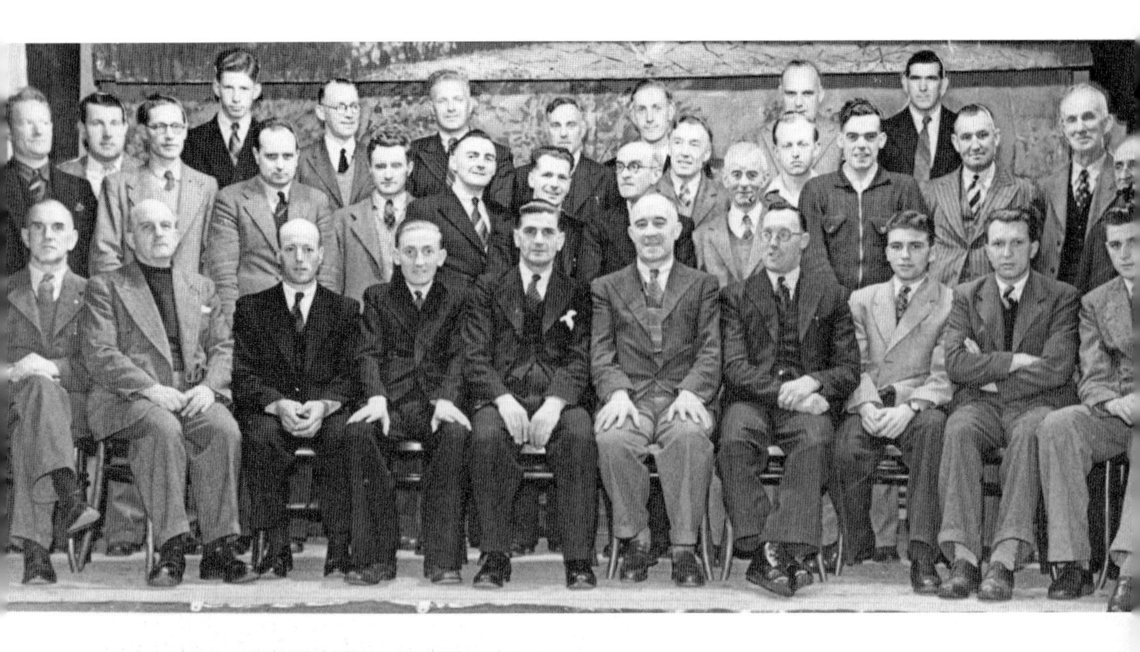

This photograph shows a rather smartly dressed Golborne Male Voice Choir, and was taken during the 1950s.

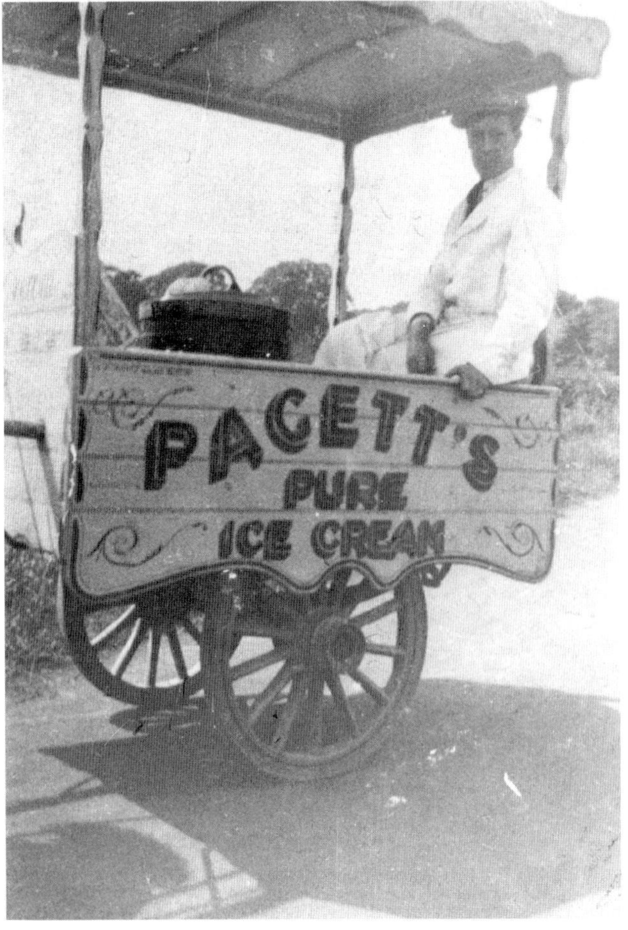

Featured in this picture is Pagett's ice-cream cart. Mr Pagett, the owner, was based in Legh Street.

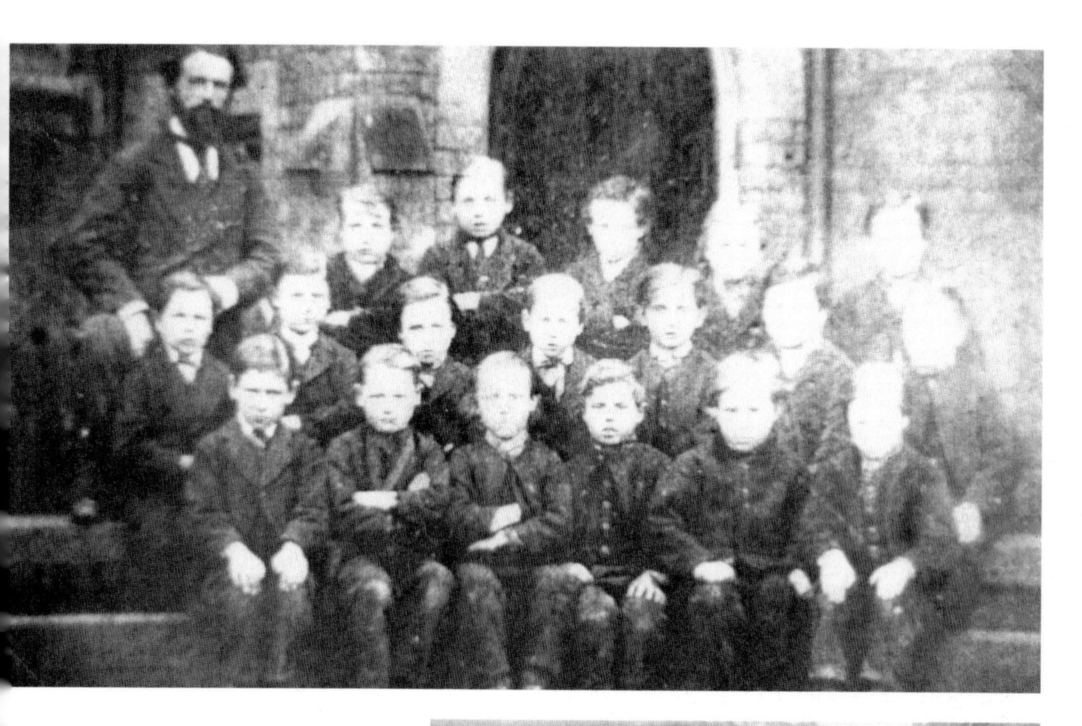

This photograph is one of the oldest featured in this collection. It shows Golborne Church School and it was taken around 1873 and 1874. In the front row, first on the left is John Wilcock. Fourth from the left is Peter Downall, the grandfather of Golborne's famous boxer, Peter Kane. Somewhere in the picture is James 'Charles' Naylor, founder of Naylor Bros Engineering Ltd.

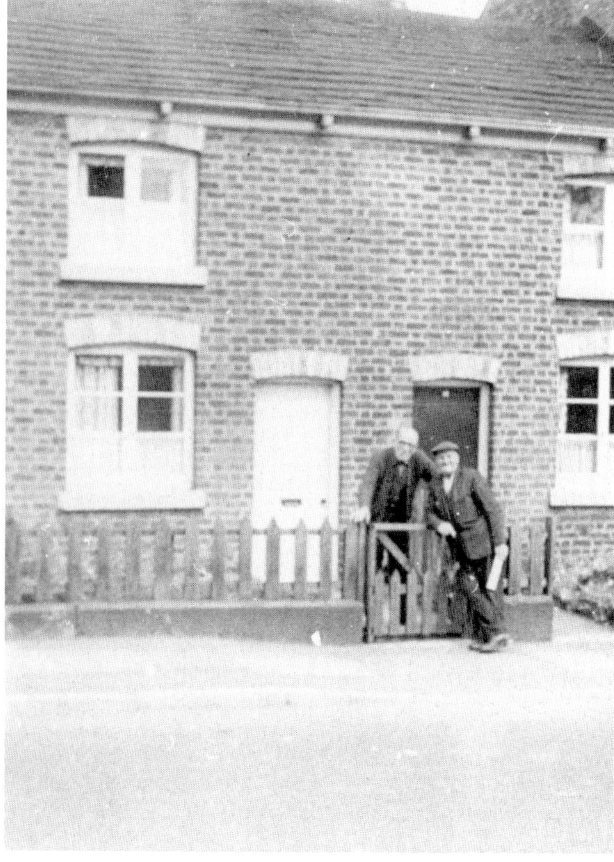

Tom Charles (without the cap) stands outside his colliery-owned cottage on Church Street with a friend.

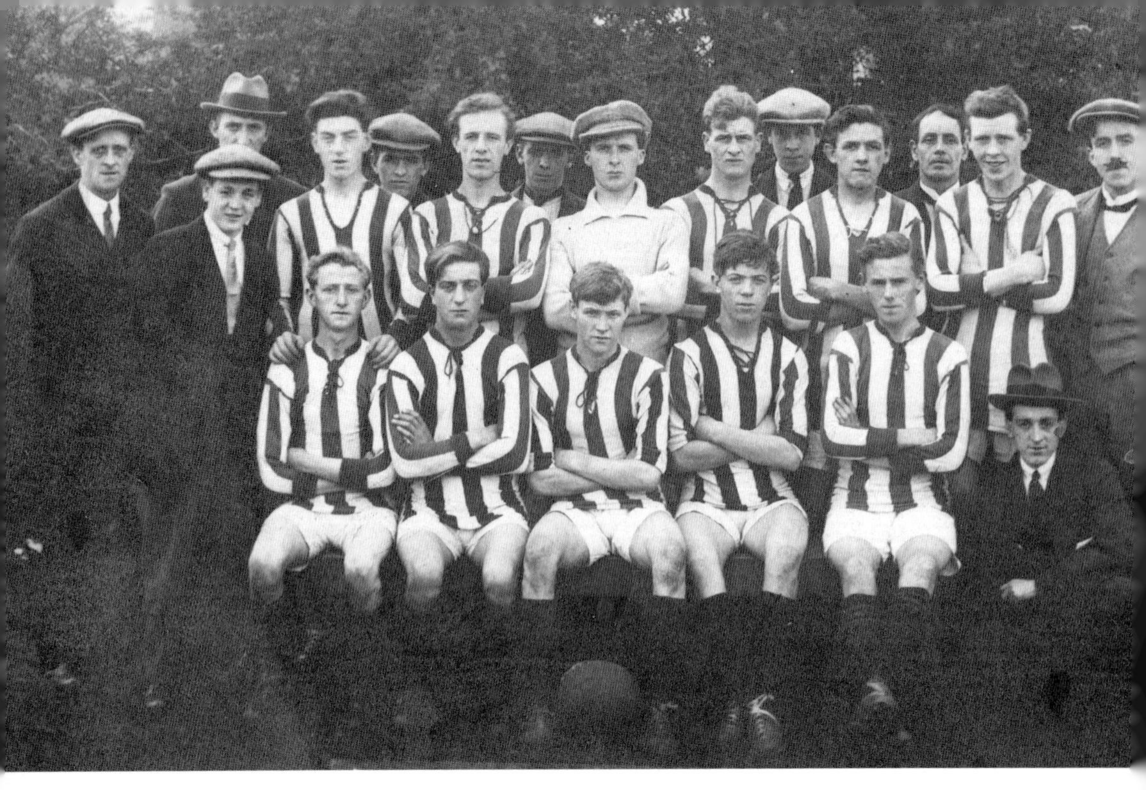

Taken during the 1930s, this picture shows the earnest-looking line-up of Golborne Baptist AFC.

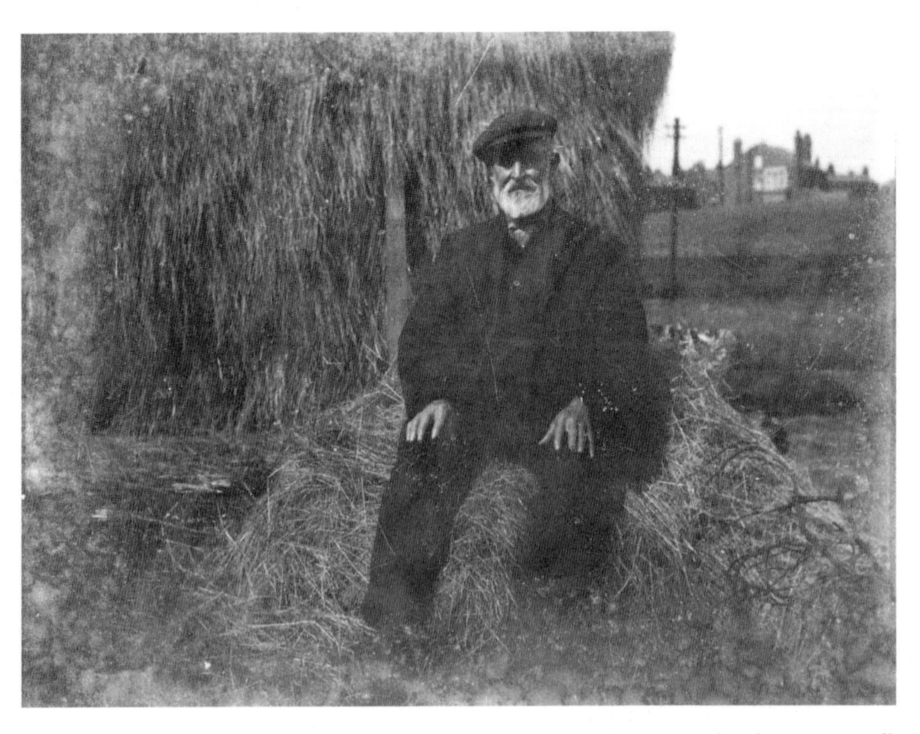

Taken in approximately 1900, this photograph features Teddy Last. He lived at Upper Mill Farm in Barn Lane and farmed all the fields down to the brook. He came from Suffolk and was born in 1830. He died at the farm in 1915.

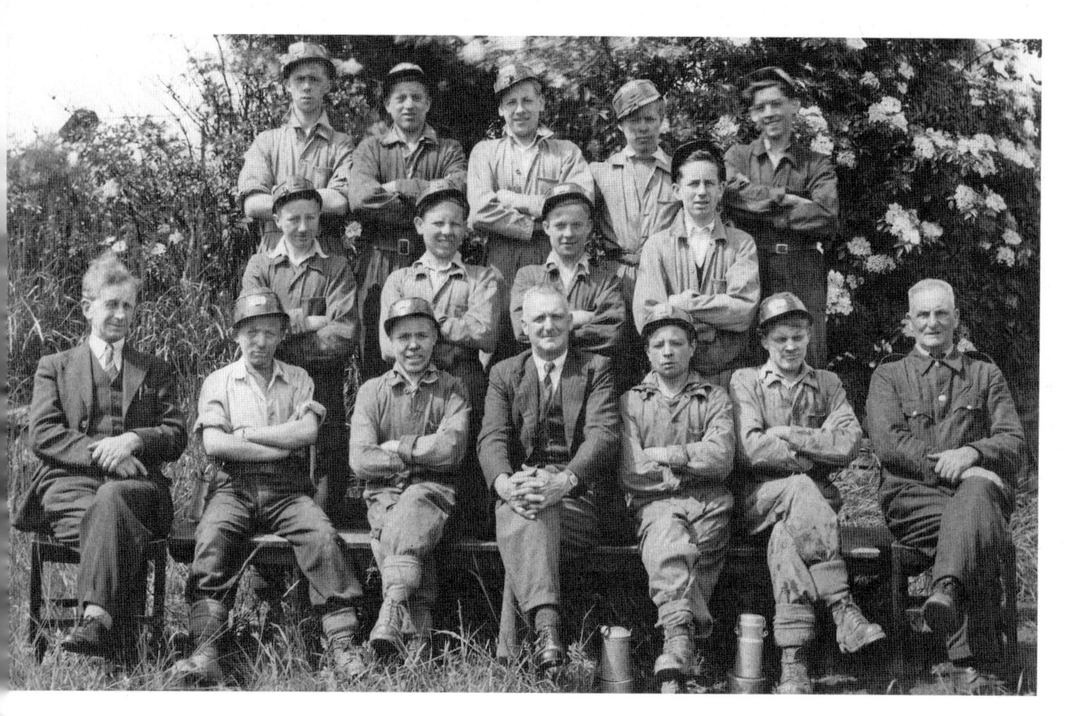

ʻThis photograph shows NCB Trainees from the Wigan area and was taken in 1949. This group of men, ʻt one time or another, all worked at Golborne Colliery. Back row, from left to right: B. Oliver, O. Wright, \. Dickinson, W. Birges, J. Birke. Centre row: W. Olerton, S. Roper, T. Gagan, J. Johnson. Seated: J. McCalfe, ‹. Dunn, J. Marsh and E. Simms. The men dressed in suits were the trainers.

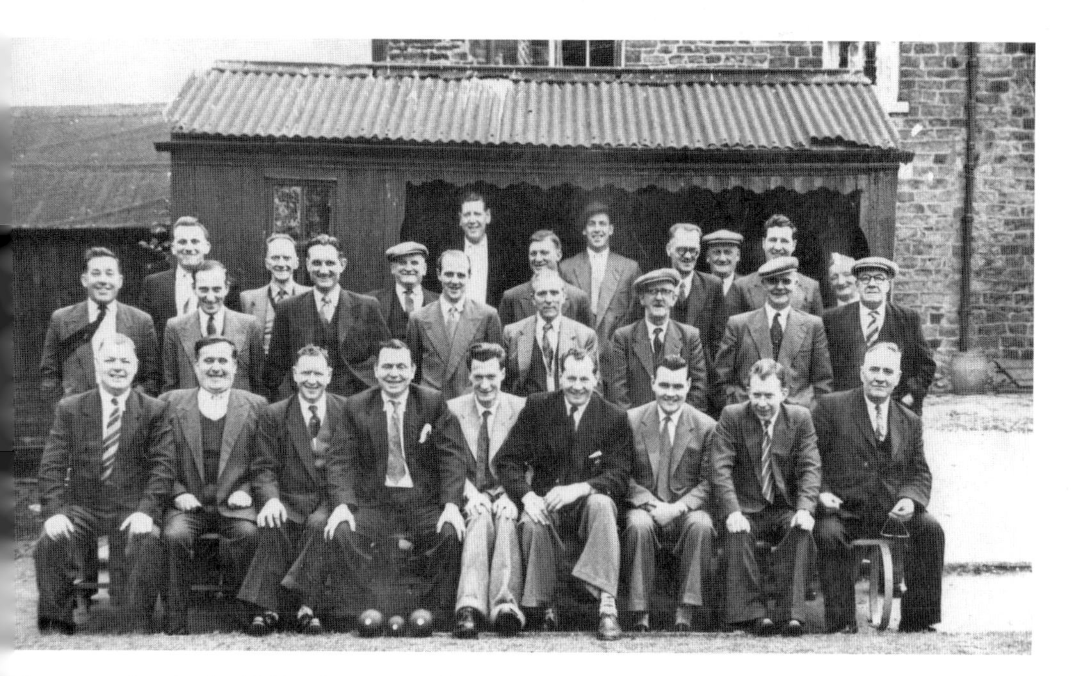

aken some time in the 1950s, this picture shows the Millstone Bowlers on an outing, all looking rather ›lly! The Millstone is a pub in Golborne, and this was their bowling team.

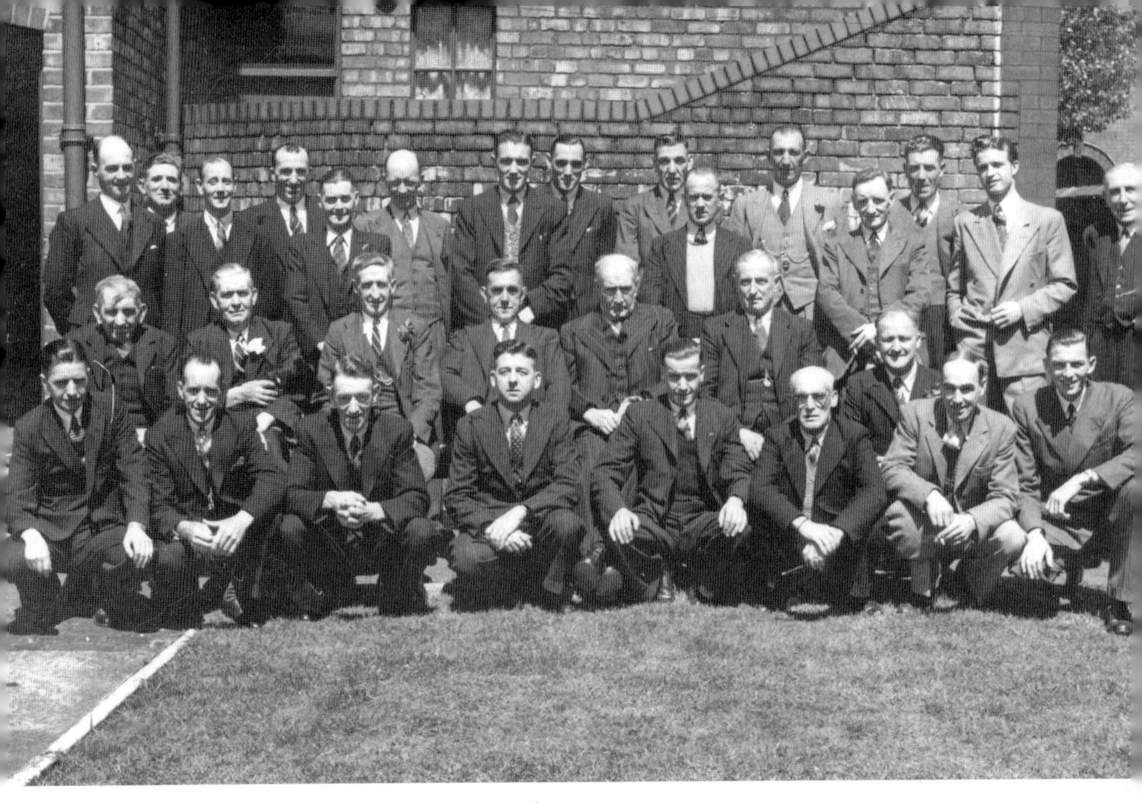

Another photograph of the Millstone Bowlers, taken in the 1950s.

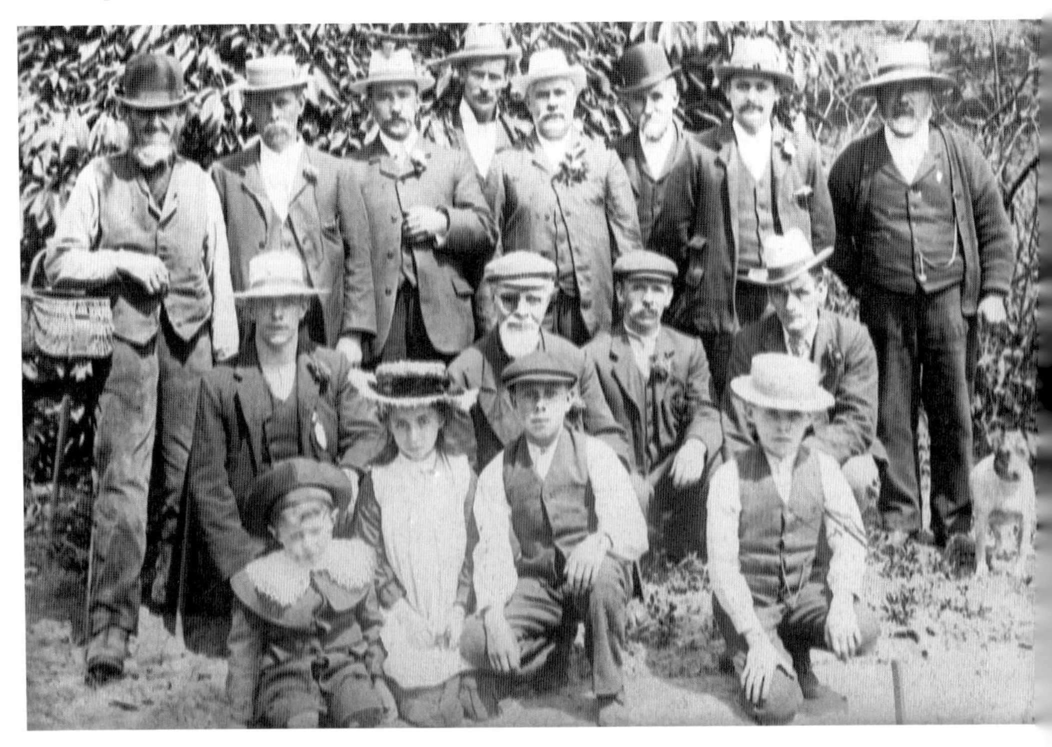

Captured in around 1870, this image shows a group of men from Golborne, most probably farmer
Presumably, the children kneeling at the front are the children of the farmers.

This is a photograph taken in approximately 1908 outside the old All Saints Church on Church Street. They are a very famous music hall dance troupe of the time called The Eight Lancashire Lads, not all of whom are here in this photo. They were founded by Bill Cawley and J.W. (William) Jackson (1863–1940) of Golborne. The young man in the centre is, in fact, deceptively, a girl. If you think you recognise the gentleman on the left-hand side of the picture, you'd be right, because this is a young Charlie Chaplin! The world-famous comedic actor and silent movie star joined the Eight Lancashire Lads before joining the esteemed Fred Karno troupe in 1910. By 1913, he had left Golborne long behind him, and was making movies for the Keystone Film Company in The United States. A fascinating claim to fame for the area, I'm sure you will agree!

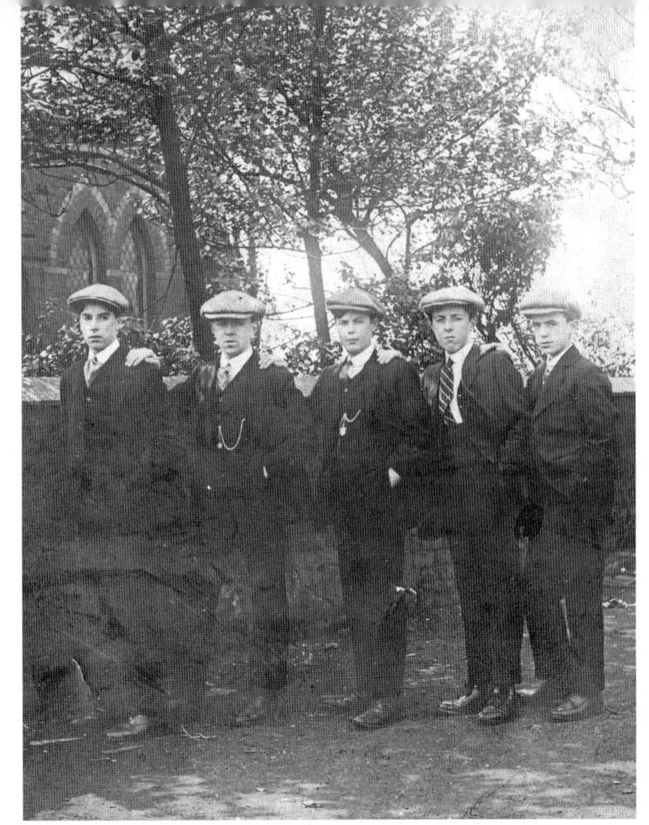

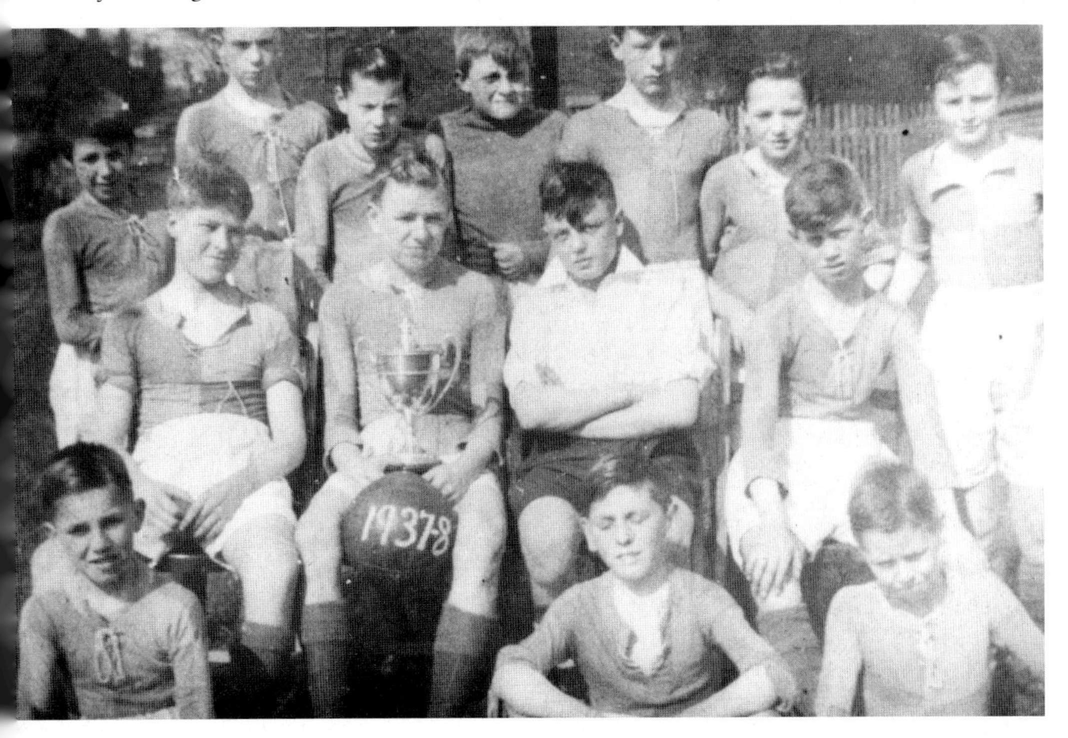

This image shows Golborne FC in the 1937/38 season. Among those in the back row are W. Barnes, F. Minton, S. Harrison, D. Stanley, J. Blackburn, J. Norris. Middle row, F. Watkinson, R. Sherman, D. Woodcock, G. Taylor. Front row: F. Johnson, J. Simpson, J. Young.

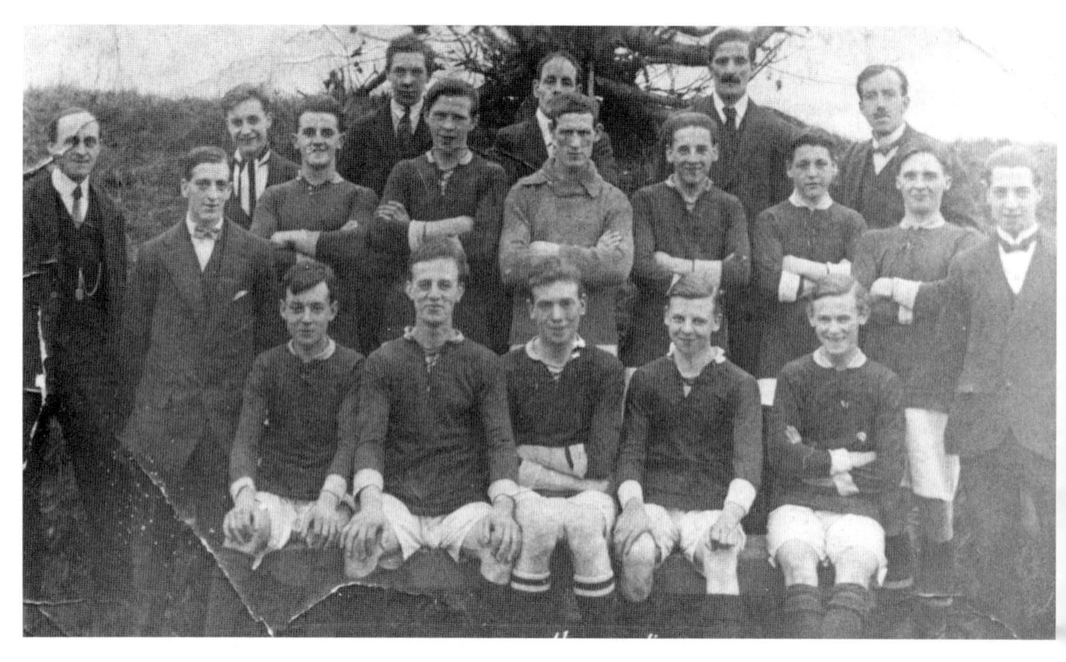

Again taken in the 1930s, this picture shows the line-up of Golborne AFC.

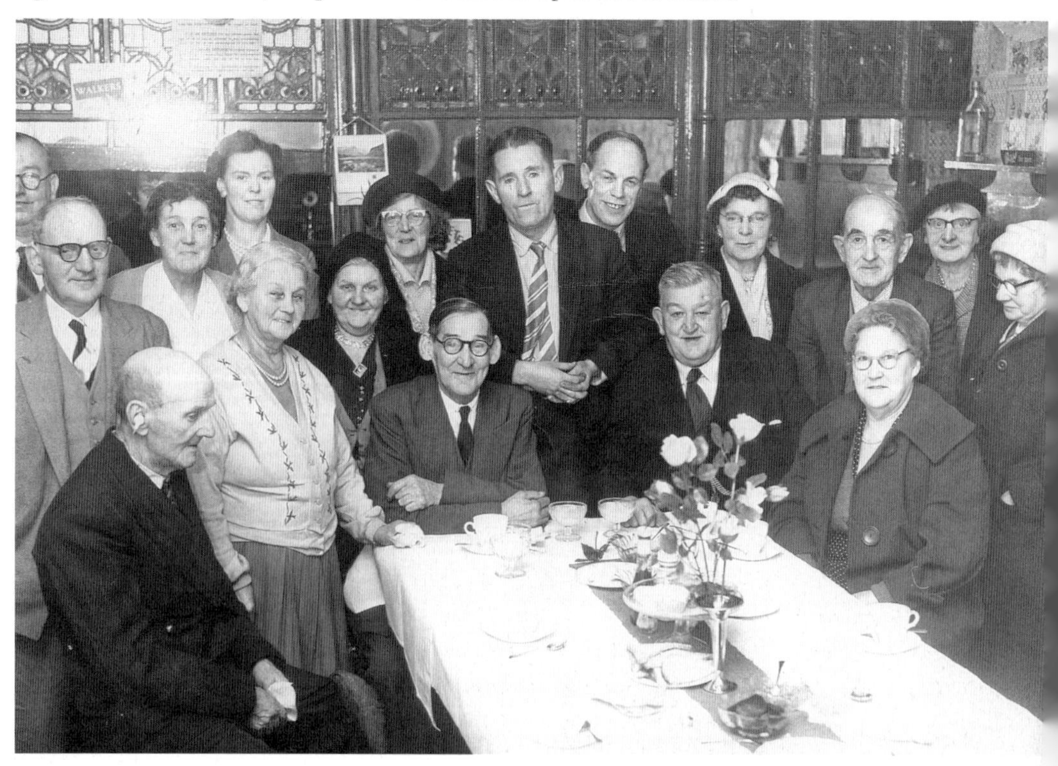

Taken in around 1960, this picture shows Charles Napier (Tippins) old folks' Christmas party. The tall lady at the back on the left with the pearl necklace is Anna Tippin, the landlady at the time. This is why the public house is referred to as Tippins, or Tipp's, still to this very day.

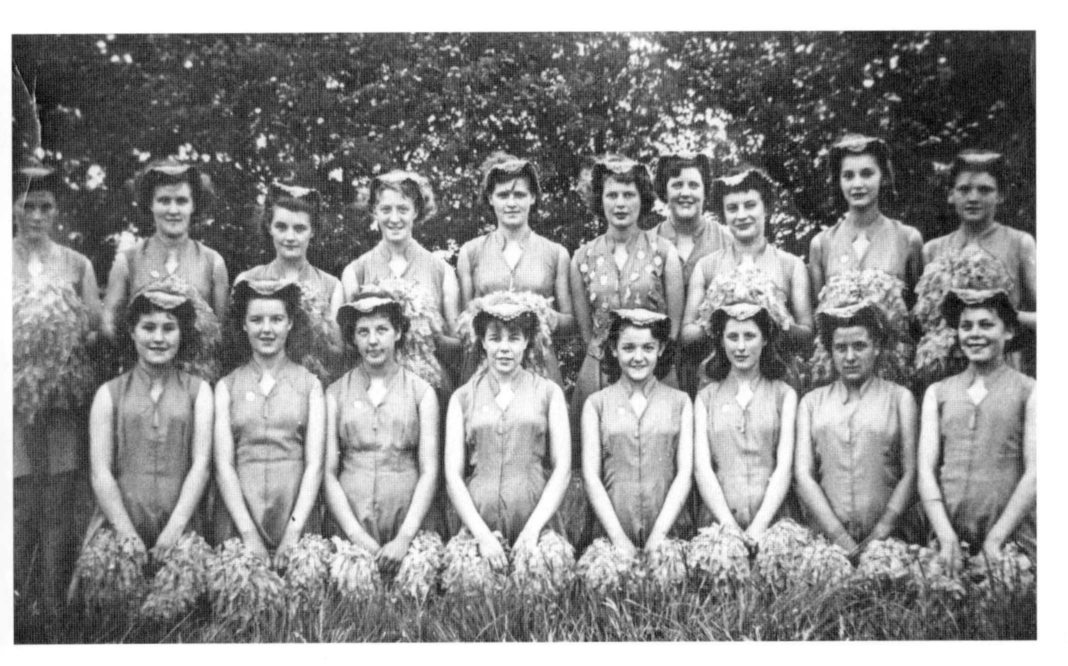

Captured in the 1950s, this picture shows a group of young morris dancers in costume.

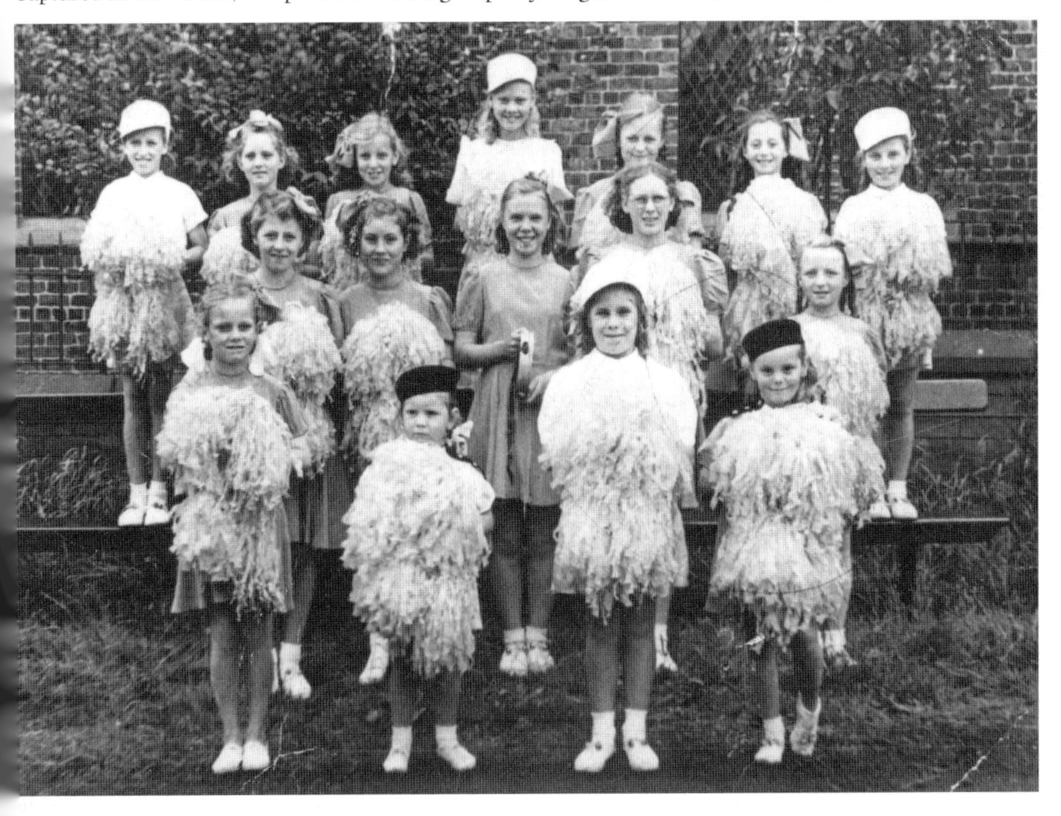

Taken between 1952 and 1953, this photograph features a group of young Morris dancers from Golborne Baptist Church.

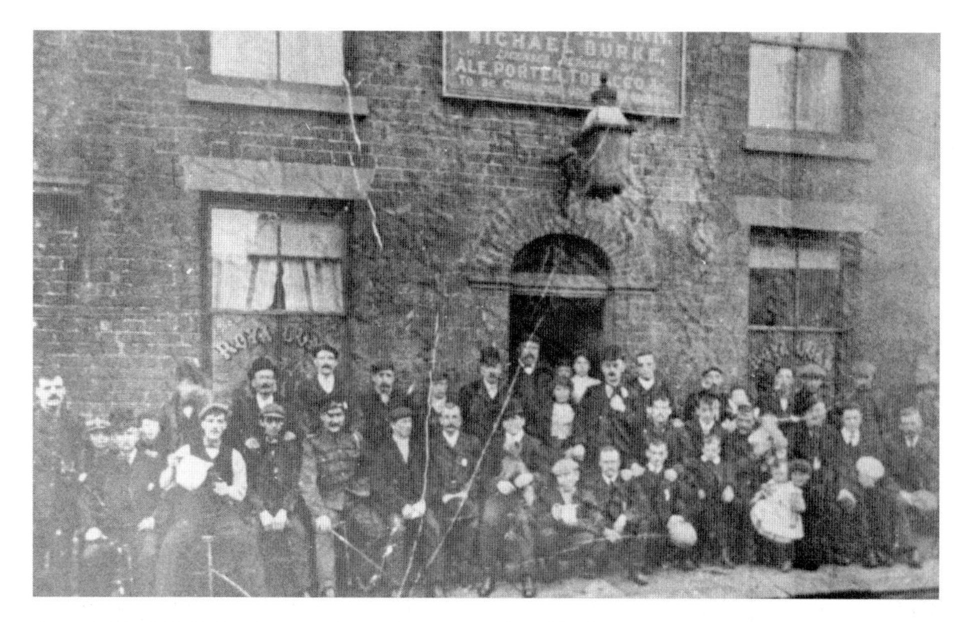

Captured in 1907, this picture shows the Royal Oak public house and its regulars from Golborne Council. This building later became the cinema called the Pavilion, locally known as 'The Bug Opera'. Then it was used as a bingo hall until the 1990s, at which point it was demolished to make way for modern housing.

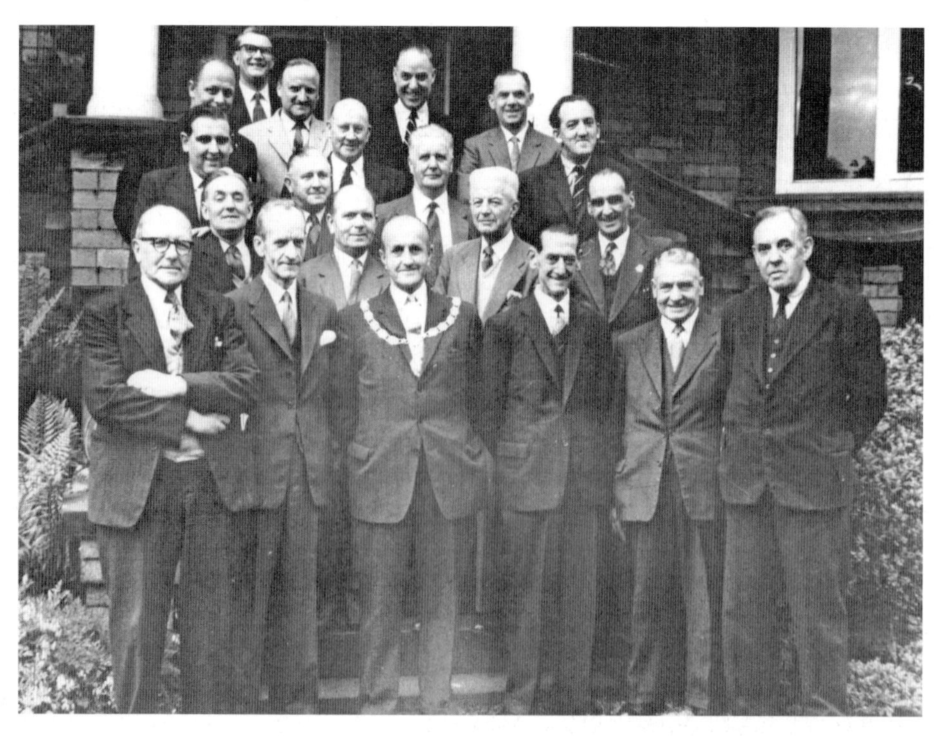

This rare picture consists of members of Golborne Council posing outside the Royal Oak public house in the 1950s. Among the group are Jack Barwell, Reg Thwaites, Bill Naylor and Tommy Ralph. Mr and Mrs Ralph had the White shop on the corner of nearby Heath Street and Peter Street.

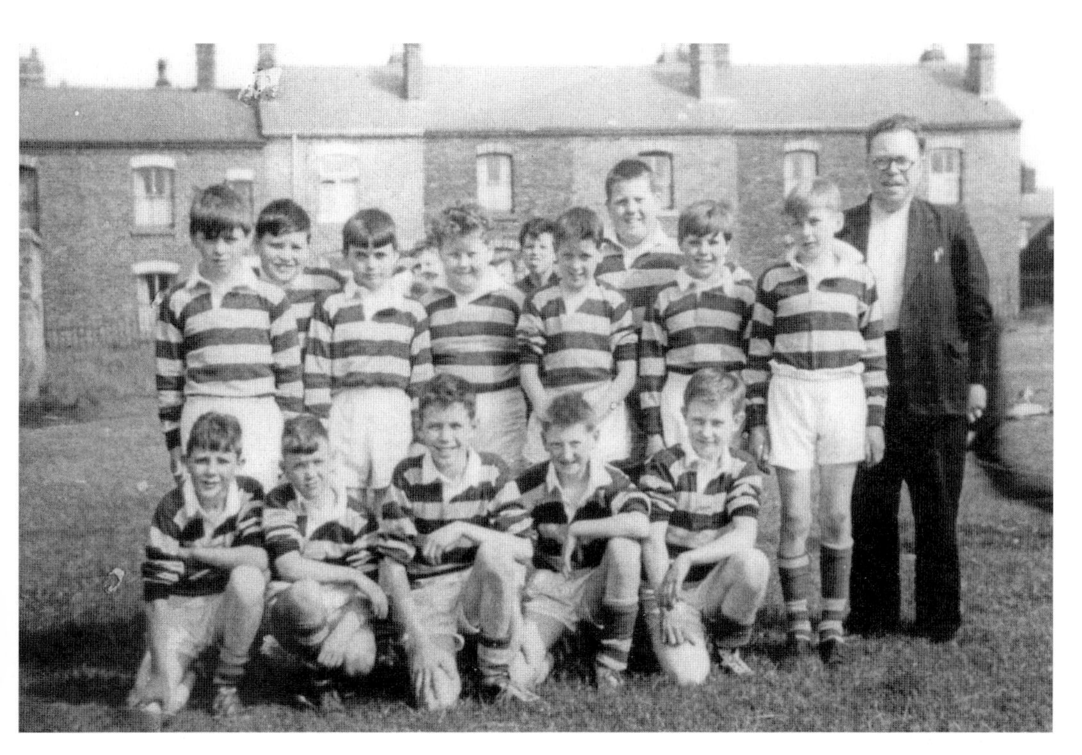

Taken in the early 1960s, this image features the young Golborne All Saints' Rugby Team. Tom Richardson is on the far left in the back row.

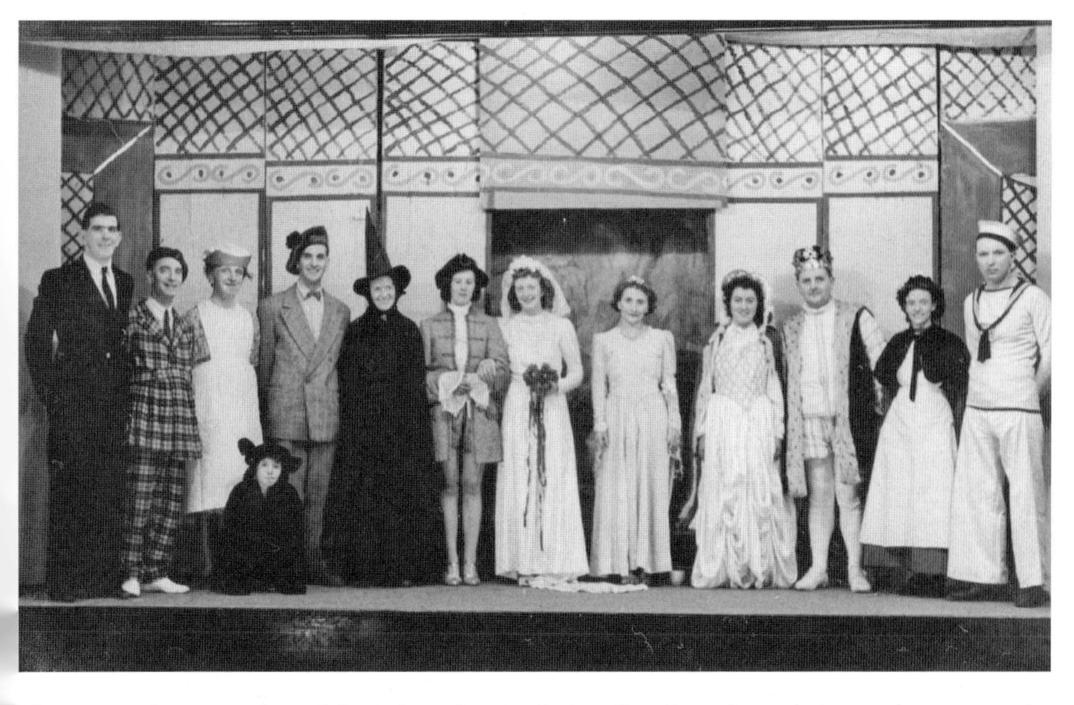

This picture shows members of the Independent Methodist Church on the High Street taking part in the annual pantomime which was performed in the 1950s. The sailor on the far right-hand side is Bill Cartridge.

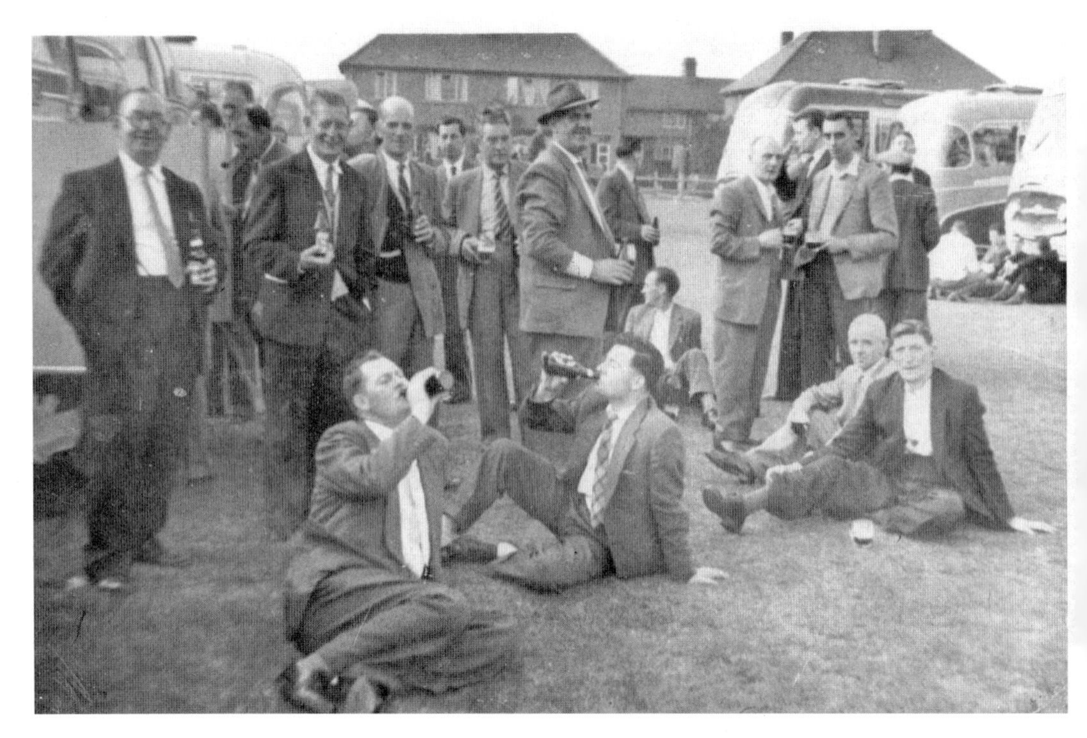

Taken in the early 1960s, this photograph shows an outing for the Charles Napier race meeting. As you can see, the men sitting on the floor are thoroughly enjoying some liquid refreshments!

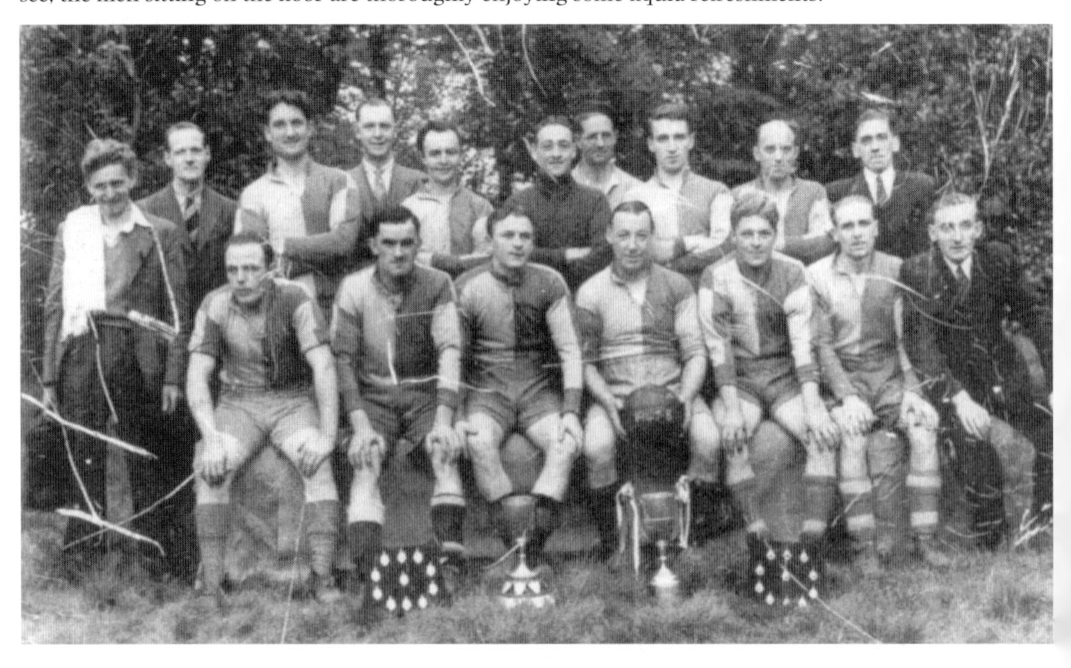

This picture shows the Harbens Football Team in the 1947/48 season, photographed here at Golborne Sports Club. Jack Casey is the gentleman second from the right in the front row and Johnny Simpson is on the far right in the back row; the Sports club 'Simpson's Fields' were named after him.

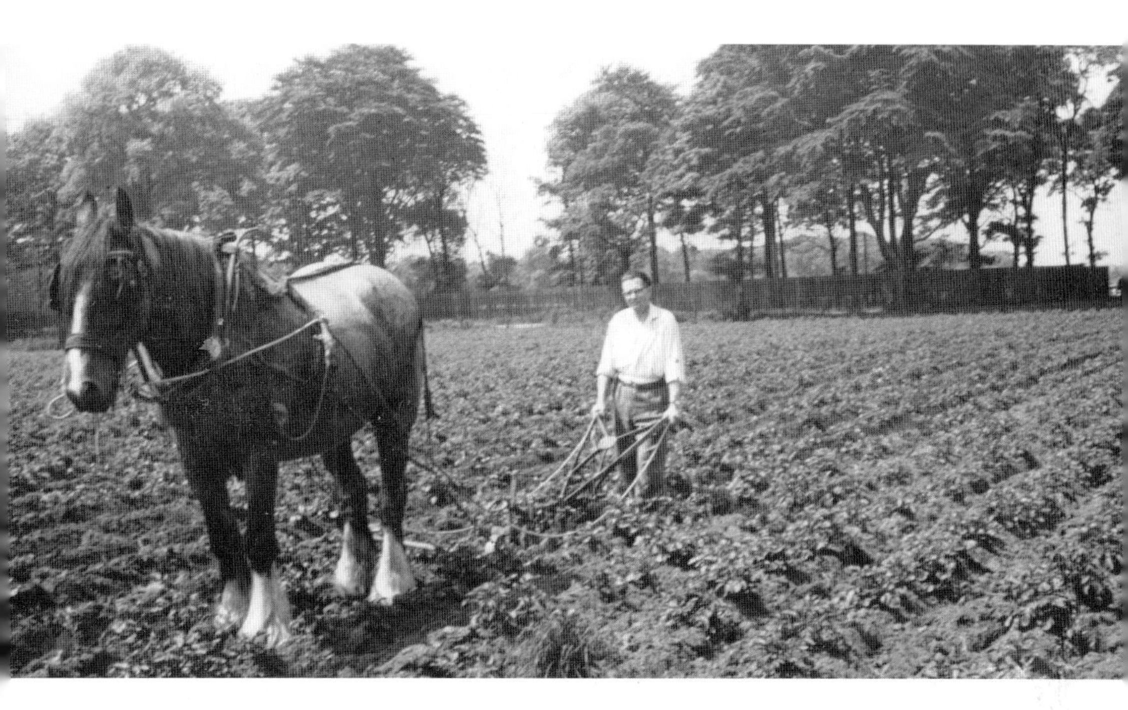

This photograph, captured in the 1950s, shows Jimmy Bridge ploughing his field at the top of Harvey Lane with a trusty shire horse.

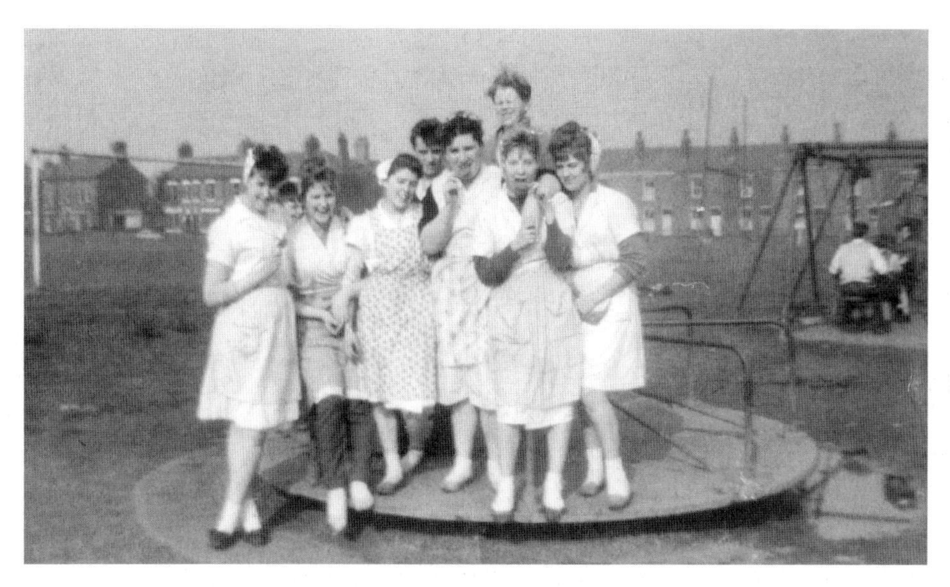

This picture shows the Sun-Pat girls taking a well-earned break on Legh Street Park in the 1960s. Mr William Mitchell founded a wallpaper manufacturing business in 1850 at Brookside Mill in Legh Street. The mill was burned down in 1886 but was rebuilt and became a major success. In 1940, H.S. Whiteside and Company took over the mill, although they were probably better known as the company Sun-Pat. By the mid-1950s, Sun-Pat employed over a thousand people. The factory unfortunately burned down on 10 March 1963. There is now a housing estate on the site.

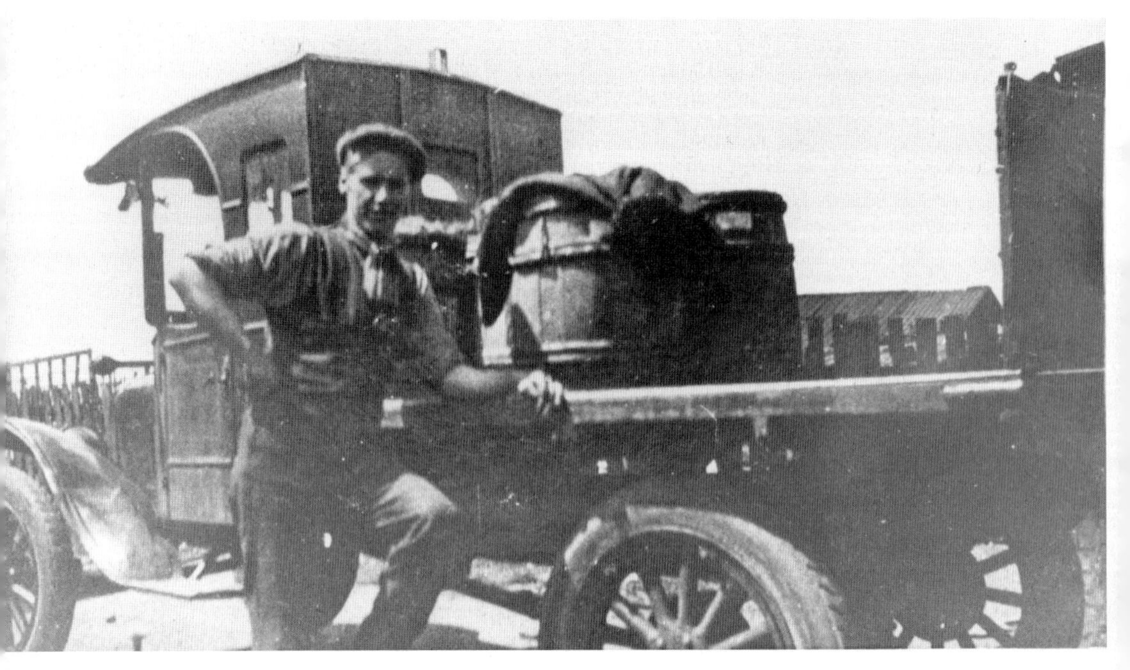

This is an employee of Bob Barrow, a fruit and vegetable wholesalers, whose shop is where Alan Jones' Funeral Parlour is situated now. The gentleman is pictured with one of his flat-bed lorries. On the right-hand side of this picture is the only image of the former cotton mill on Lowton Road. This is why the road was named Factory Lane before they renamed it to Lowton Road.

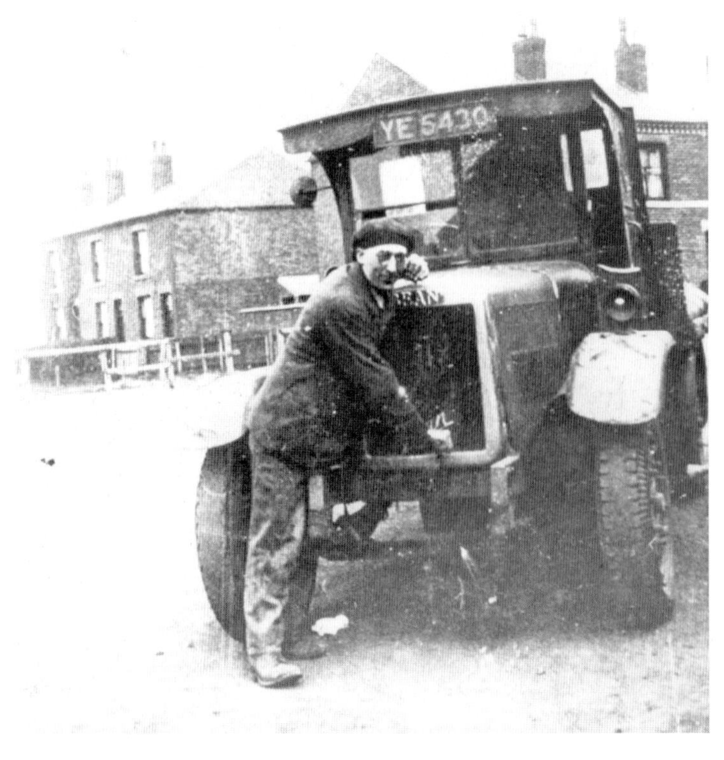

This picture shows another Bob Barrow's employee. This photograph was taken on Factory Lane, and in the background is the top of Taylor Street.

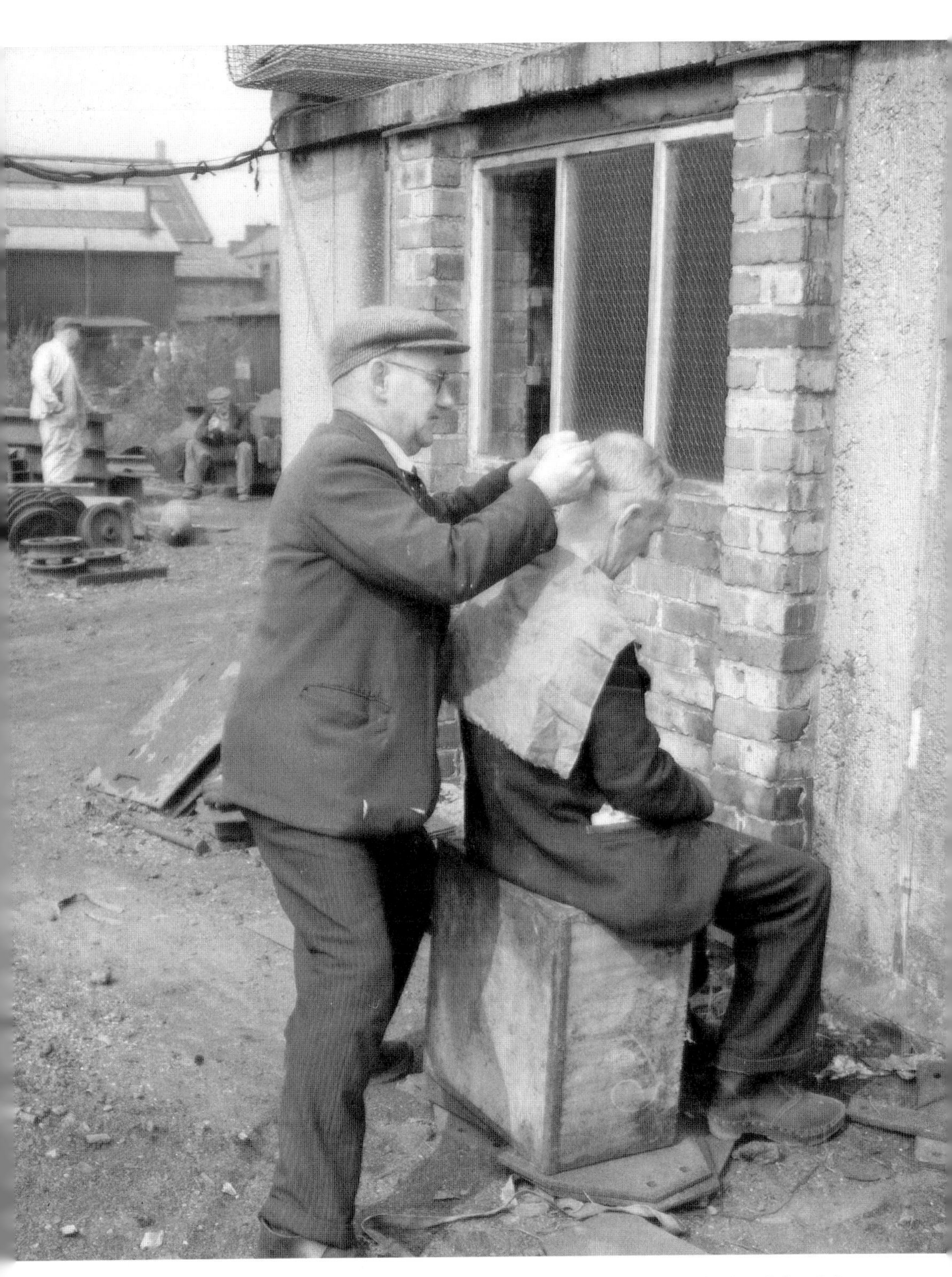

Taken in the 1950s, this photograph shows a gentleman receiving a free haircut on his lunch break from a fellow employee of Naylor Brothers engineering.

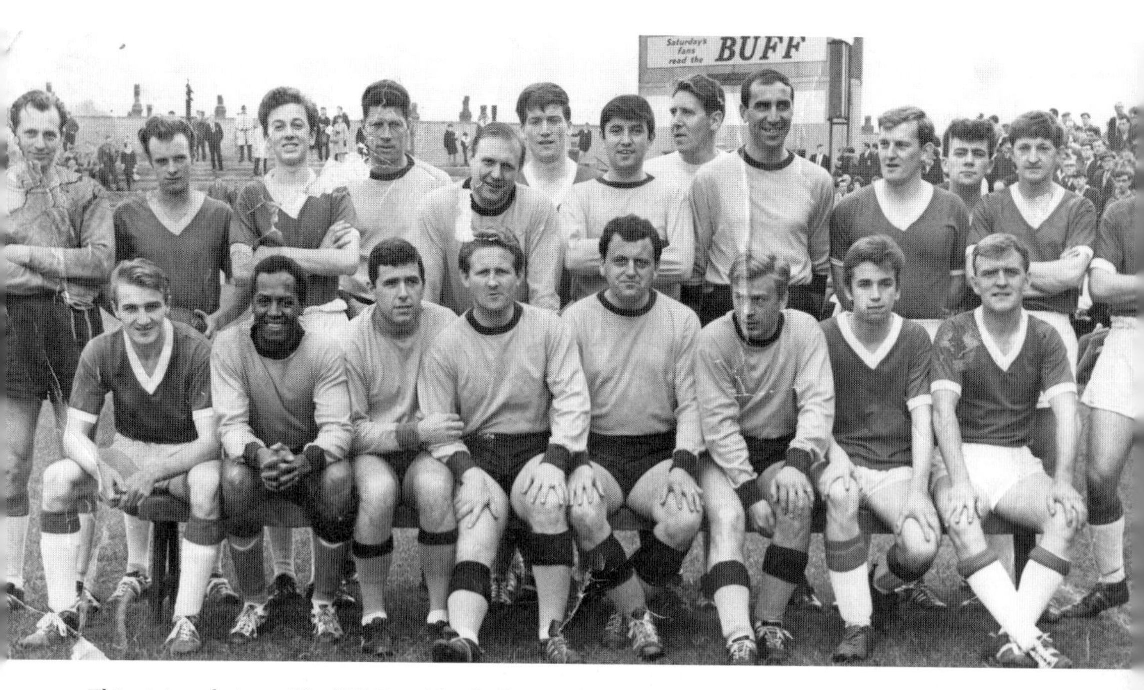

This picture features The 'TV Stars' football team in the light-coloured shirts and the William Tatton team in the darker shirts. Jimmy Tarbuck is in the centre of the back row with his arms folded. The place and date of this photograph are sadly unknown.

4

EVENTS AND CELEBRATIONS

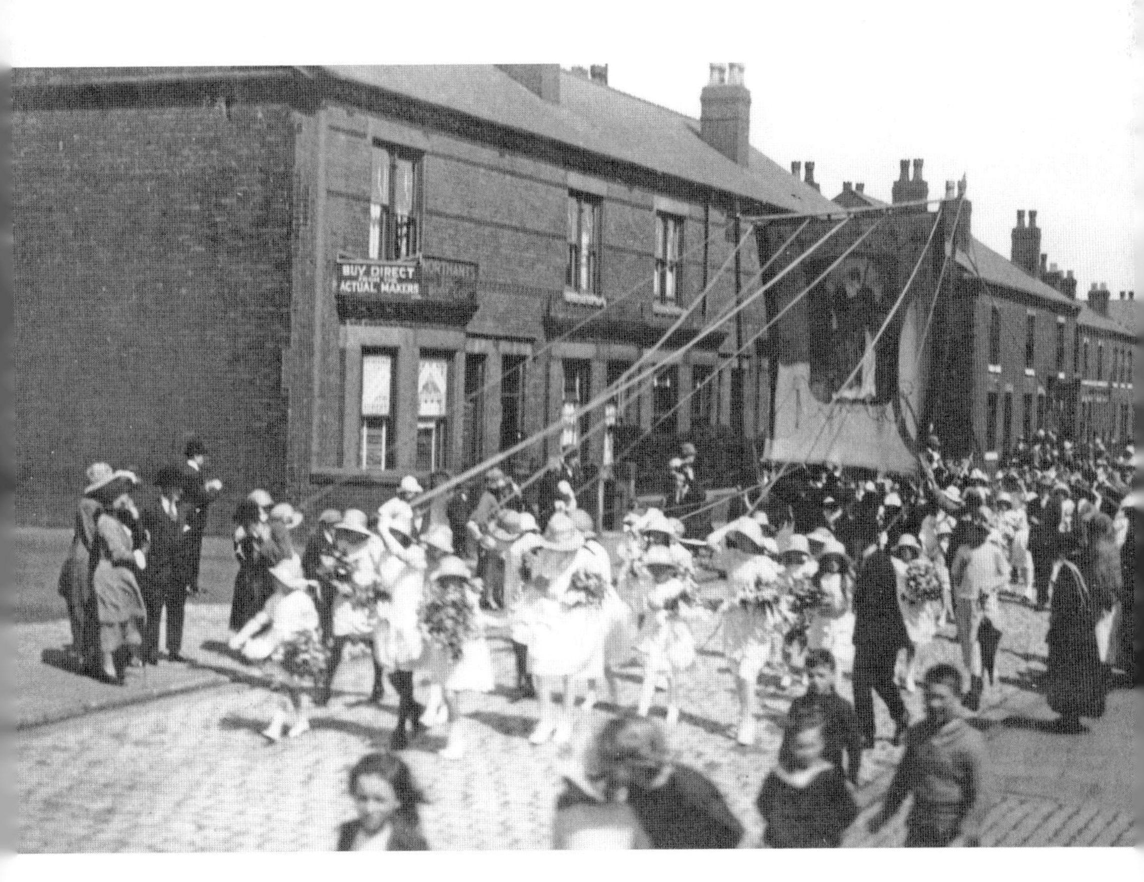

Taken in 1922 on Heath Street, Golborne, this picture shows the St Thomas' Walking Day procession passing Northant's shop.

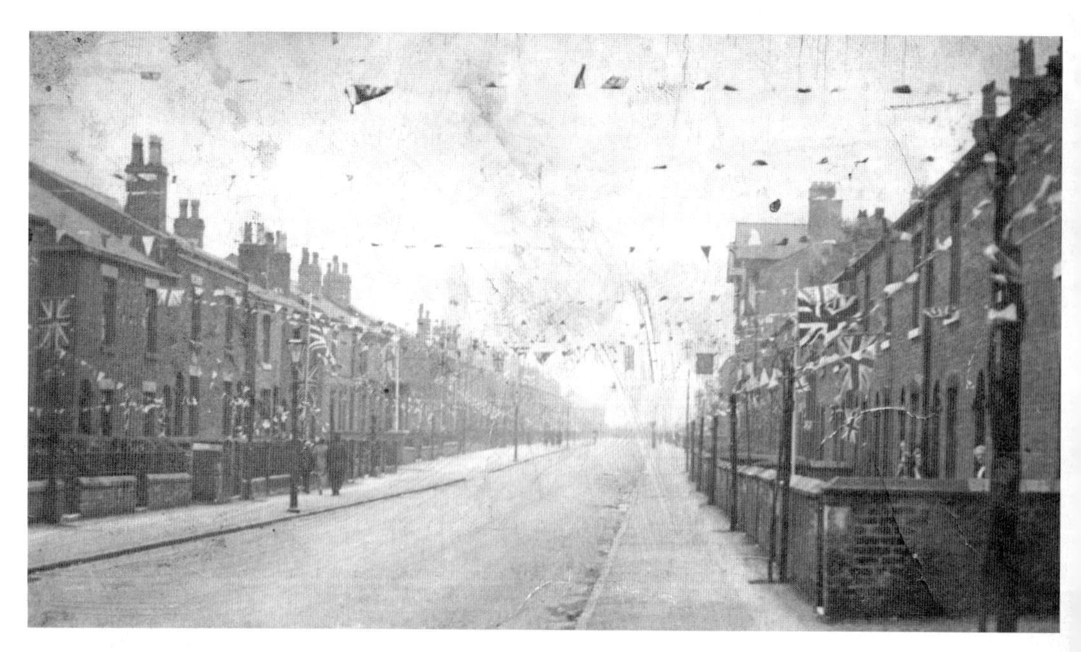

Captured in 1953, this image shows a decorated Bank Street, decked out with bunting and flags for the Coronation celebrations for Queen Elizabeth II.

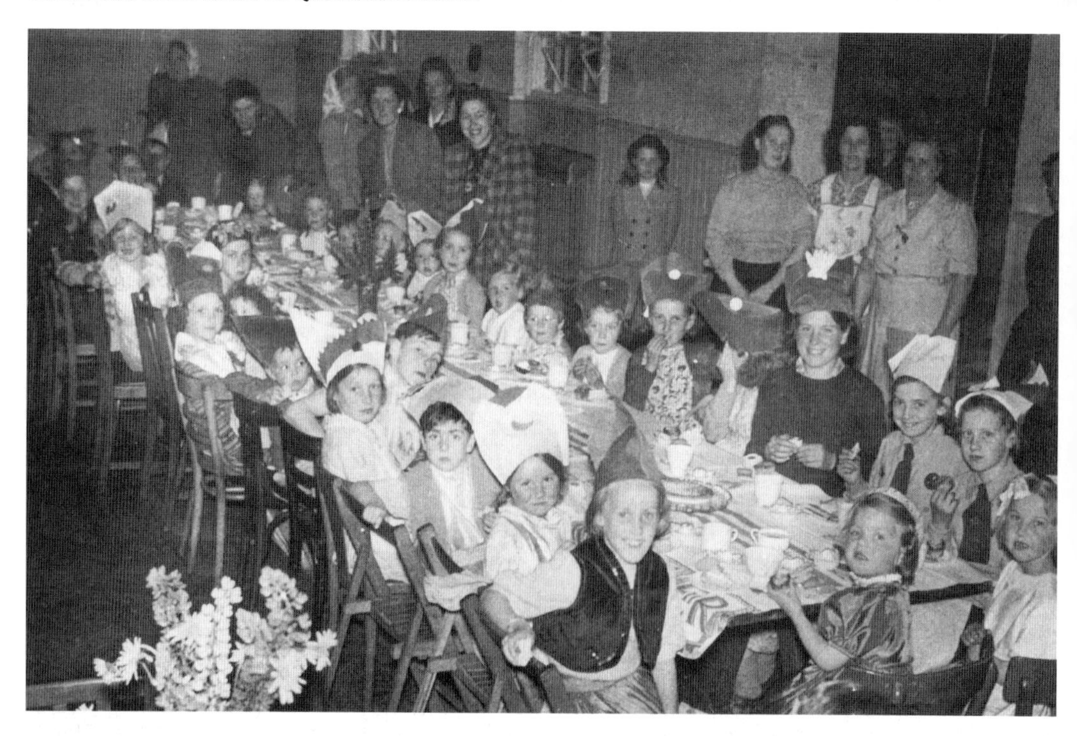

Taken in 1953, this picture again shows Bank Street's Coronation celebrations. The children of Bank Street are at the British Legion Club, the drill hall doubling as the dining hall for the celebrations. As you can see by all the smiling faces, a good time was had by the children and adults alike! This building used to be used to train recruits for the army.

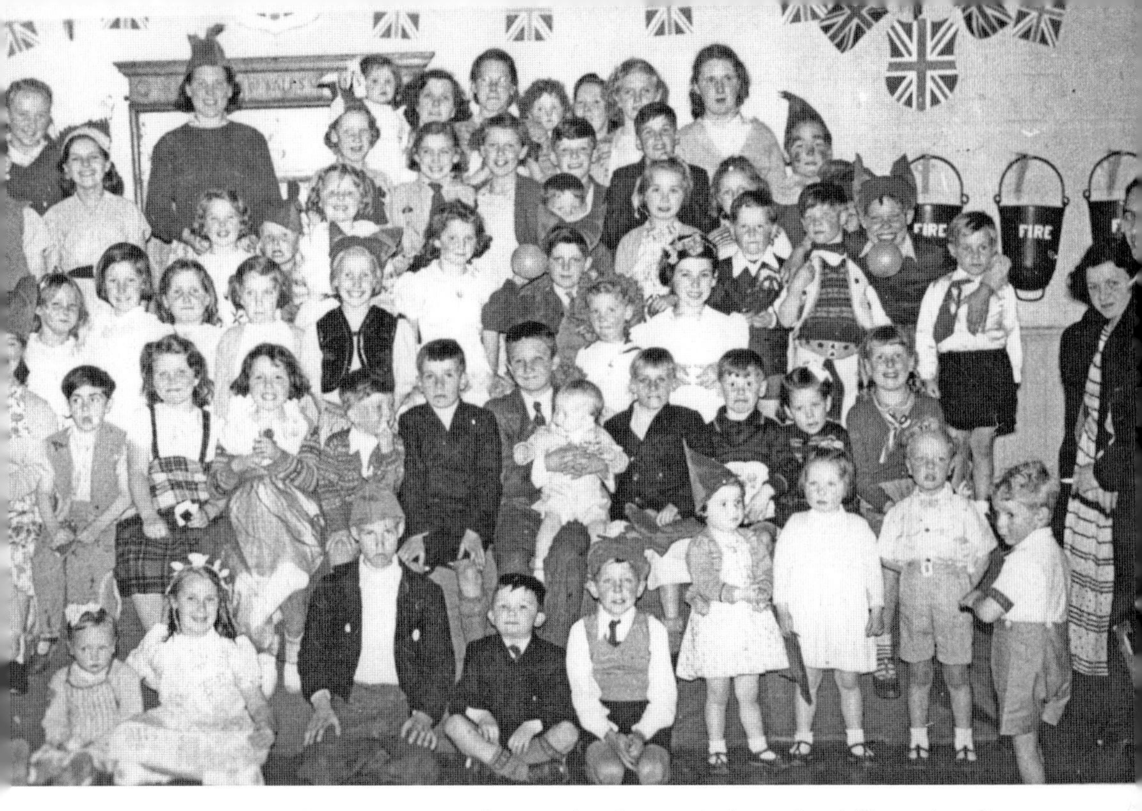

Taken on the same day as the two previous photographs, this image shows the children of Bank Street posing for a photograph to mark the occasion of the Coronation after their celebration lunch.

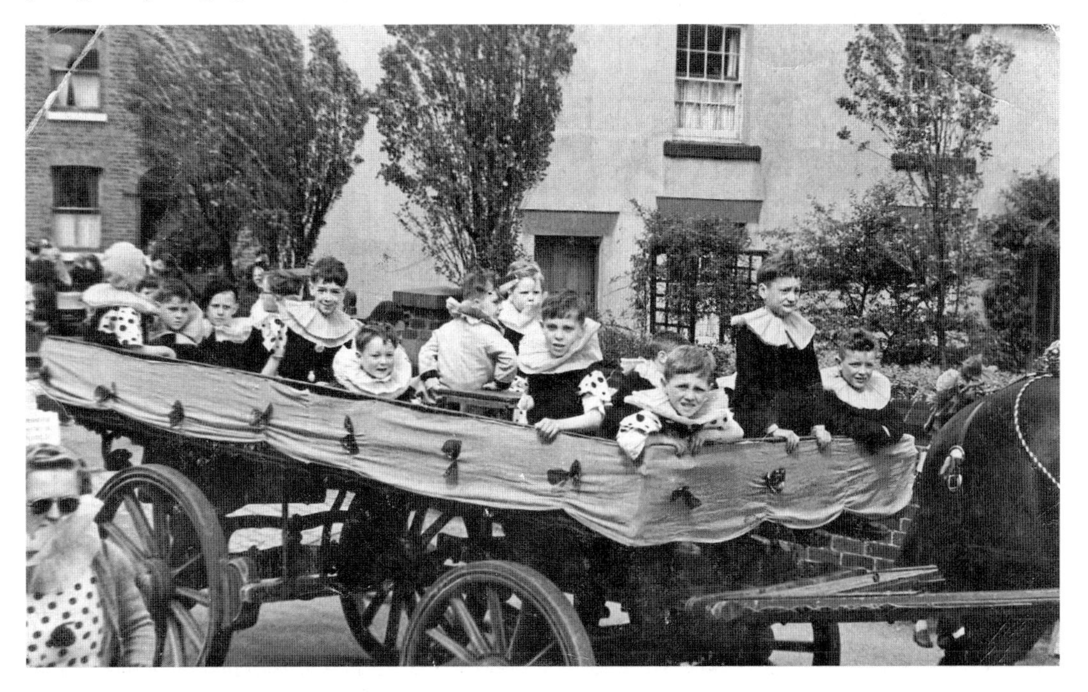

This photograph shows a group of children looking like they are having a lot of fun on a truck in Peter Street. Behind the truck is Heath Street. The white building used to be Mrs Ralph's corner shop, and is today a private house.

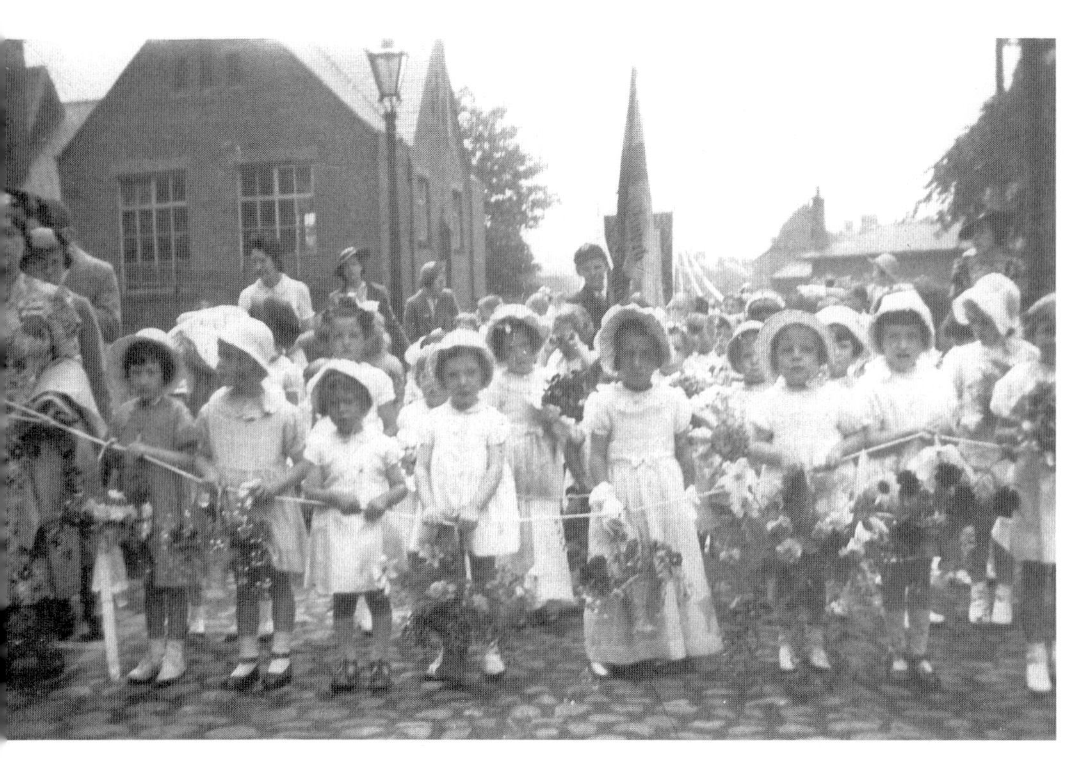

This picture shows St Thomas' Walking Day in 1939, and was taken just outside the church and school. I'm sure you'll agree the children look quite angelic, clad all in white with their bonnets.

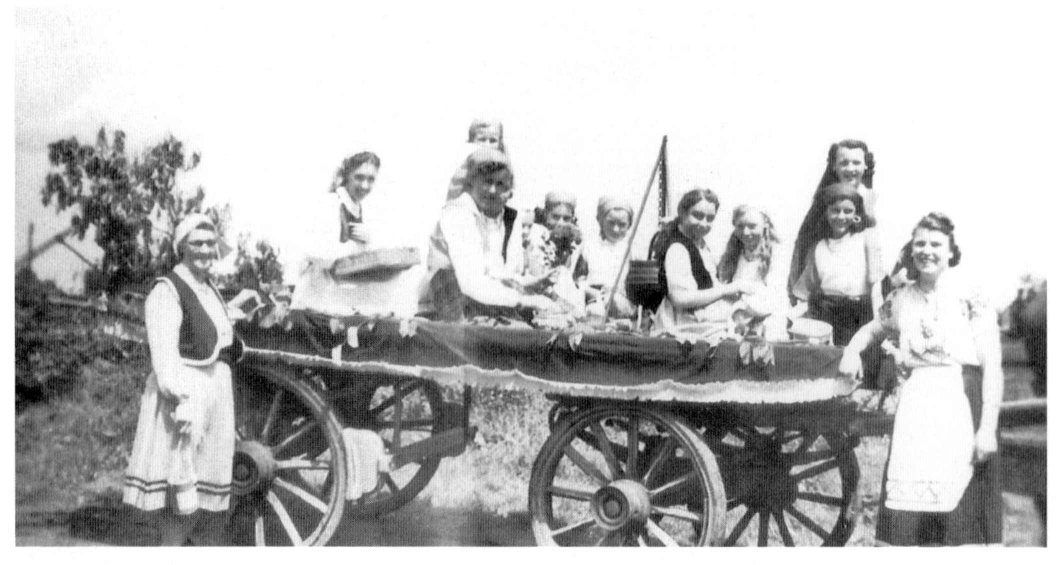

Taken in 1949, this image shows a carnival float by a farm, which today is Beech Road off Charles Street. The lady on the right is Mrs Jenkinson, farm owner, and her daughter, Barbara, is at the back on the right-hand side.

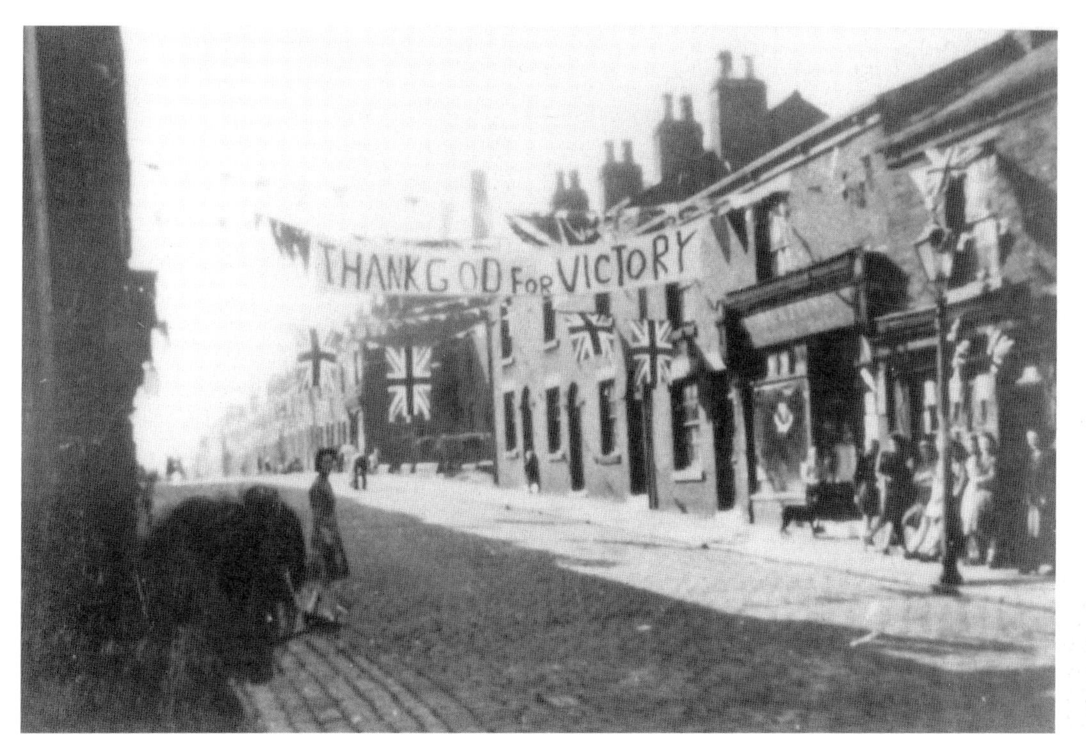

Captured on 8 May 1945, this picture shows the VE-day celebrations on Legh Street. Celebrating the end of the Second World War, the whole of Great Britain showed her relief by staging street parties. With rationing still in place, the residents of Legh Street managed to produce a worthy and enjoyable celebration.

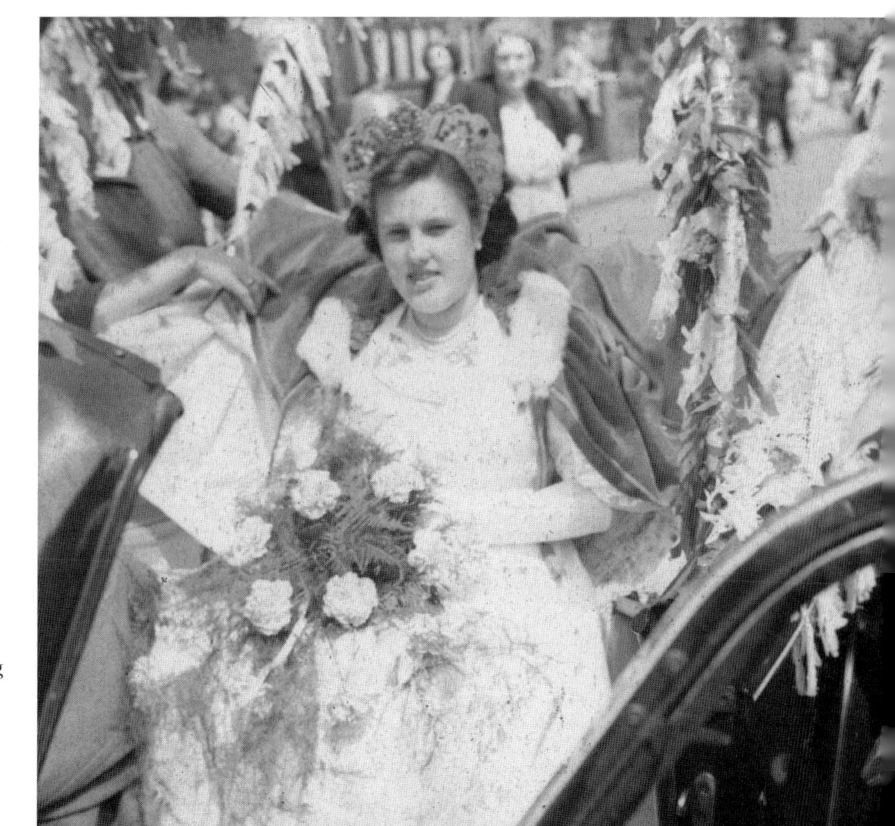

This rather lovely photograph shows the 1951 Golborne May Queen, a Miss Pauline Rubottom. She was crowned by Mrs I. Lang of Ealing.

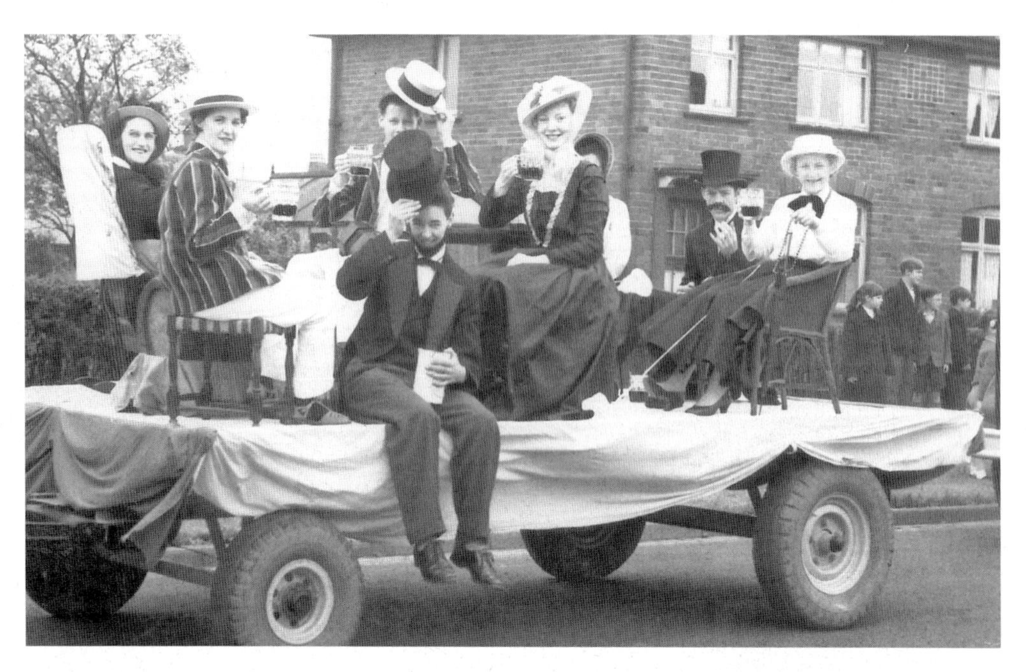

This is St Thomas' Amateur Dramatic group's carnival float in 1959 or 1960. Parked in Derby Road, the group are preparing to begin the carnival procession, in costume no less!

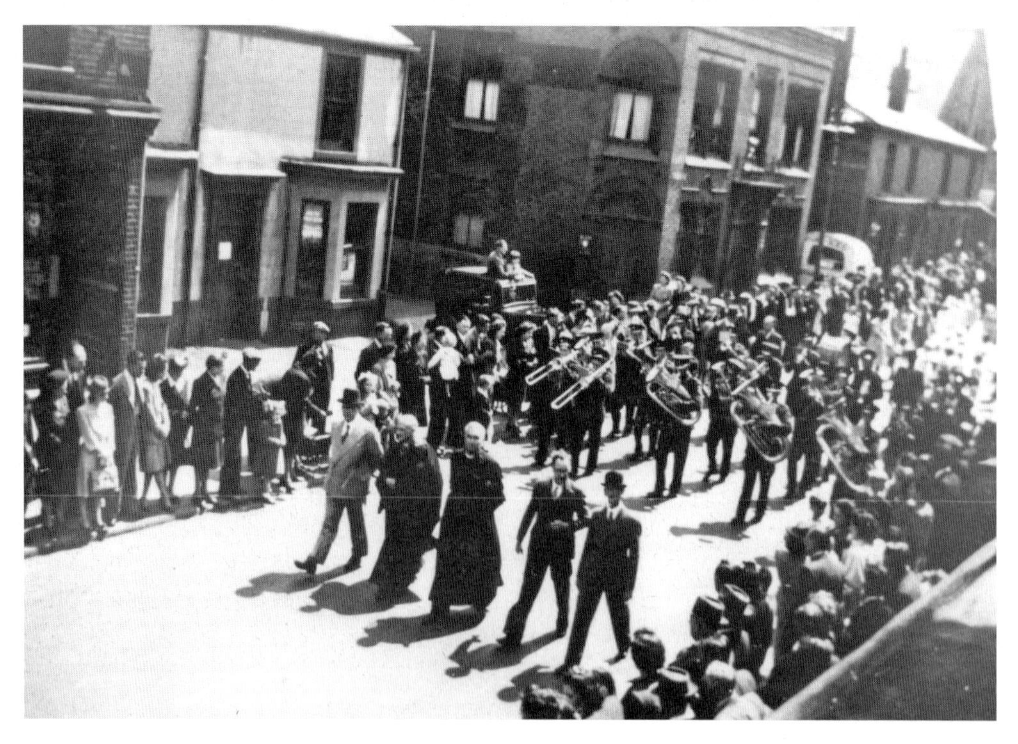

This photograph shows the first Walking Day after the end of the Second World War. The Prince of Wales public house can be seen here, but nowadays the site has changed completely, as it has been demolished. The picture was taken on High Street.

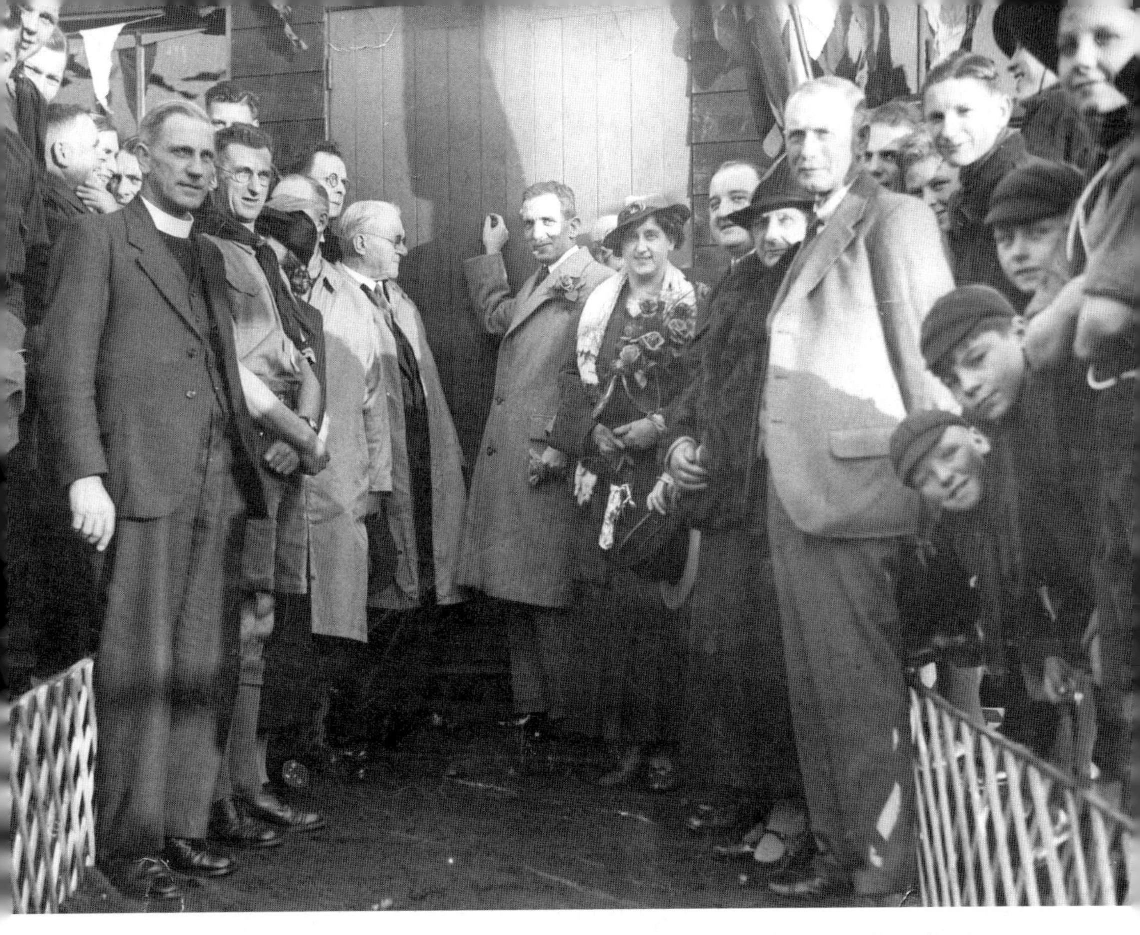

This photograph shows the opening of the scout hut on Church Street in about 1935. In the picture are Elaine Pilling, Revd M. Gaskell (rector) and Harold Bailey (Scout Master).

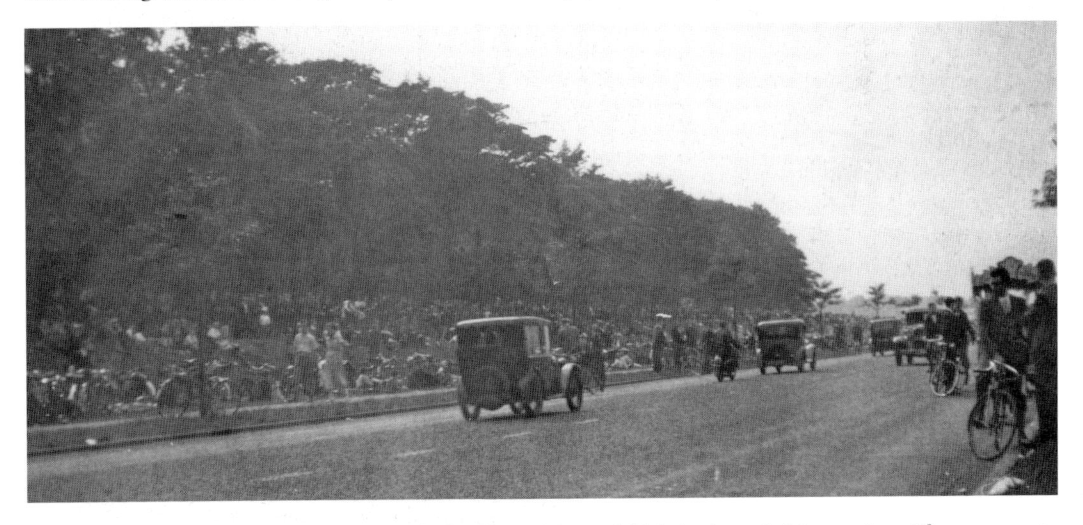

This picture of the East Lancashire Road, dated 16 August 1936, is shrouded in mystery. There seems to be a large gathering of people, presumably waiting for a big name to pass by. Is it royalty? A sporting hero perhaps? Or maybe even a movie star of the time? I'm sure after seeing this picture, someone's memory might be jogged.

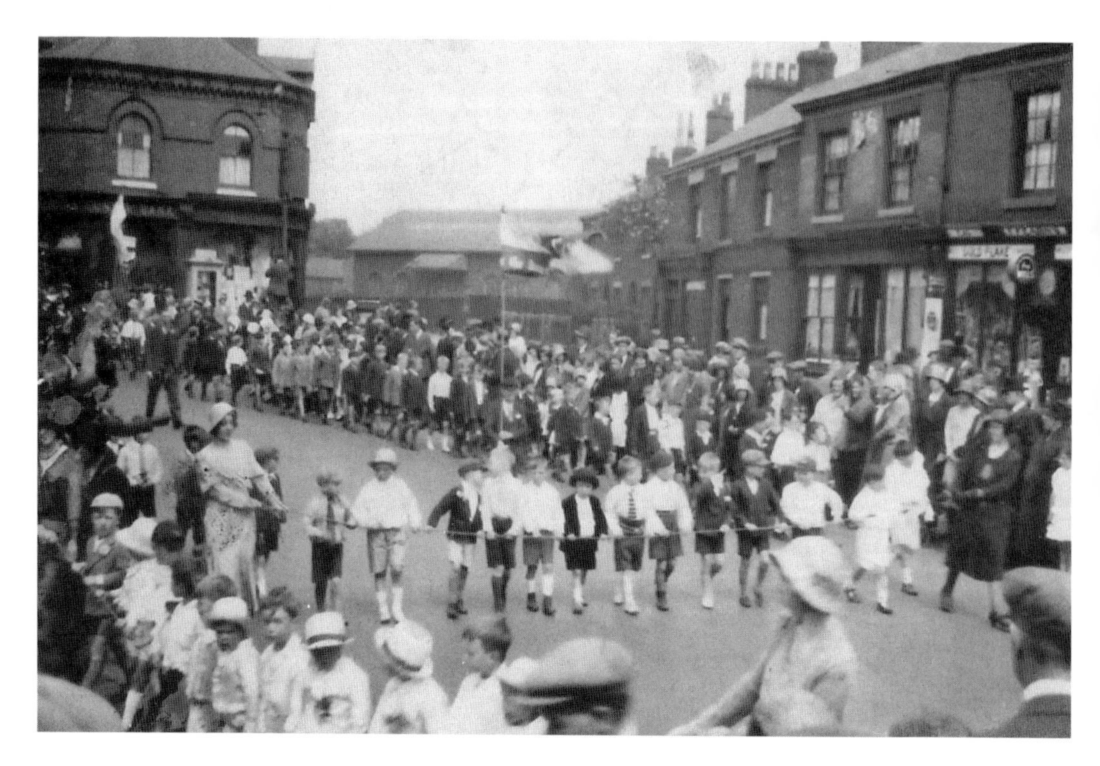

Possibly taken during the early 1930s, this picture captures another St Thomas' Walking Day. Clearly a lot of people turned up to spectate.

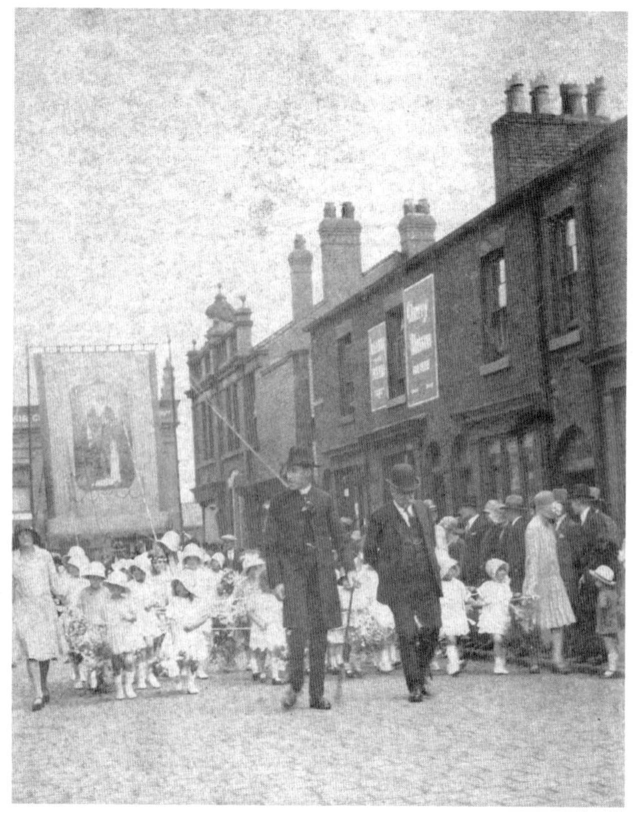

This photograph again shows another St Thomas' Walking Day from the early 1930s, passing up Heath Street. As was typical with the route at the time this picture was taken, the procession would have started from the church on Church Street, going through Heywood Avenue and Lowton Road to the Red Lion public house, then back through Church Street again, followed by Charles Street, Bank Street, Heath Street, High Street and Church Street again. Finally, the procession would rest in the church or on the field where Cottesmore Way is now.

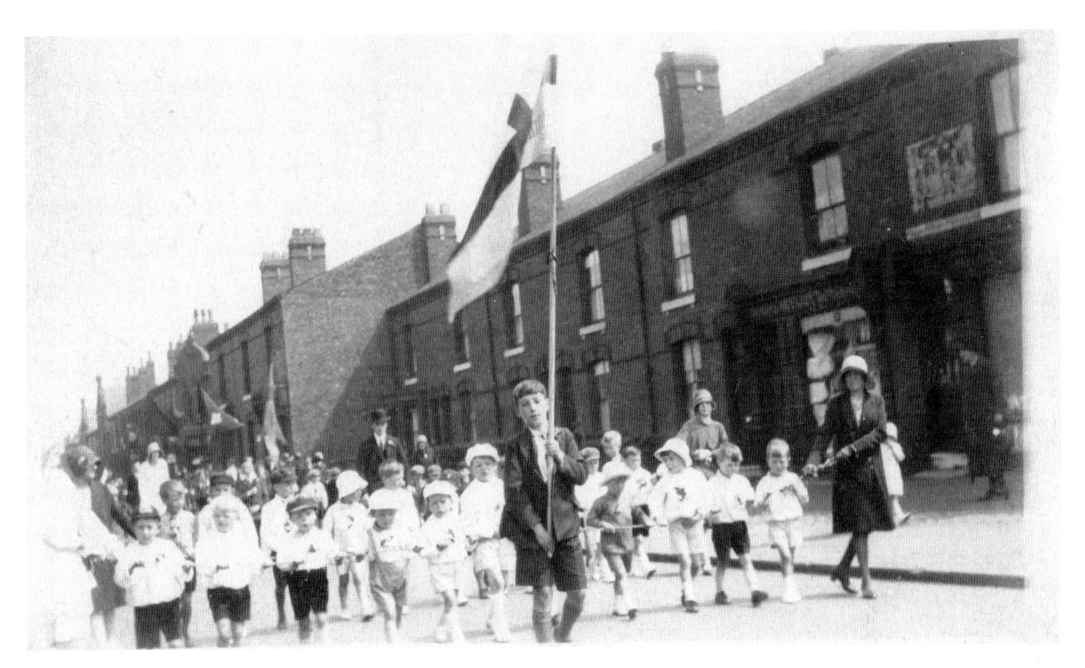

This photograph, dated 17 June 1930, features another Walking Day parade passing through Heath Street, typically being led by a young gentleman wielding a flag. Mylott's shop can be seen on the right-hand side of the picture.

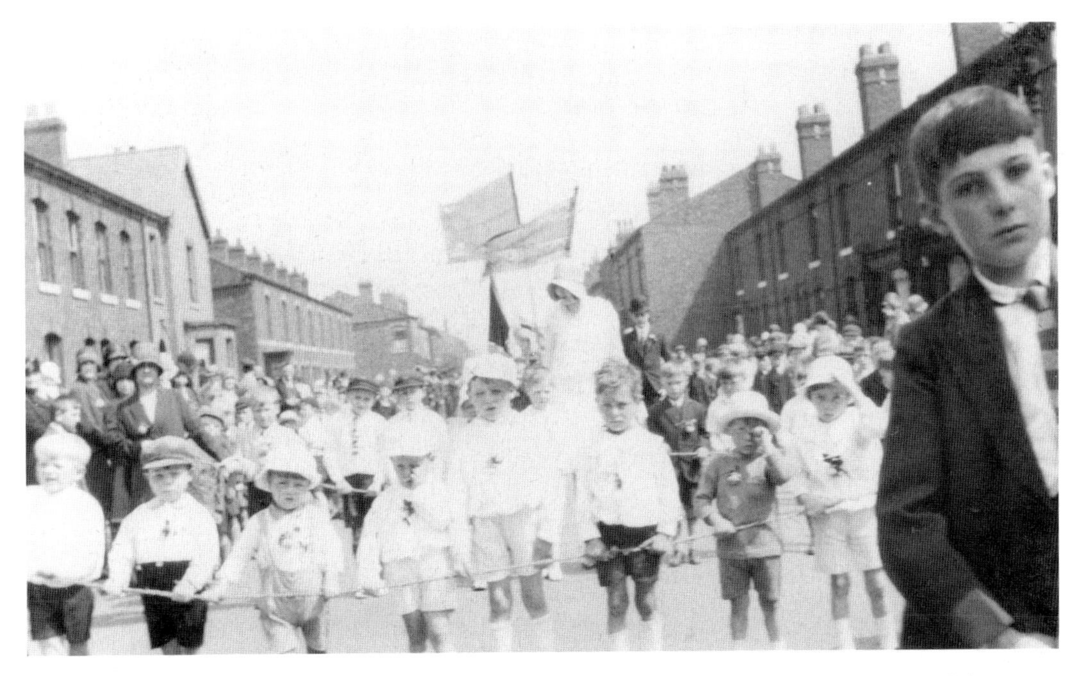

This photograph was taken on the same day as the previous picture, this time in the middle of the action by the front rope of children, who all seem very curious as to why they are being photographed!

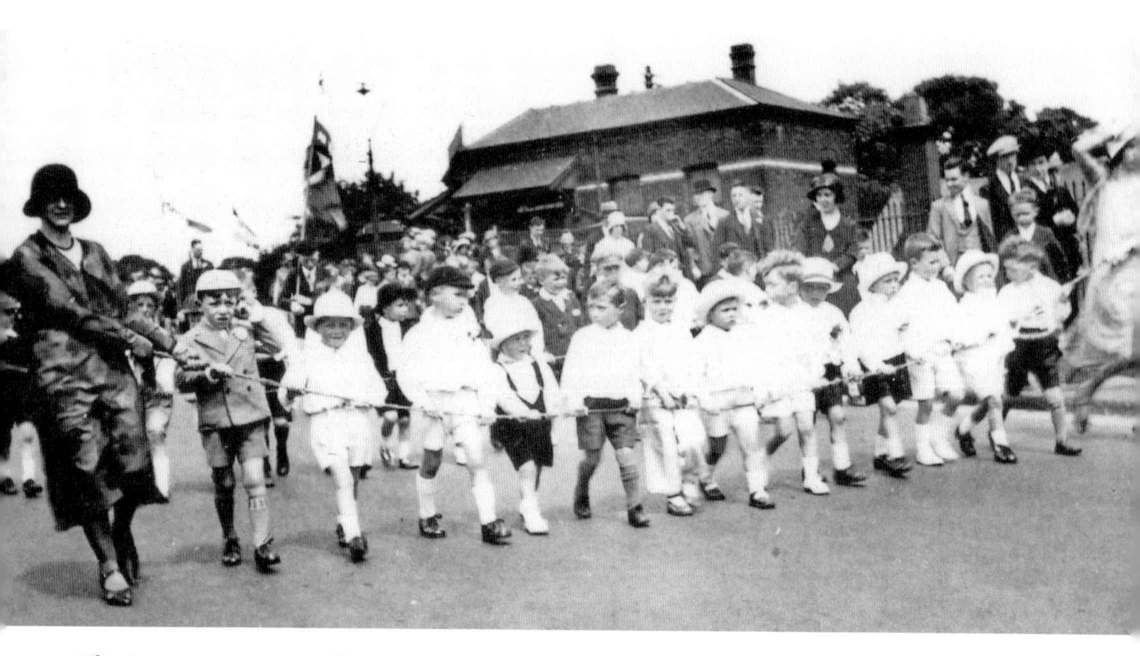

This image captures a Walking Day, this time in the 1920s. The location of the picture is on the railway bridge outside the railway station.

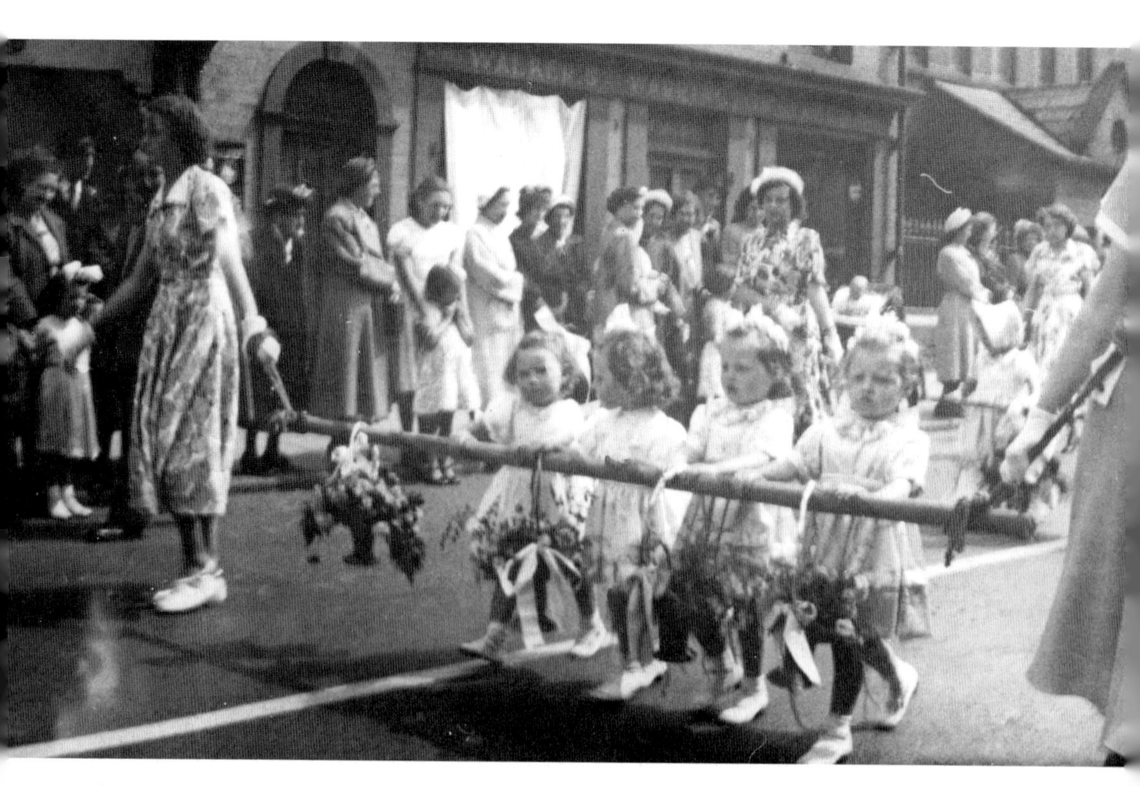

A beautiful photograph of a Walking Day procession in 1953. You can see 'Auntie Nellies' shop, as it was affectionately known, in the background.

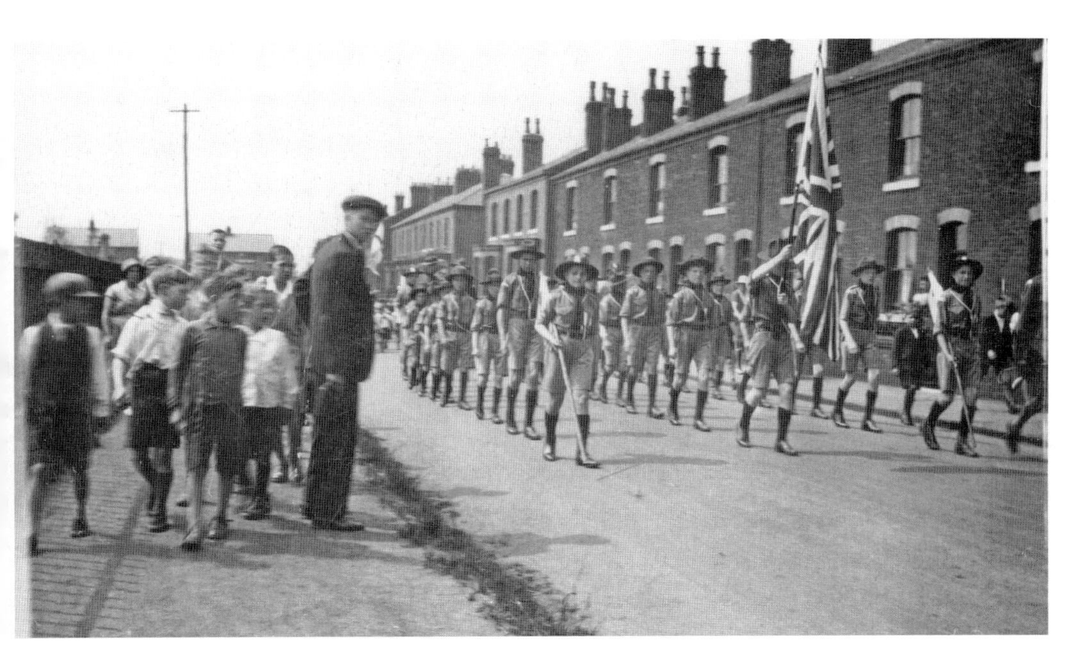

Dated 3 July 1933, this picture shows the local scouts walking down Legh Street on Walking Day, with a few spectators on the left-hand side of the photograph.

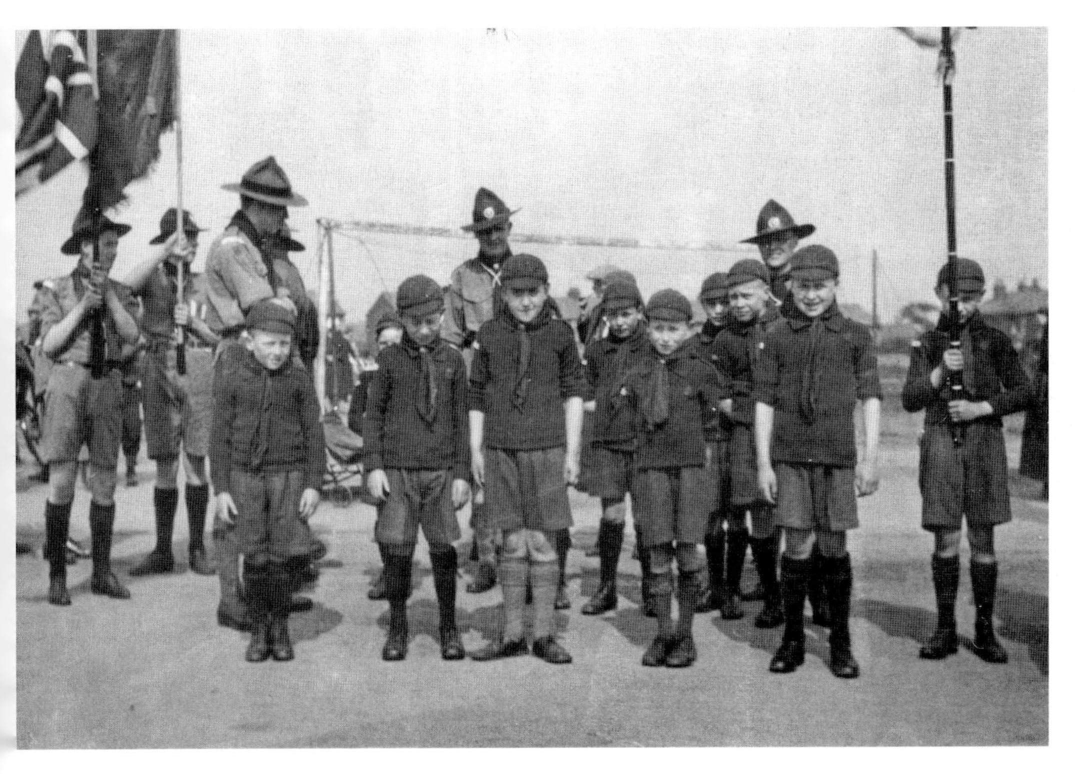

Captured on 6 May 1935, this image shows a group of scouts in Legh Street park, possibly having a rest after the Walking Day.

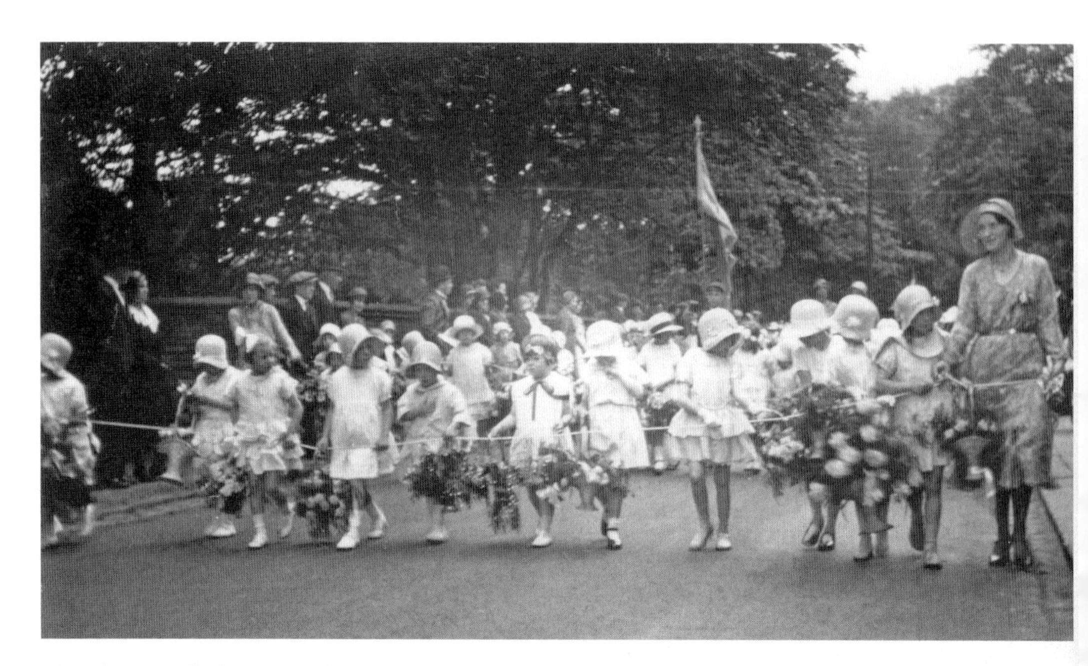

This photograph shows a Walking Day parade in the 1930s, venturing down Bridge Street towards High Street.

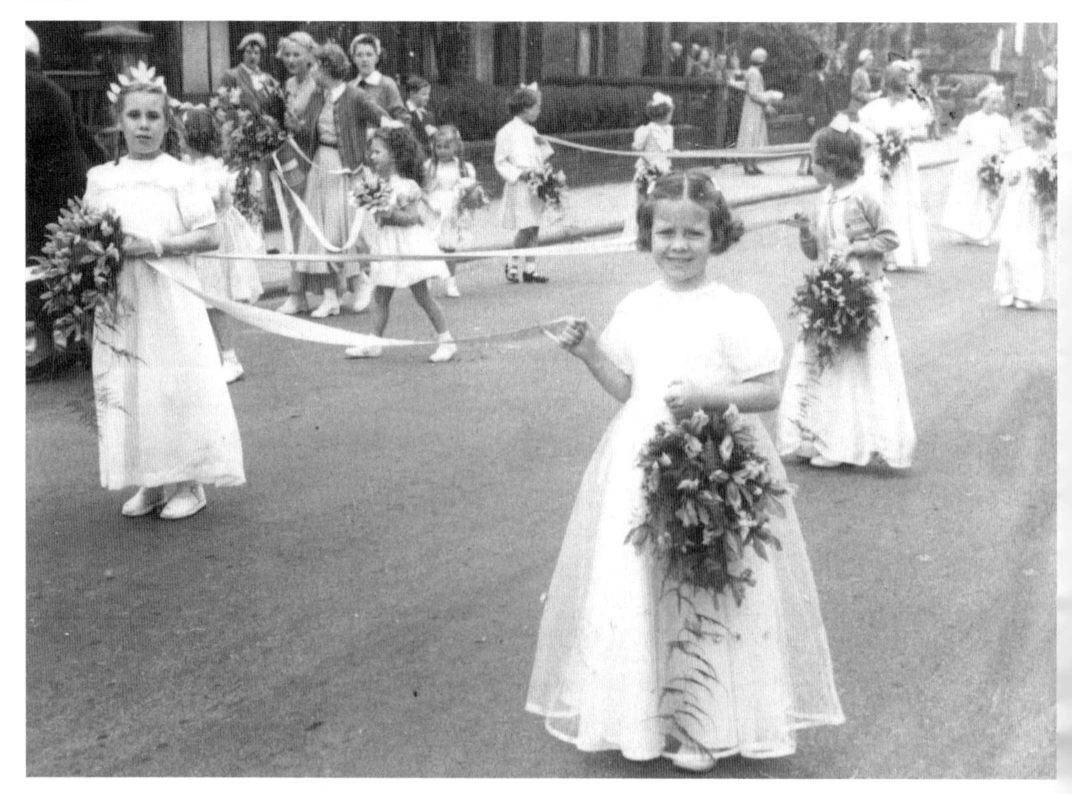

Taken in 1954, this picture shows a Walking Day parade passing the Baptist Church in Charles Street, with the girls in traditional dress.

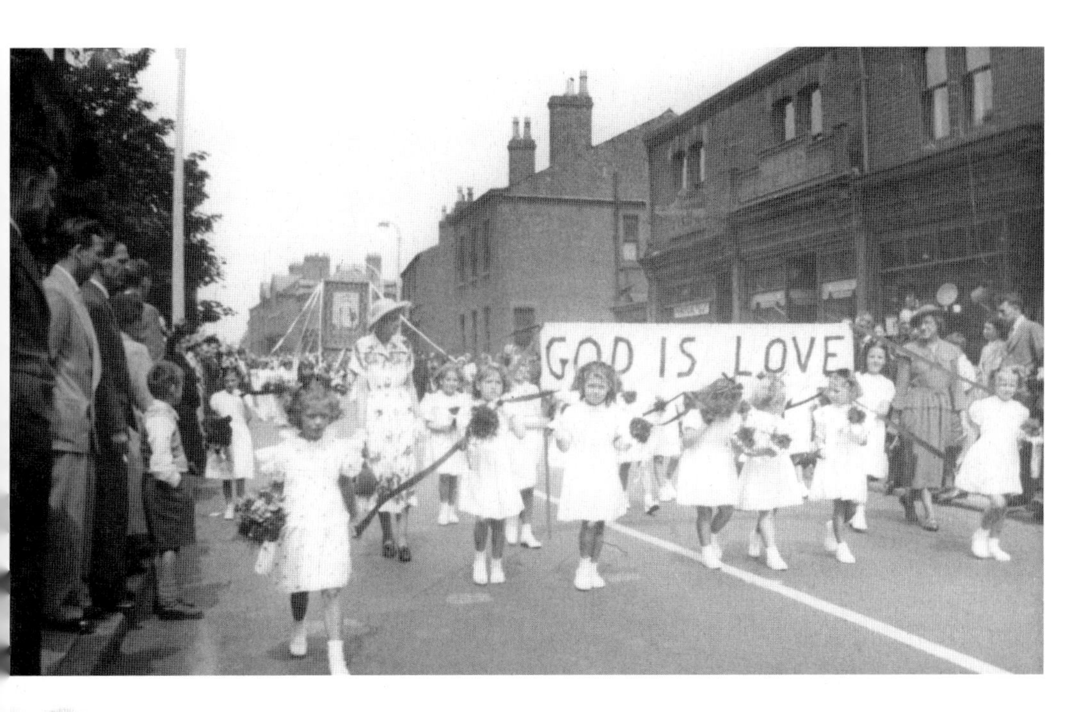

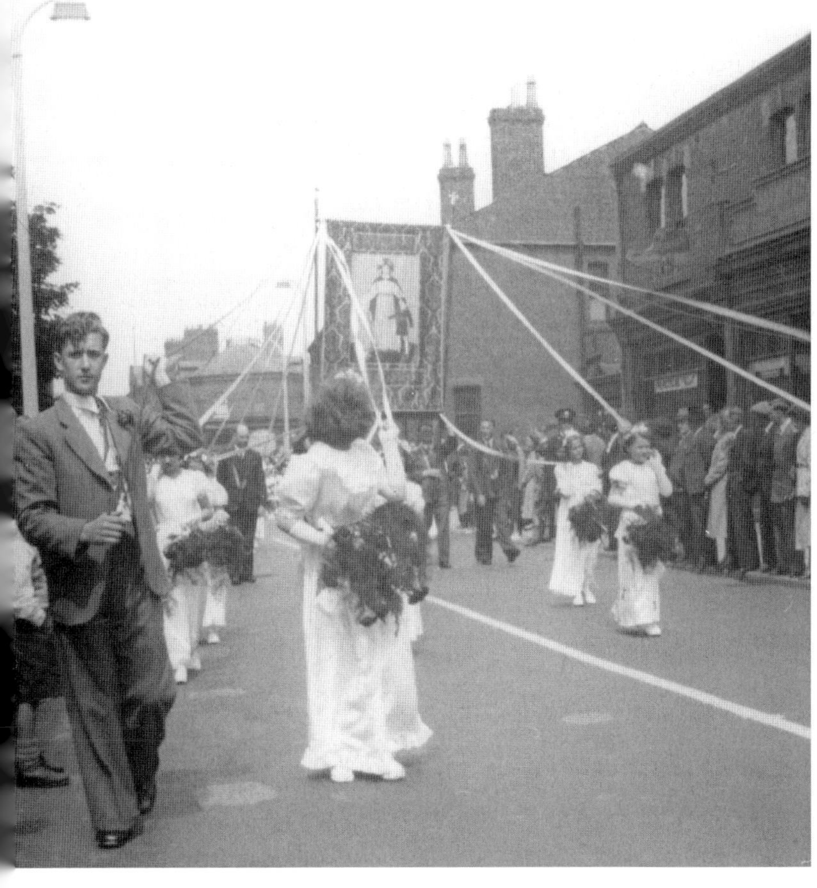

Taken in the 1950s, this picture shows the Walking Day parade on their procession down High Street. You can see Mort's shop and Howarth's to the right of the photograph with the crowds in front of them.

An alternative shot of the same Walking Day parade.

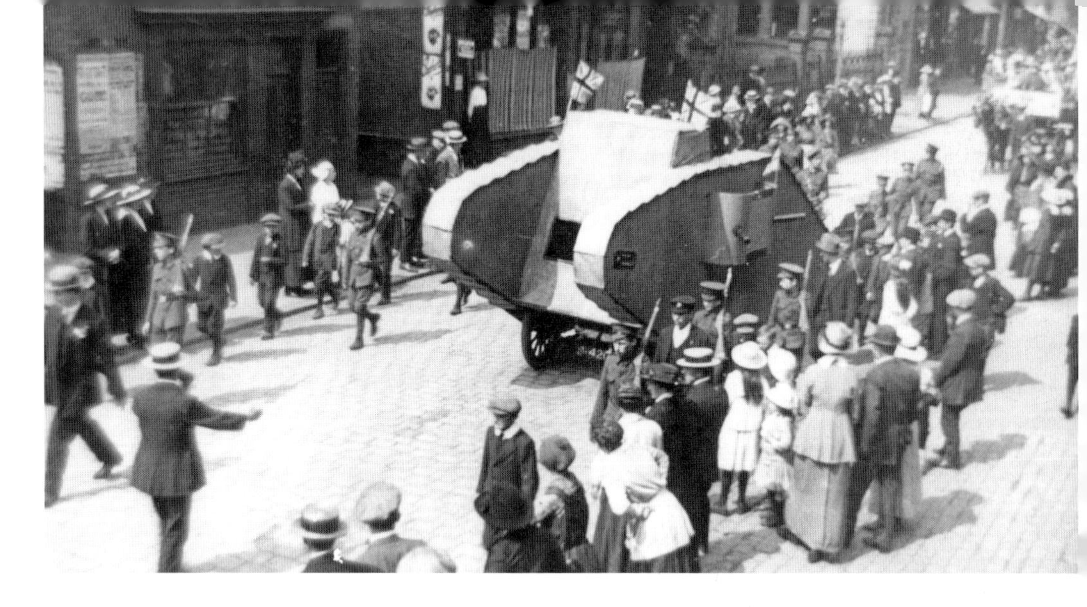

This photograph shows Naylor's tank at the carnival on 20 May 1918. The tank was built out of wood by brothers Joe and Ernie Richards, who worked at Naylor's engineering, and the pair named it Humpy Joe's tank. This nickname was given to Mr Joe Unsworth, who, unfortunately, was born with a humped back. Not considered fit for active duty in the Great War, he was somehow called up to fight in March of 1918. The Richards brothers went to see Mr Unsworth's mother and asked if they could borrow Joe's car to place the frame of the tank over. Mrs Unsworth said yes but there was no petrol in it. Fuel was obviously in short supply with the war on. They managed to acquire some petrol, and proudly paraded Humpy's tank in the carnival. The man in the straw boater hat at the front of the photograph is Mr Richard Walker. He had to guide the driver of the tank around the streets of Golborne as he couldn't see where he was going!

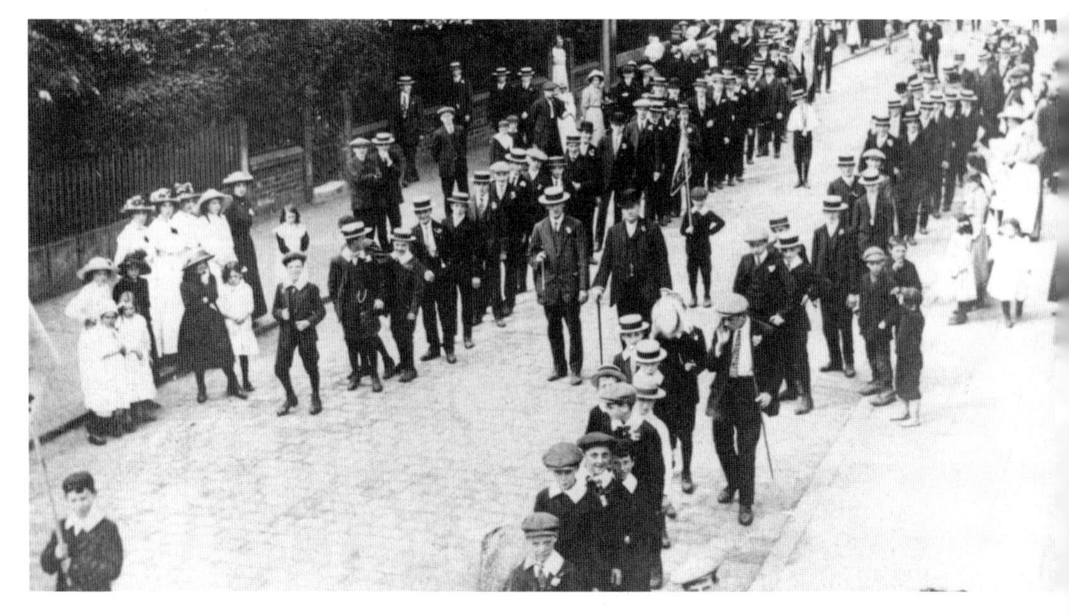

This is a photograph of the Walking Day parade from the early 1900s on the High Street. We can make an estimation as to the approximate date from the hats the men are wearing. The straw boater, or skimmer, was worn from the beginning of the 1900s by barber shop quartets, punters, schoolchildren and gentlemen of every type. This type of hat is typically used to emulate the 1920s style by modern-day fancy dress shops.

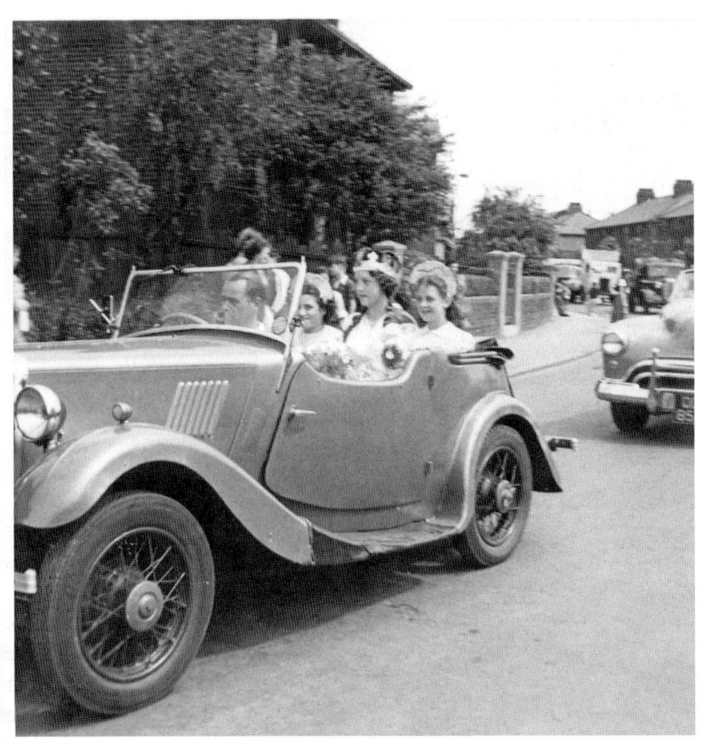

This photograph belongs to a collection possibly dating from the late 1950s, early '60s. This picture shows the new May Queen on her journey to the ceremony in a lovely old-fashioned car, where she will receive her crown for the following year.

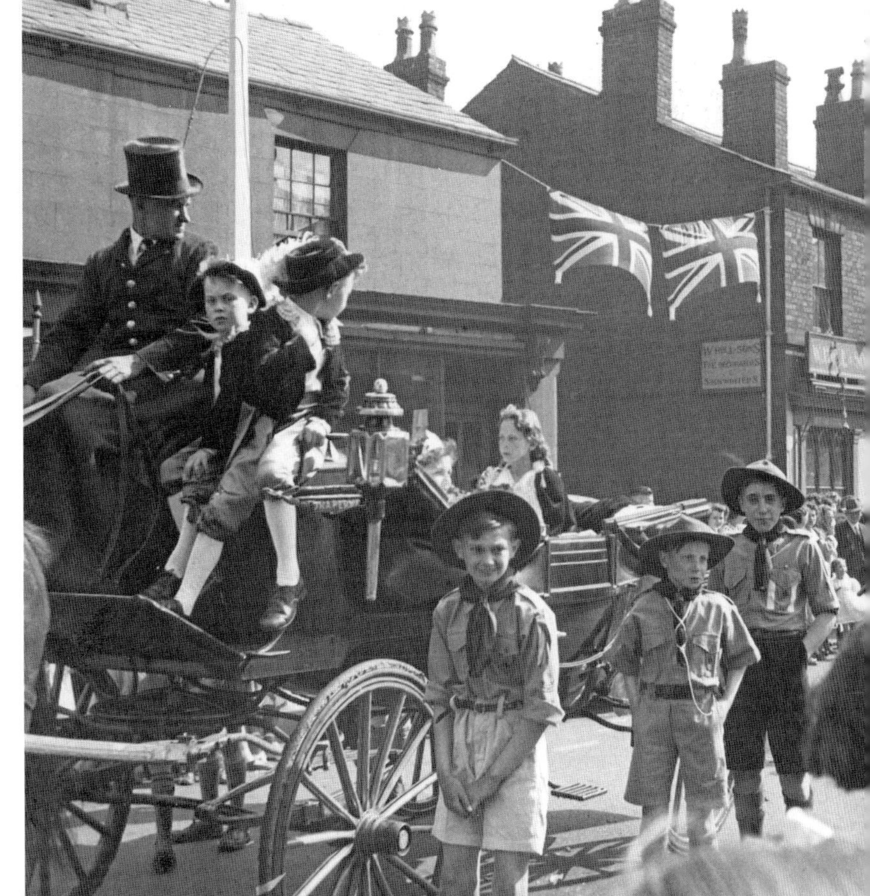

This photograph, possibly from the late 1950s, shows the carnival passing through the High Street. Visible in the background, behind the boy scouts and the float, is W. Hill & Sons, who were decorators and sign writers.

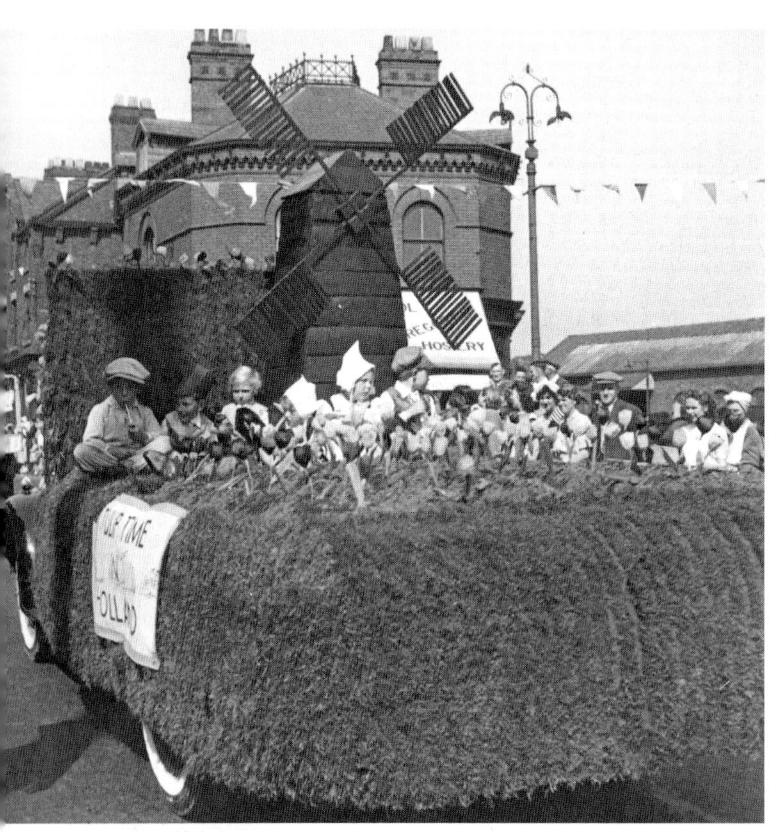

This photograph again shows the carnival, in the centre of Golborne. The building in the background to the right used to be a bacon distribution warehouse. The first May Queen carnival in Golborne was held in 1880; the first May Queen was Miss Jane Waddington. Golborne was one of the first towns in the surrounding area to have a carnival and people came from miles around to see the event.

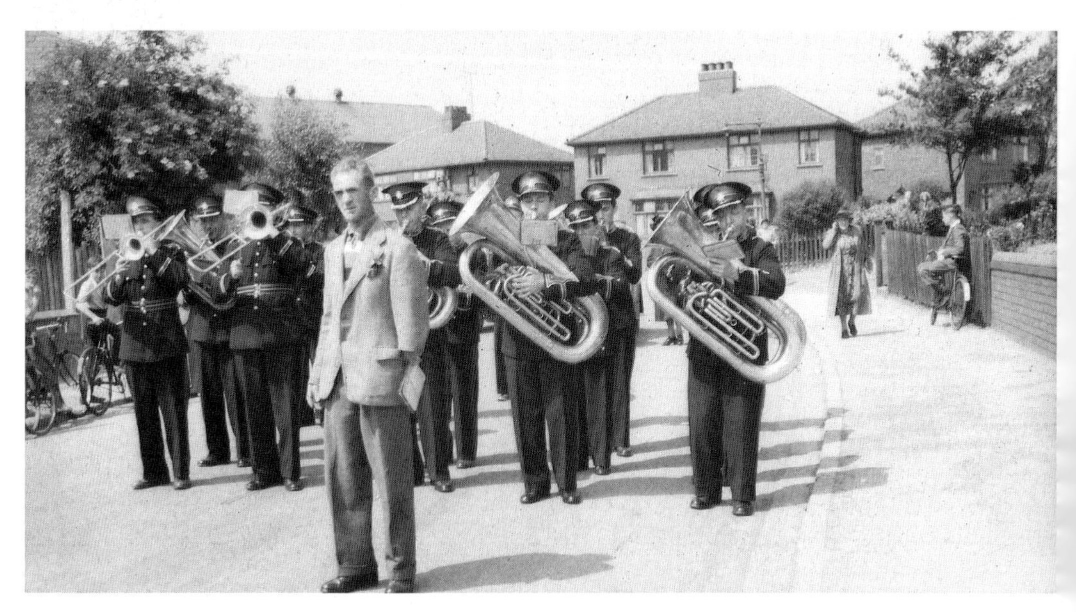

This picture, taken in 1951, shows the carnival brass band. The gentleman in front is Joe Woods; he was the drummer for quite a few years after taking over from his brother. The uniforms were bought by the Ladies' Committee. They were made from material that made the band sweat in the hot weather! James Gordon Green is in the middle somewhere as well as his brother (name unknown).

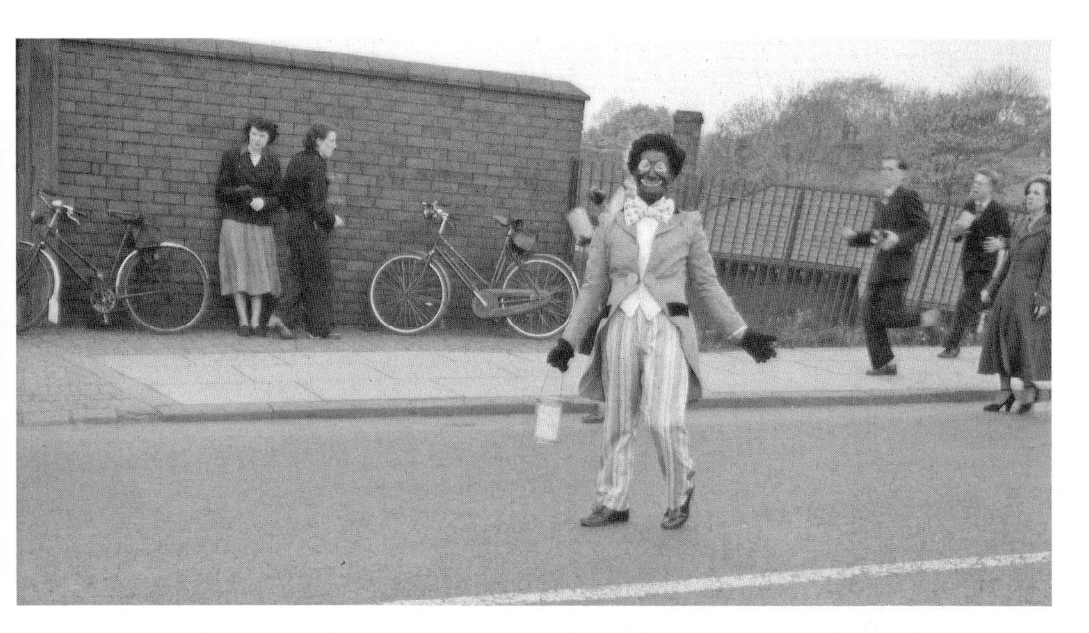

This photograph of the carnival, was again taken in 1951. Taken on the railway bridge, this character, according to the official carnival programme, is called the 'Silver Thread Golliwog'. This is not deemed as politically correct today, of course, but jam jars all over the world at the time were emblazoned with the character.

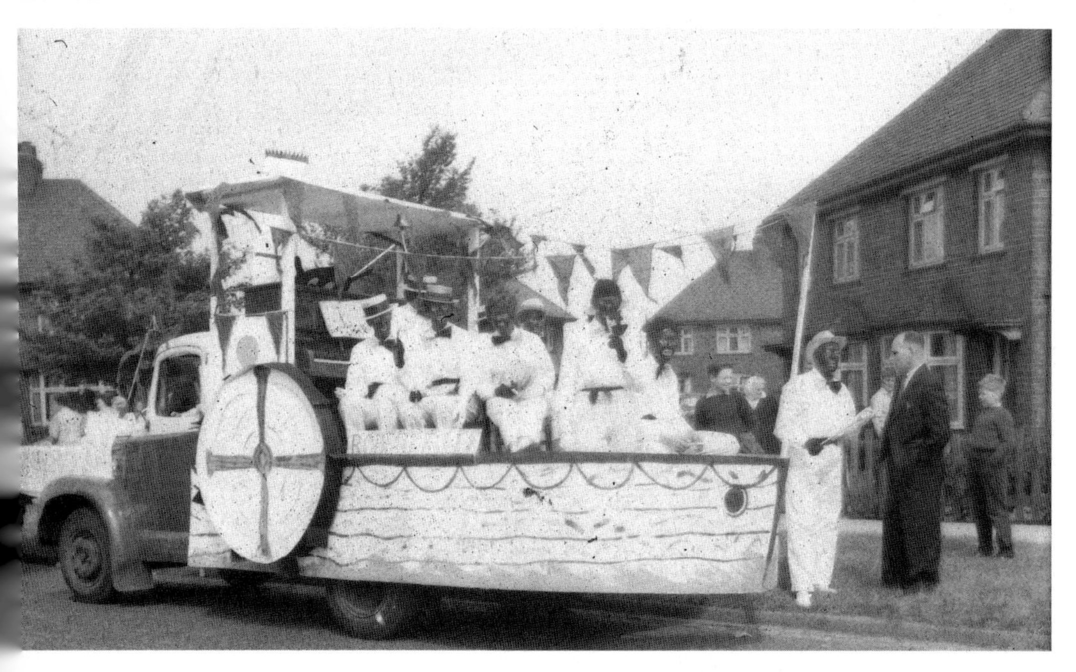

Taken in the early 1960s, this photograph shows a carnival float getting ready to start its journey in Derby Road. This picture shows a float honouring the 'Black and White Minstrel' show. This was a weekly, light entertainment and variety show, presenting traditional American minstrel and country songs, as well as music hall numbers. It ran from 1958 until 1978, but as is the case with the previous picture, the term and the act are no longer considered politically correct.

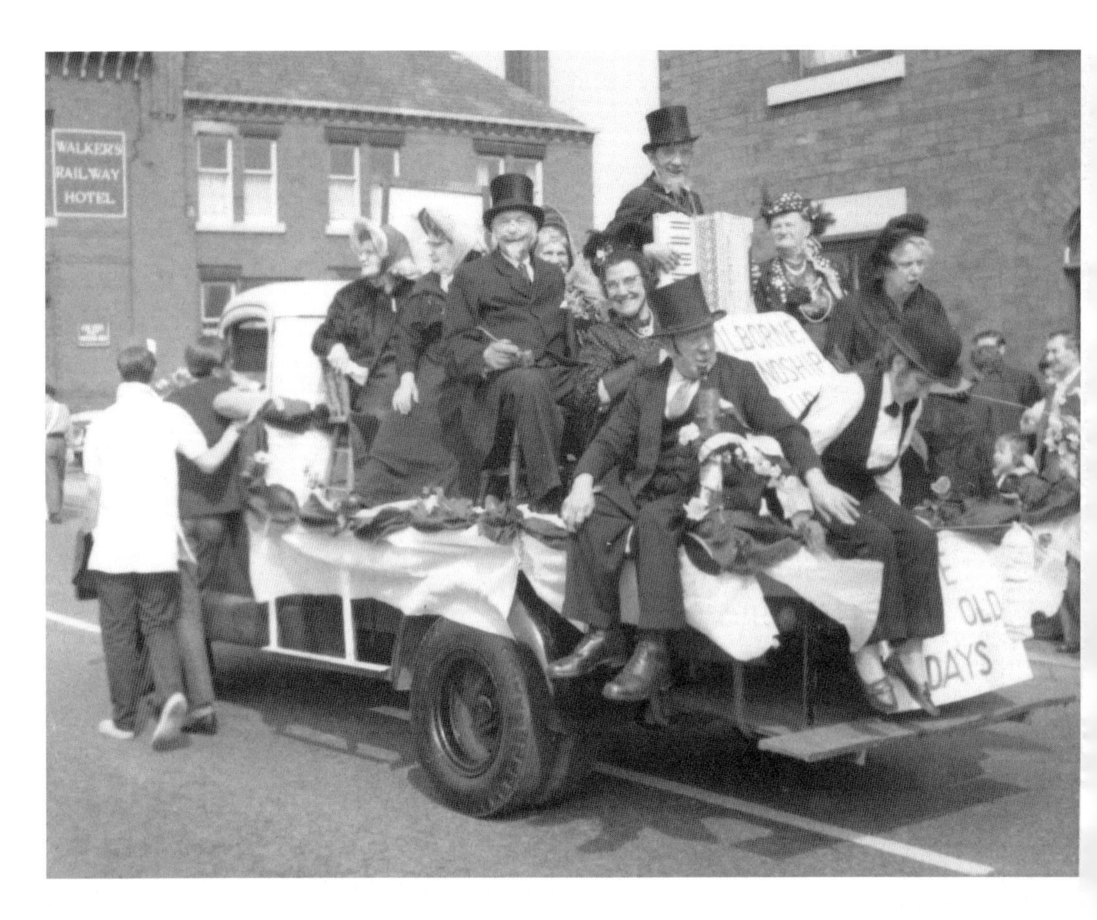
WALKER'S
RAILWAY
HOTEL
OLD
DAYS

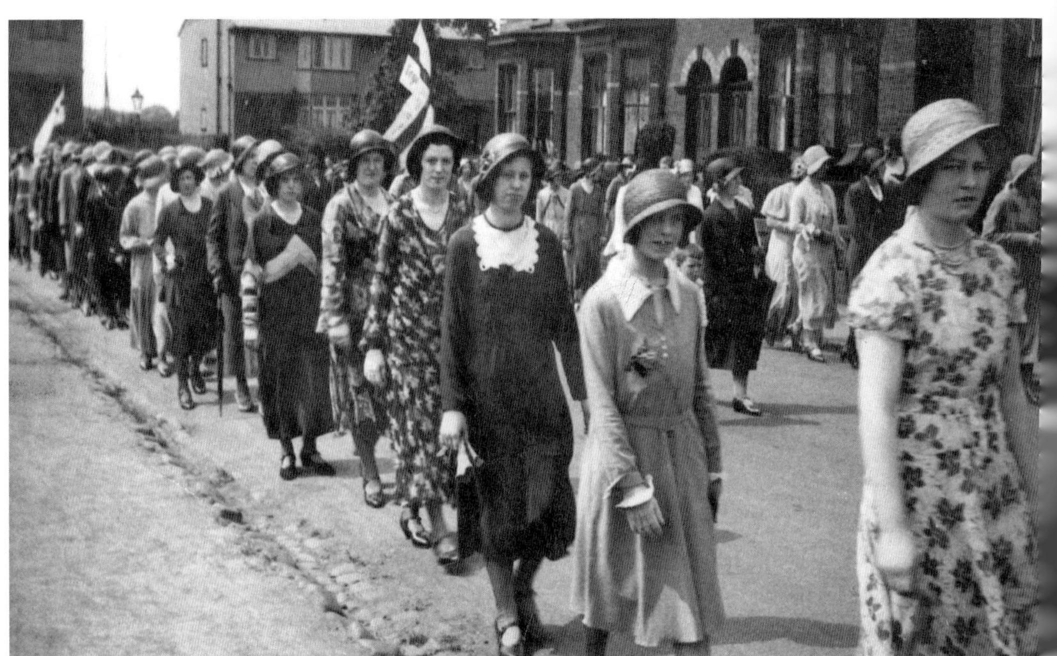

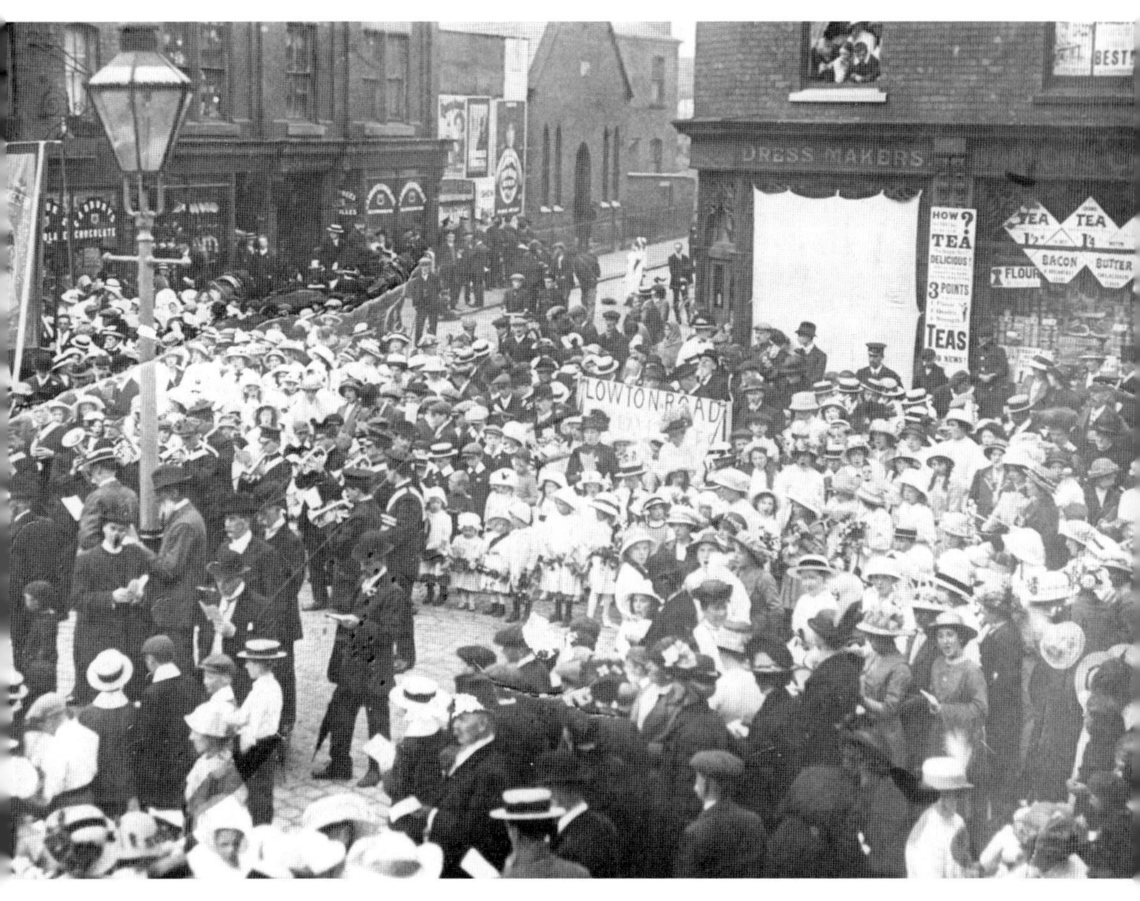

Taken around the turn of the century, this photograph shows the gathering of a very large crowd congregating by 'The Big Lamp' on carnival day. Barlow's grocery shop is visible in the background on the right-hand side.

Opposite above: This photograph captures a carnival in the 1960s outside The Railway public house. The man with the beard wearing a top hat in the centre of the photograph is a Mr Sutton. Also, in the background of the photo towards the left, is the Walker's Railway Hotel.

Opposite below: This picture was taken on a Walking Day during the 1920s, and the decade is evident from the hats and general attire of the women in the photograph. The parade would have gone down Legh Street, then head towards Bridge Street.

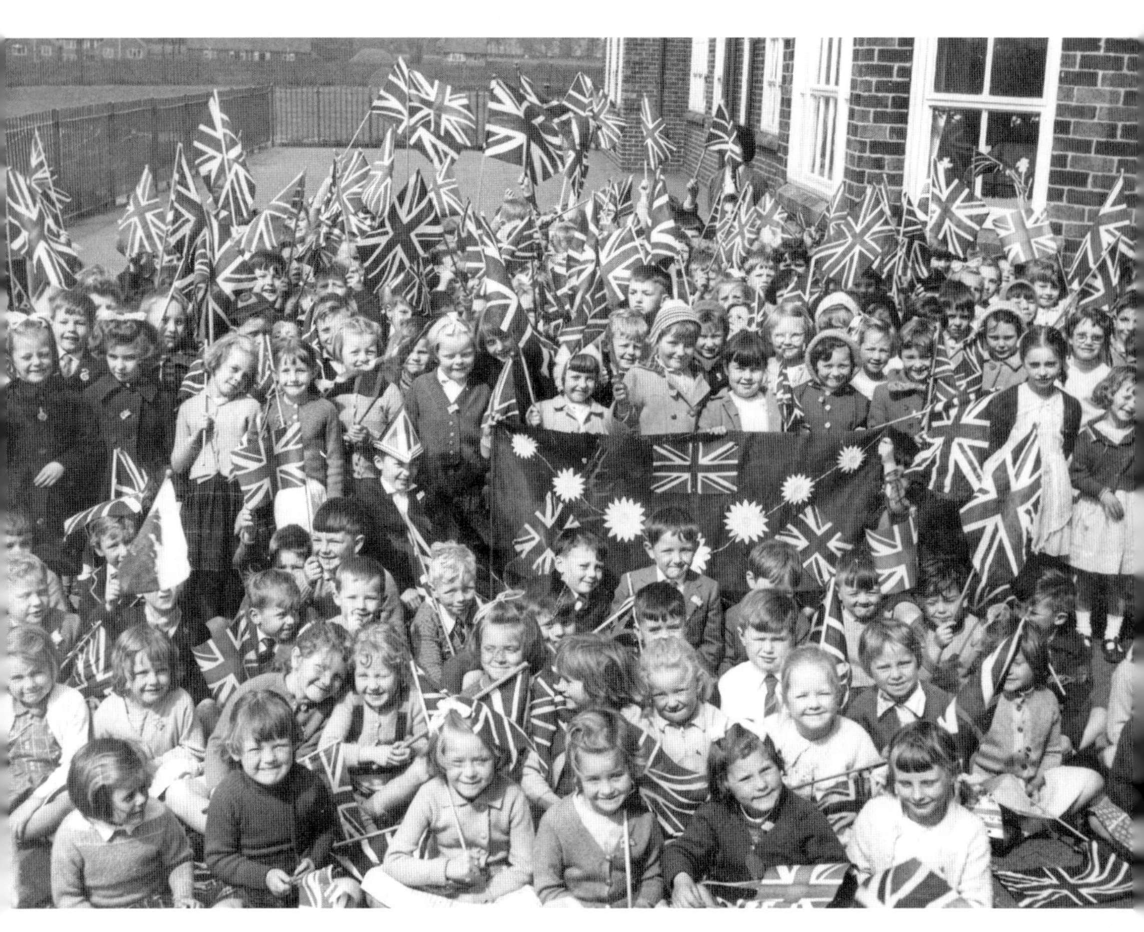

Captured in the early 1960s, this picture shows Empire Day celebrations at the Council School. The smiling childen sit amongst an abundance of Union Jack flags.

5

SCHOOL

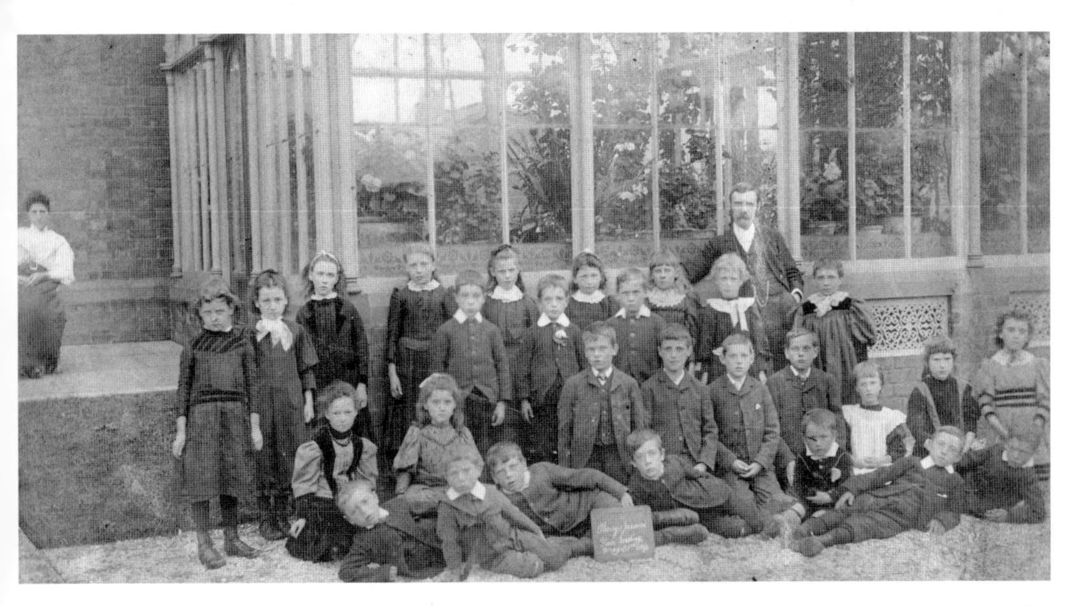

While there is little information known about this photograph, closer inspection of the small plaque at the front of the group of smartly-dressed children dictates that the picture was taken on 31 May 1893. The picture's location was situated somewhere in Park Road.

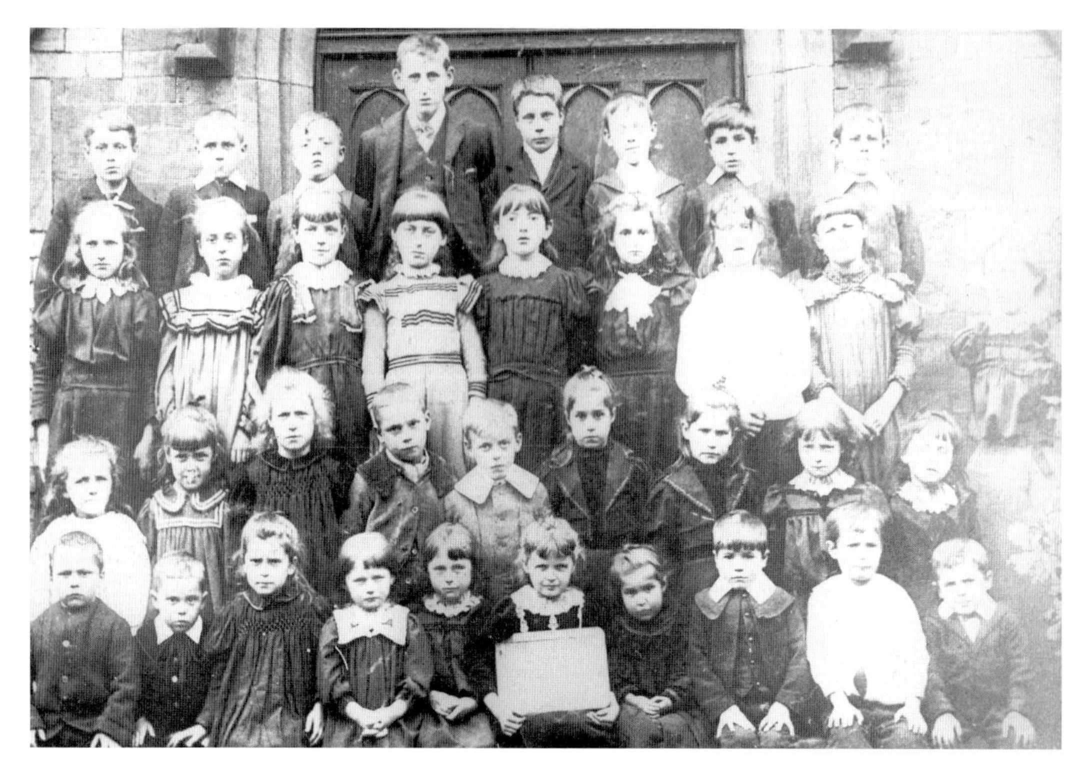

The Congregational School, 1903. Look at the children's sullen faces; a stark reminder of how times were hard back then.

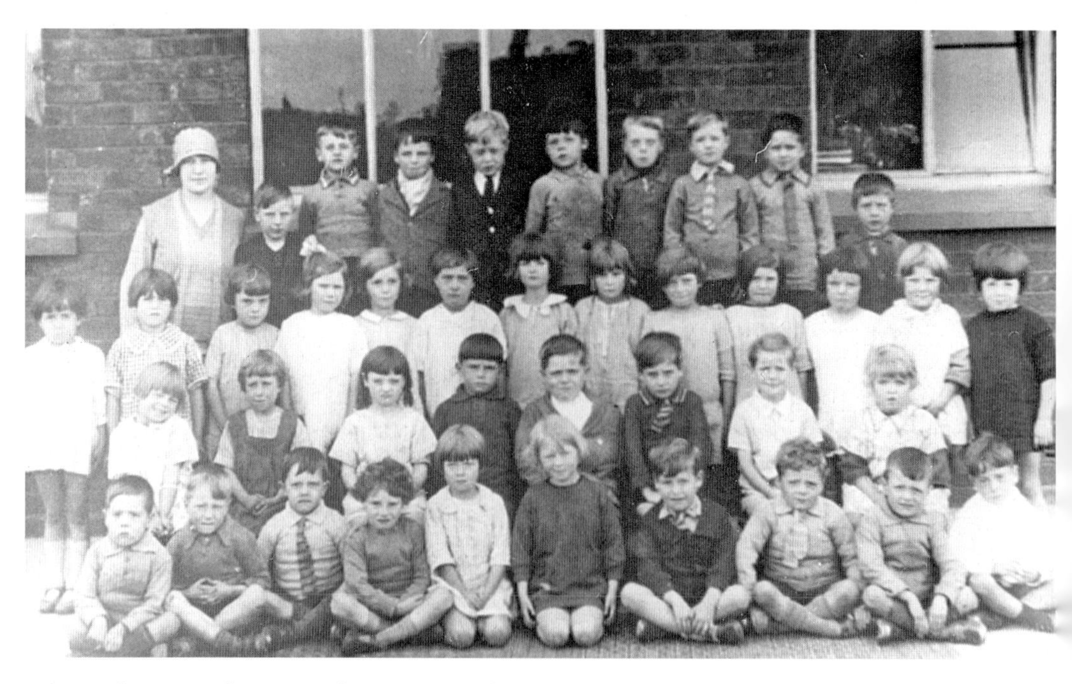

Taken in the 1930s, this picture shows a group of young students from Golborne County, or Council School, as it was known at the time.

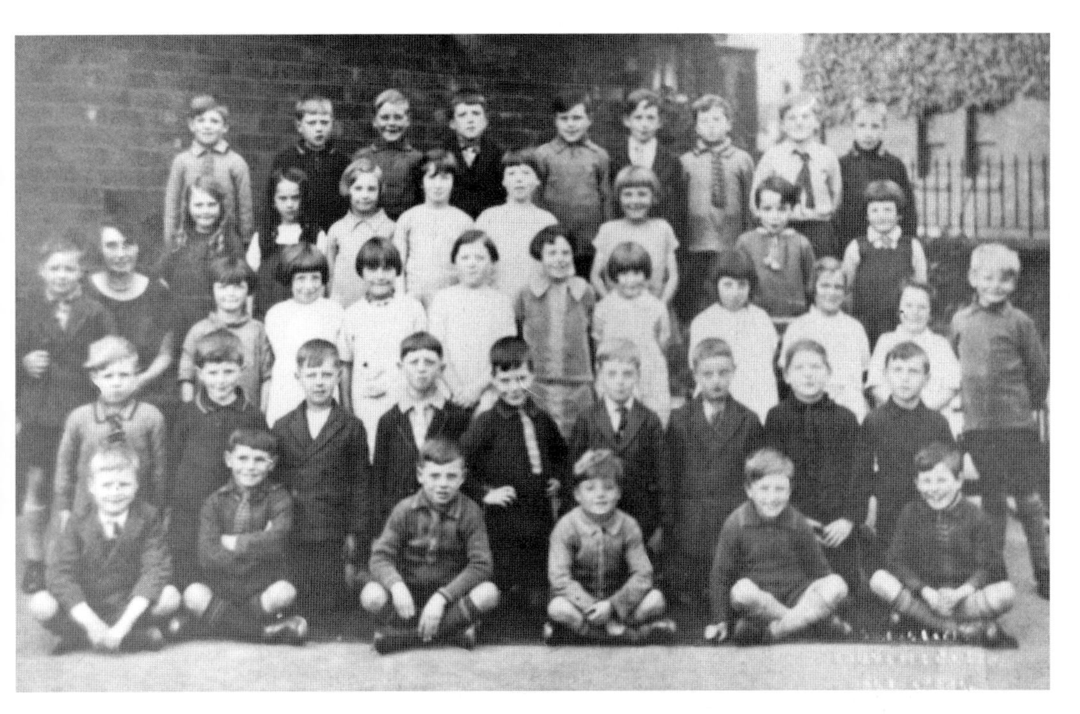

This photograph again shows pupils from Golborne County School in the 1930s, this time featuring a larger class.

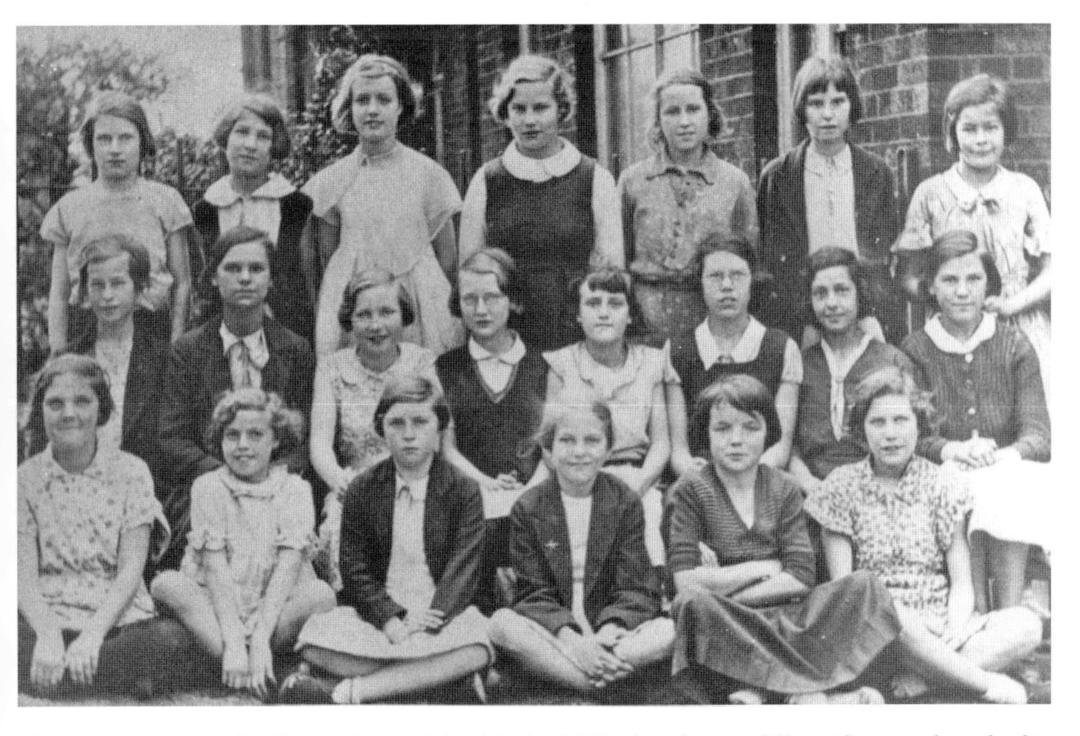

This picture is again of Golborne County School in the 1930s, but shows a different line-up of pupils, this time only girls.

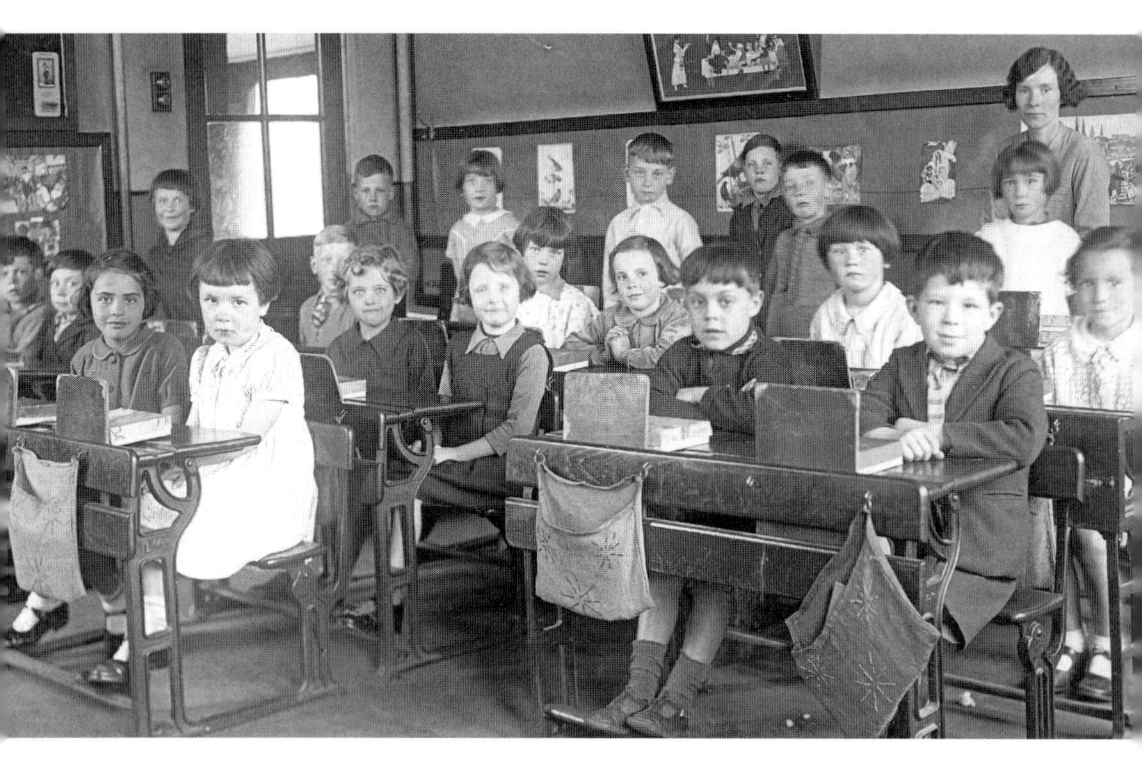

The photographs on these two pages are taken from postcards of Golborne Council School in 1936, showing classes of varied ages.

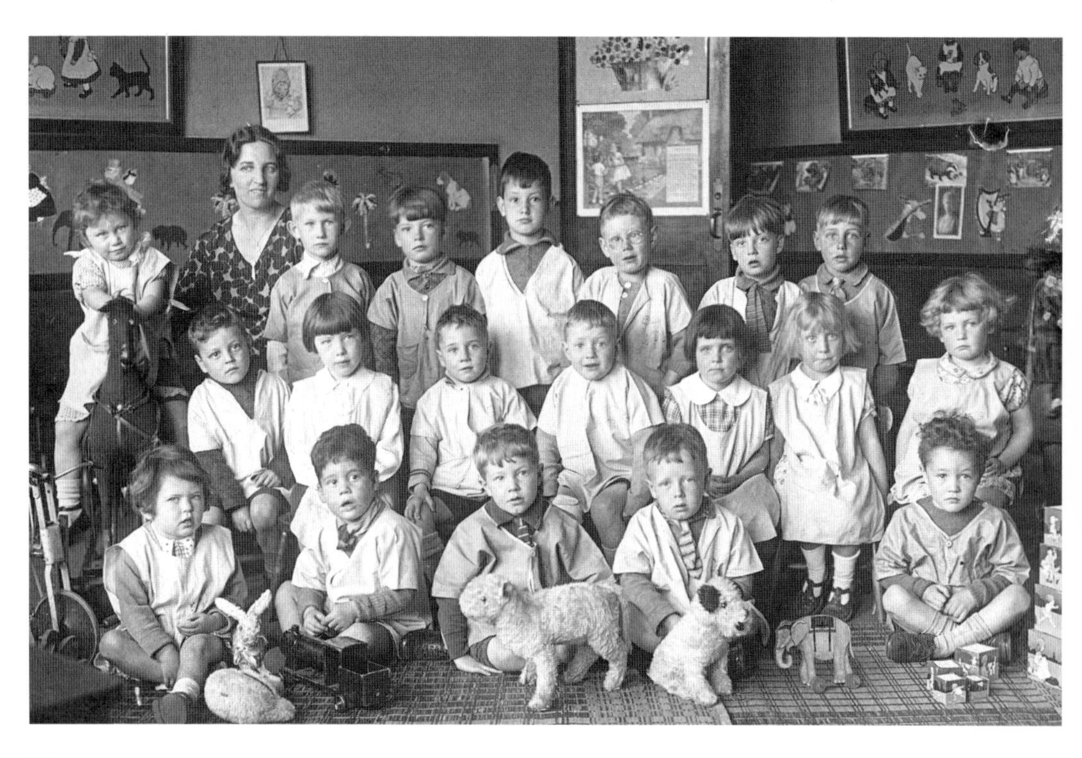

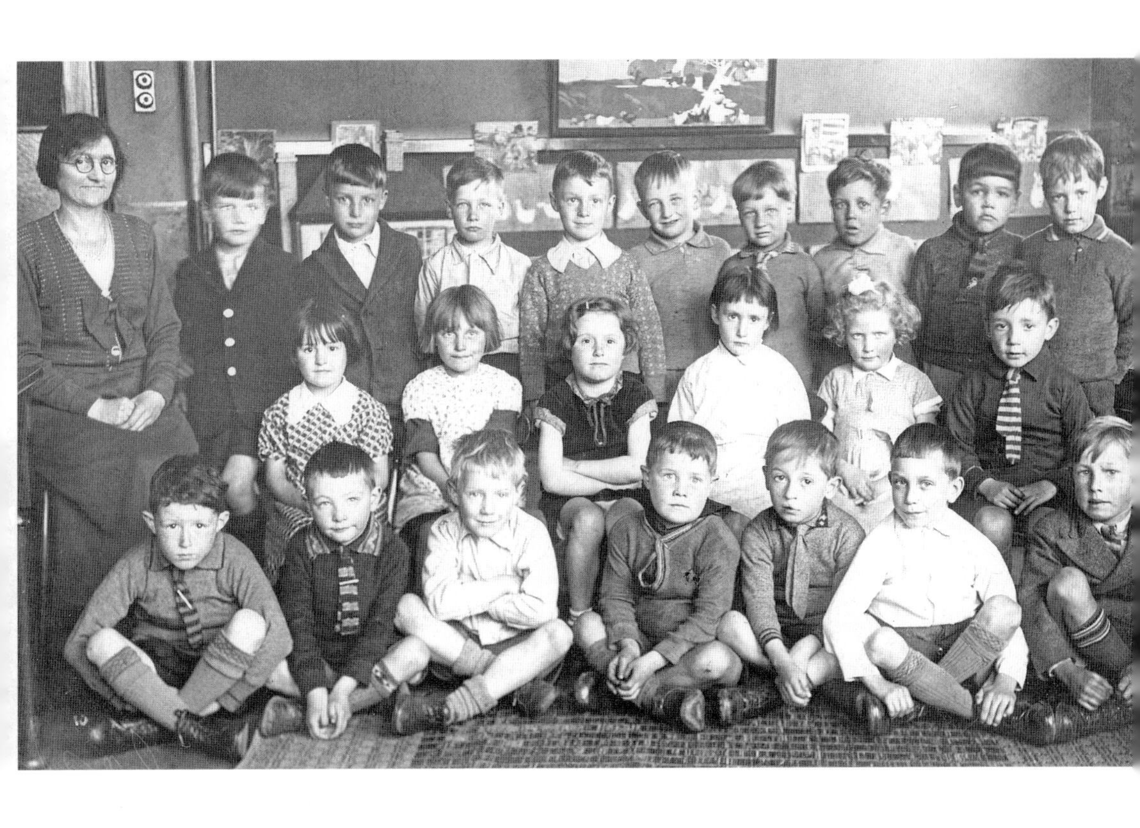

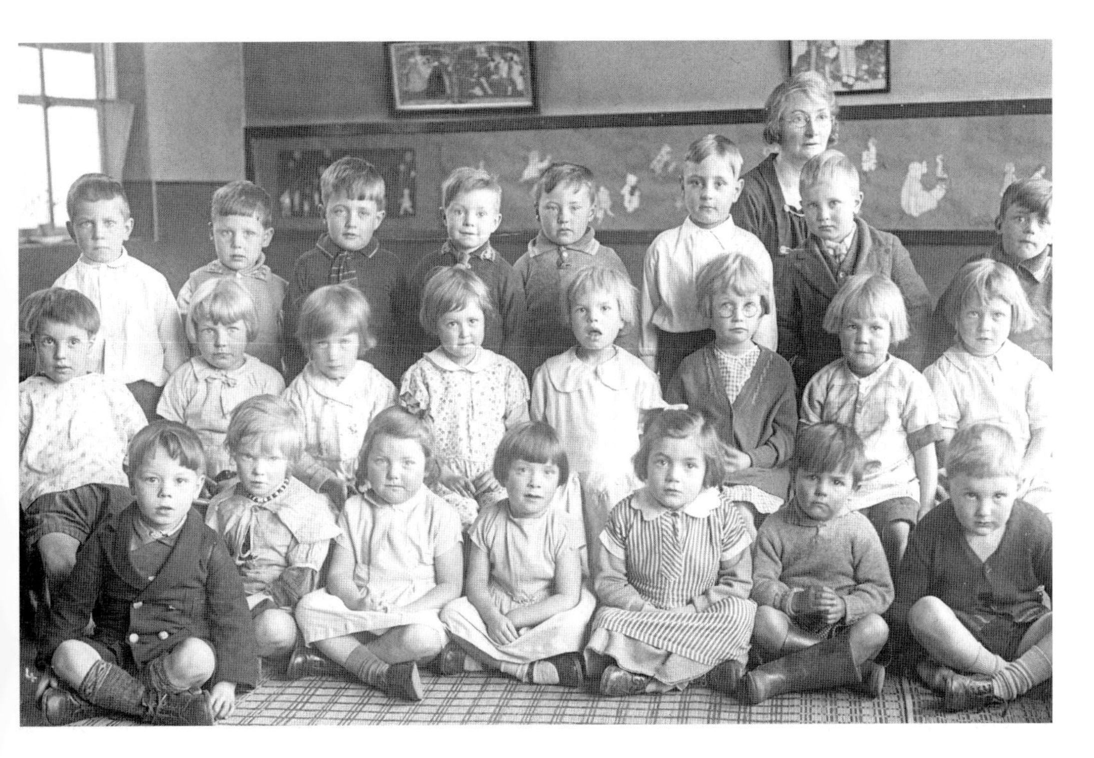

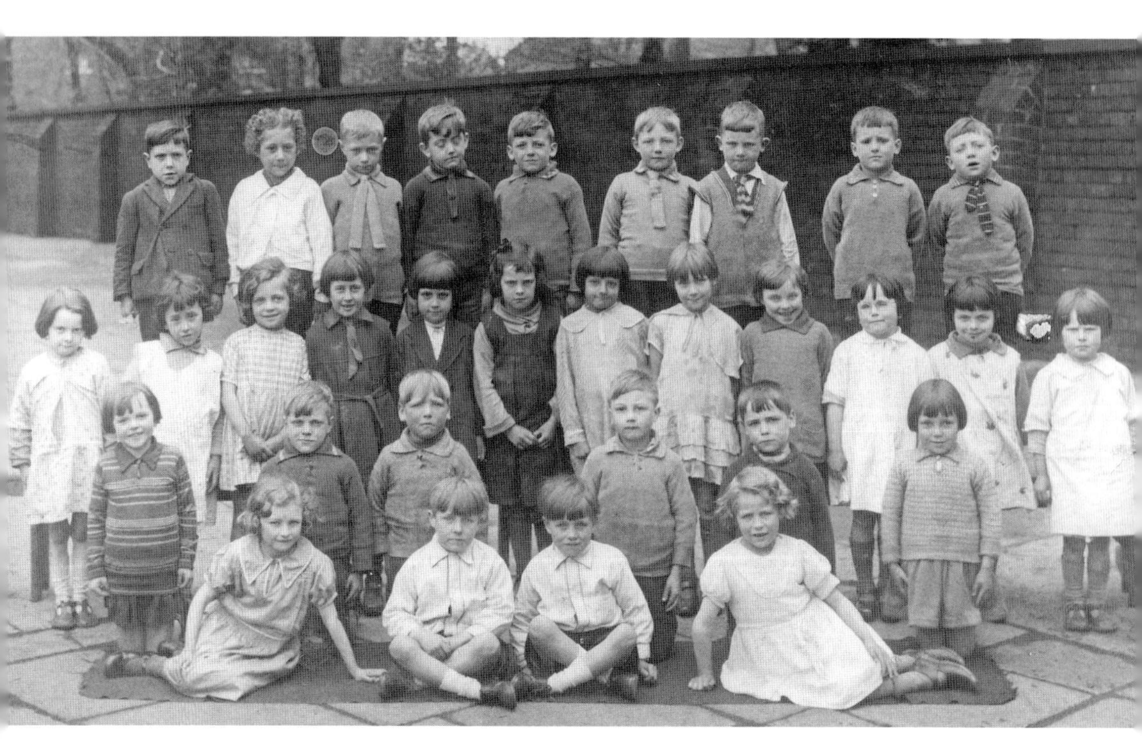

This photograph shows the Parochial School yard, though unfortunately the author was not able to discover the date on which the picture was taken. The brick wall behind the children was later replaced with a rail fence.

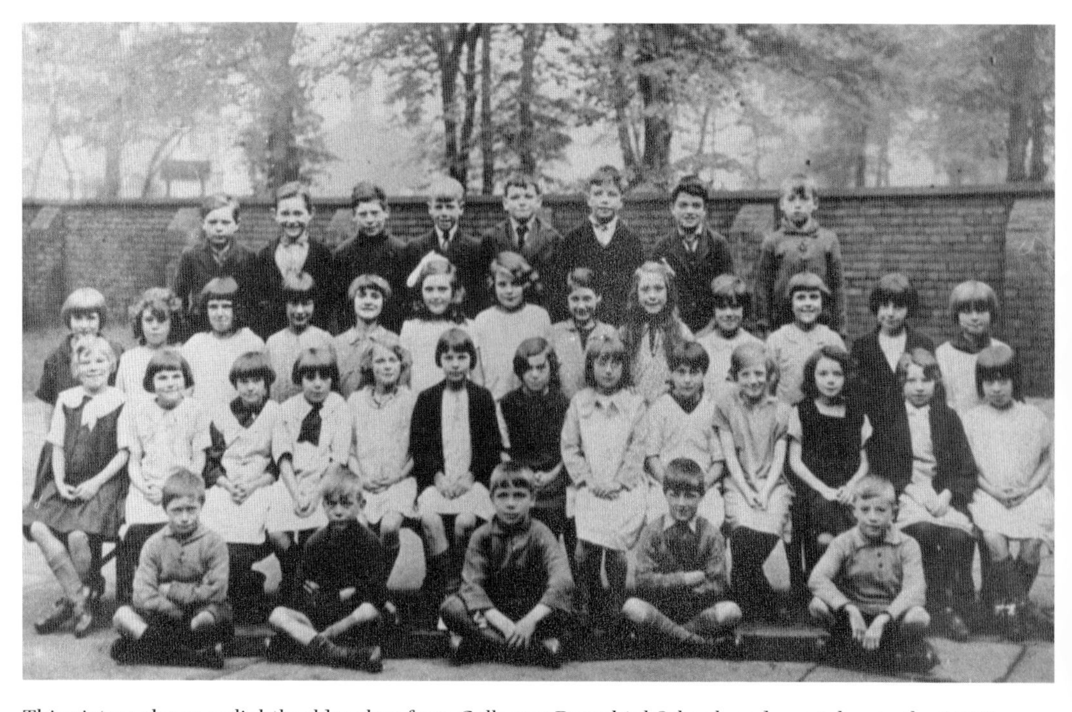

This picture shows a slightly older class from Golborne Parochial School, and was taken in the 1930s.

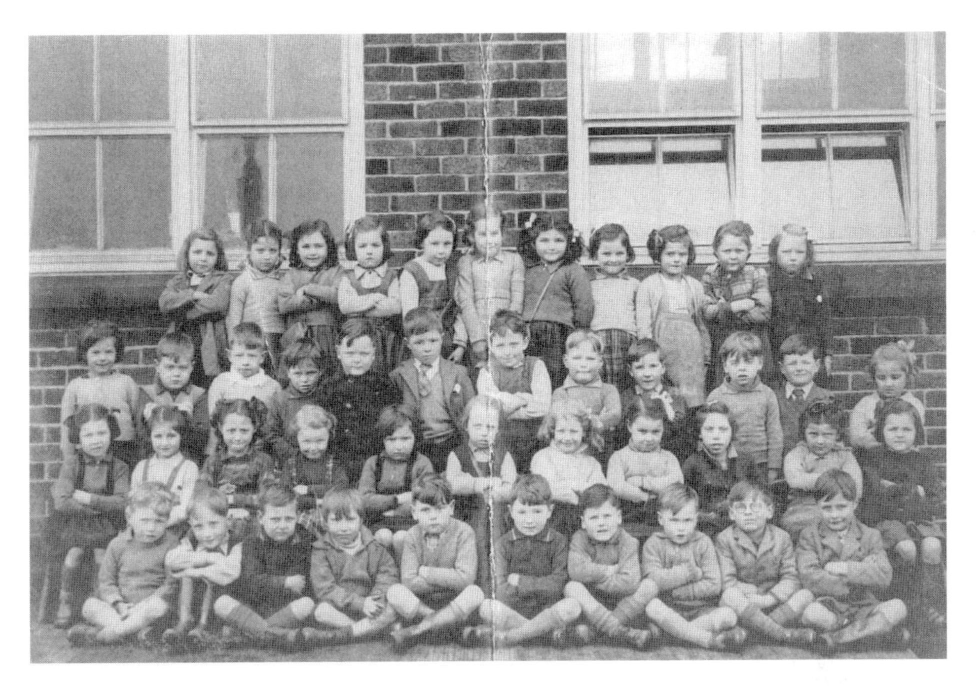

Taken in 1946, this photograph shows a rather grumpy-looking class of pupils from Golborne Council School.

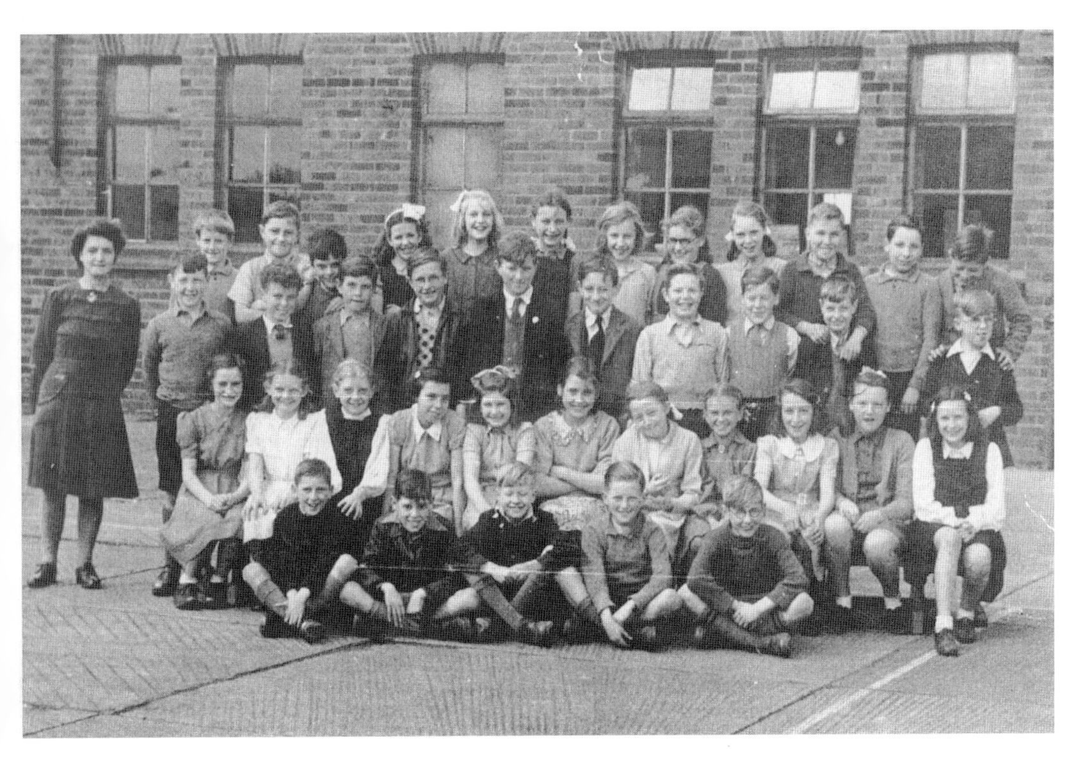

This picture shows a class from Golborne Council School in 1948.

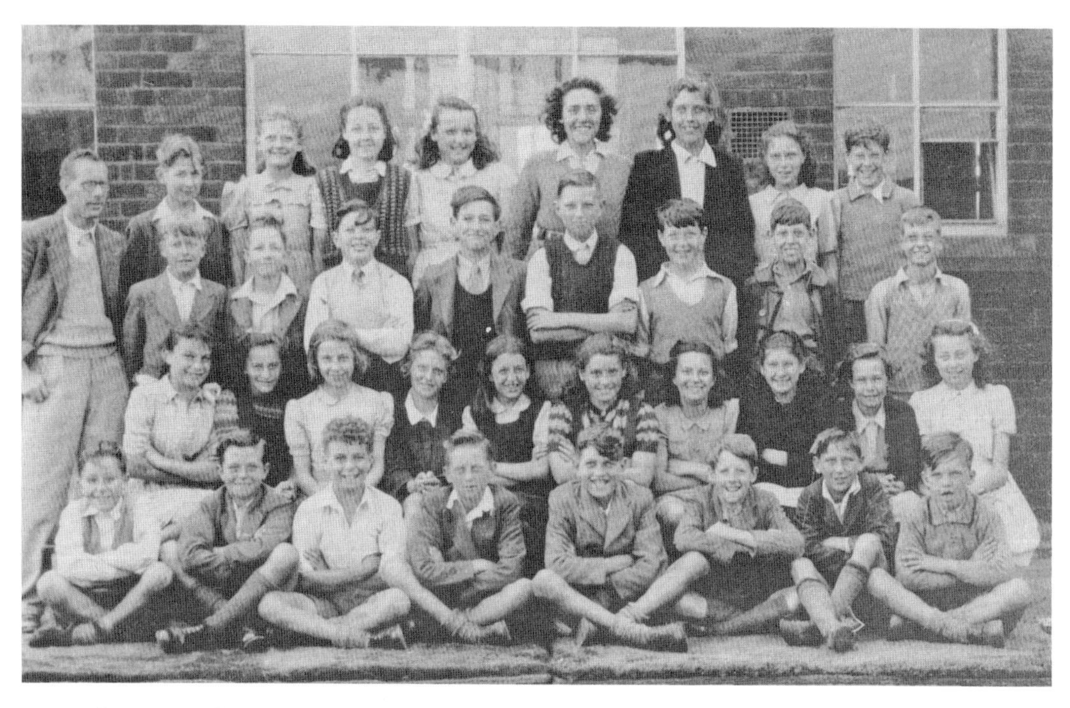

Again, this picture shows a class from Golborne Council School, this time a year later in 1949.

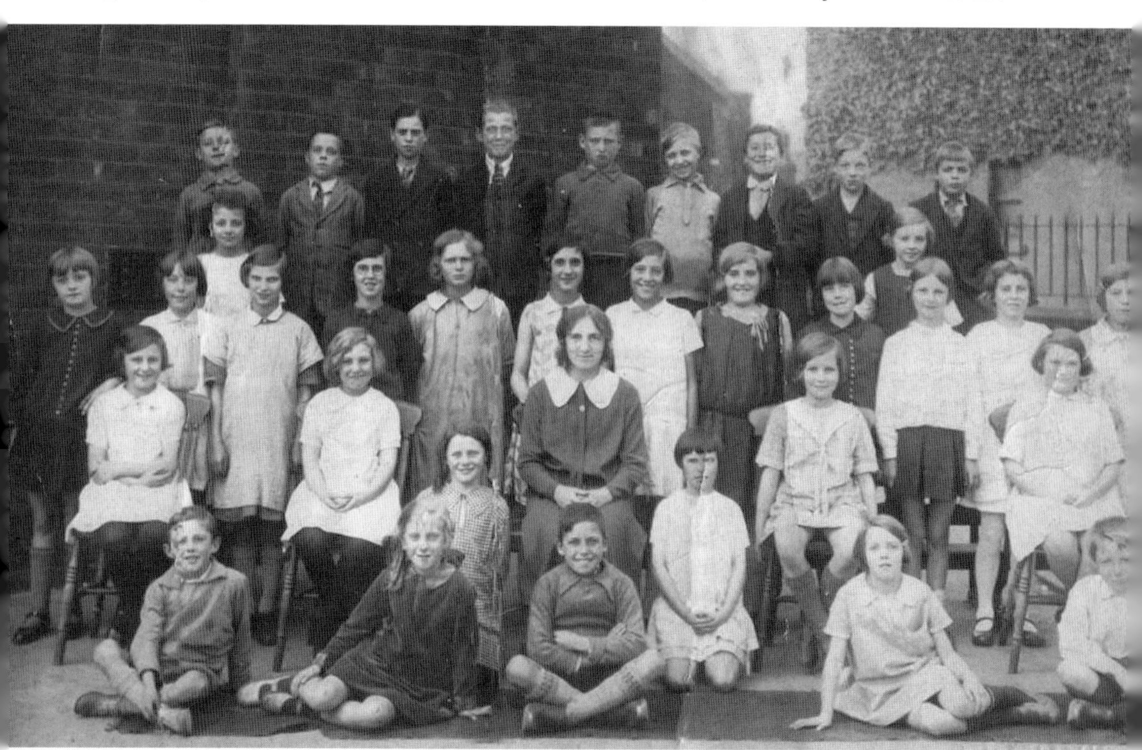

Moving on to another school, this photograph shows a class from St Thomas' Church of England School in 1930. The primary school used to be called the Parochial School.

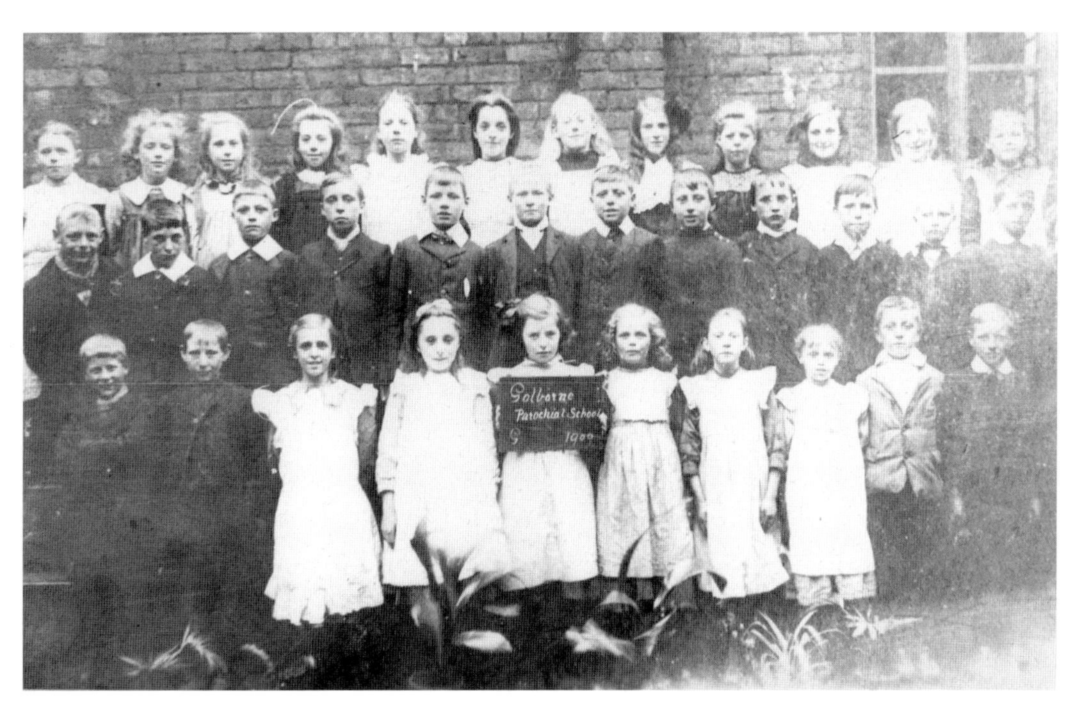

Taken in 1909, this picture shows a group of children from the Parochial School.

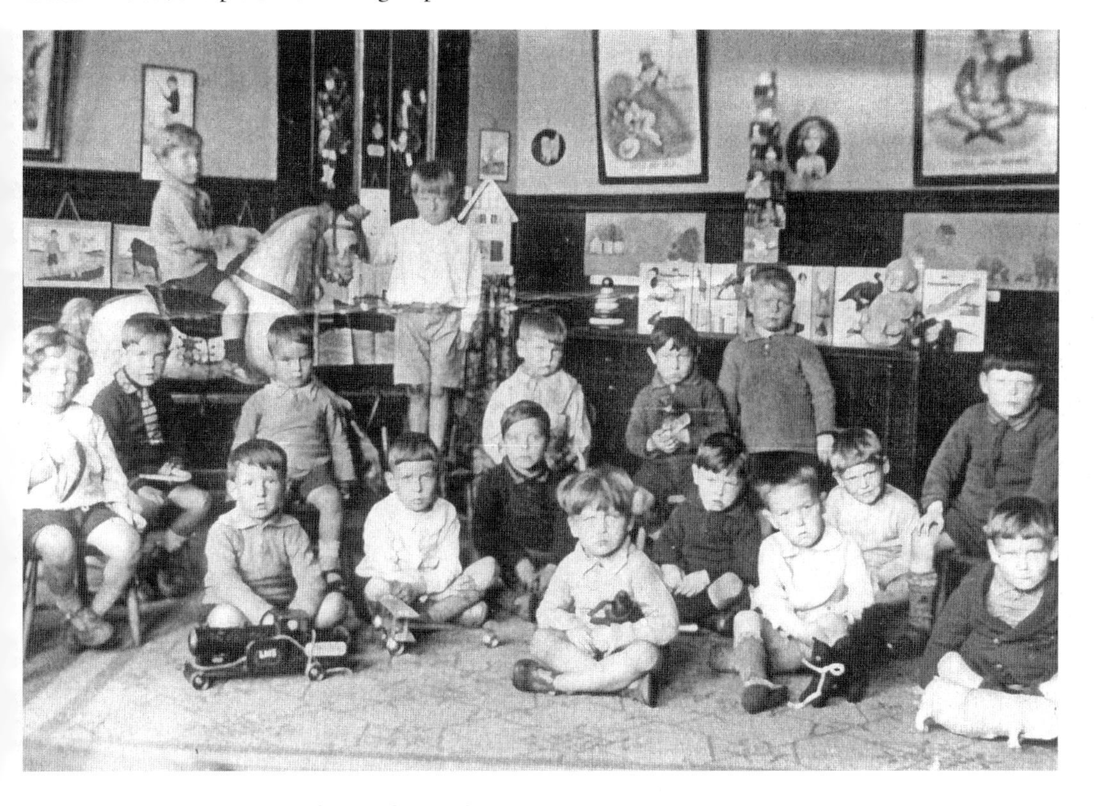

A photograph of All Saints' School, taken in the 1940s.

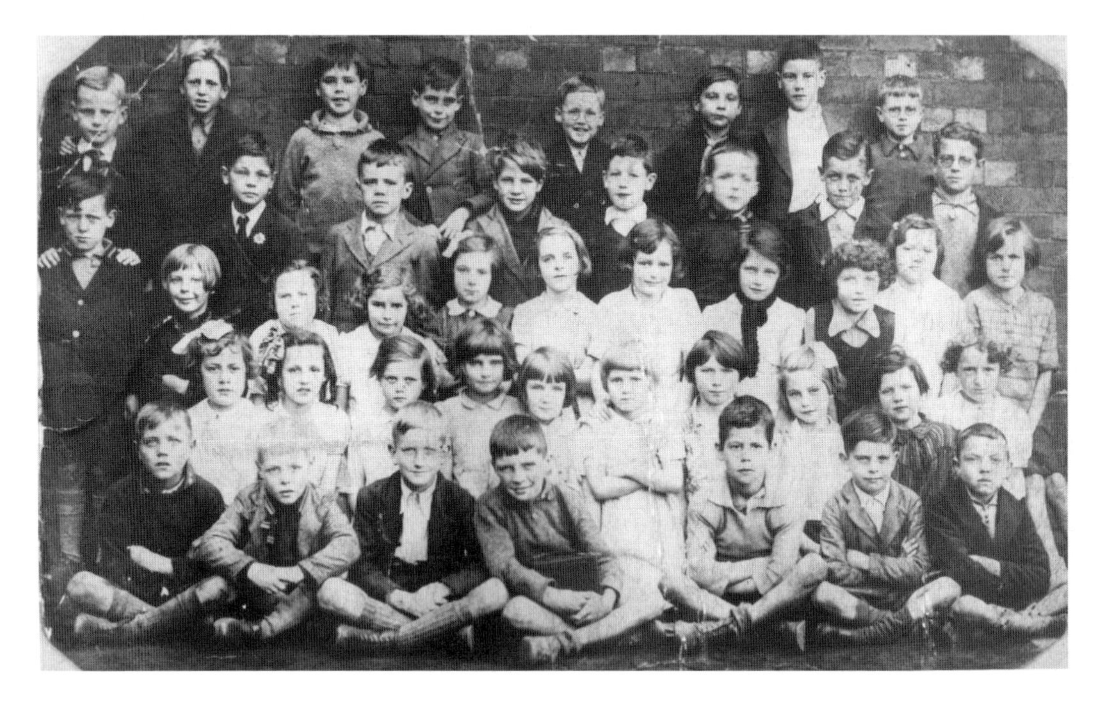

Also taken in the 1940s, another photograph of pupils at All Saints' School,

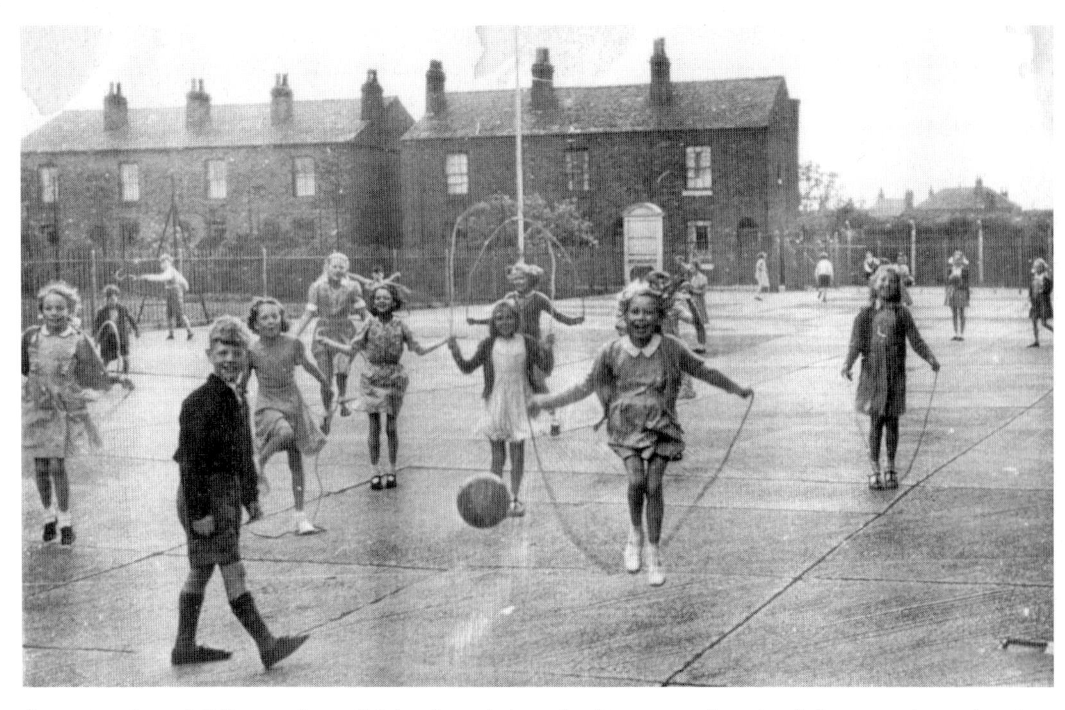

An action shot of Golborne Council School pupils happily skipping in the school playground on a break in 1954.

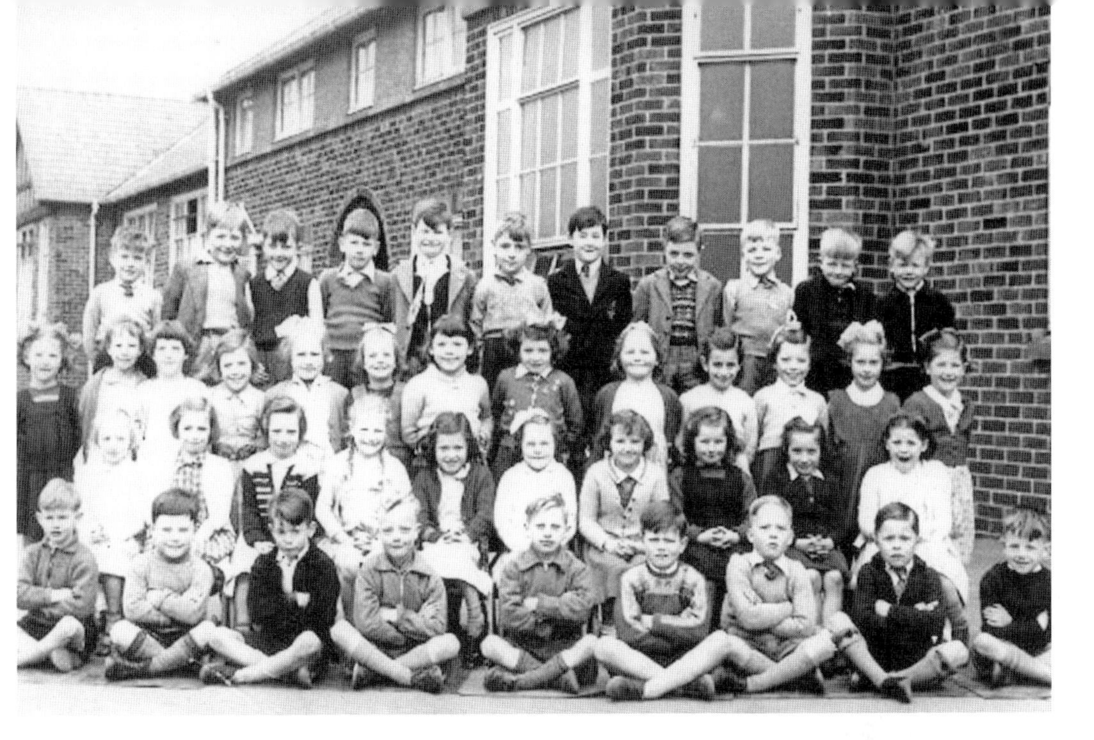

This photograph, taken in 1956, shows Golborne Council School pupils.

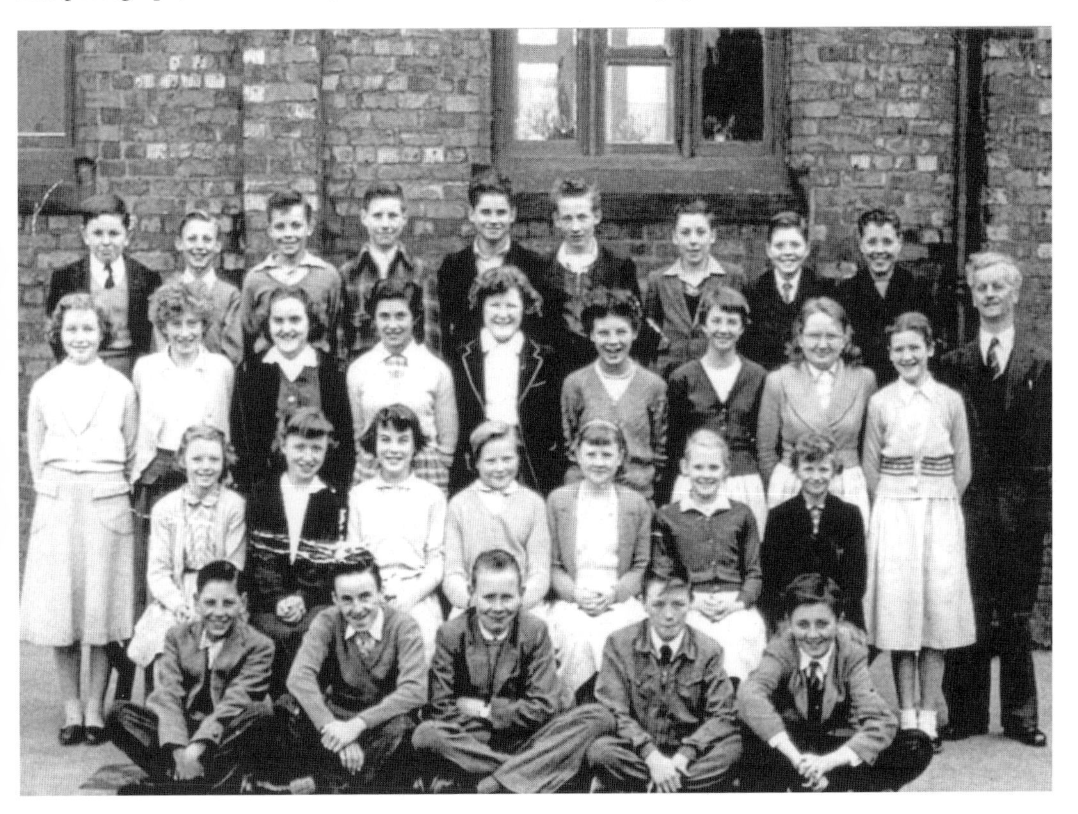

This photograph shows staff and pupils from All Saints' School in 1956 or 1957. The teacher on the far right-hand side of the picture is Austin Hardman.

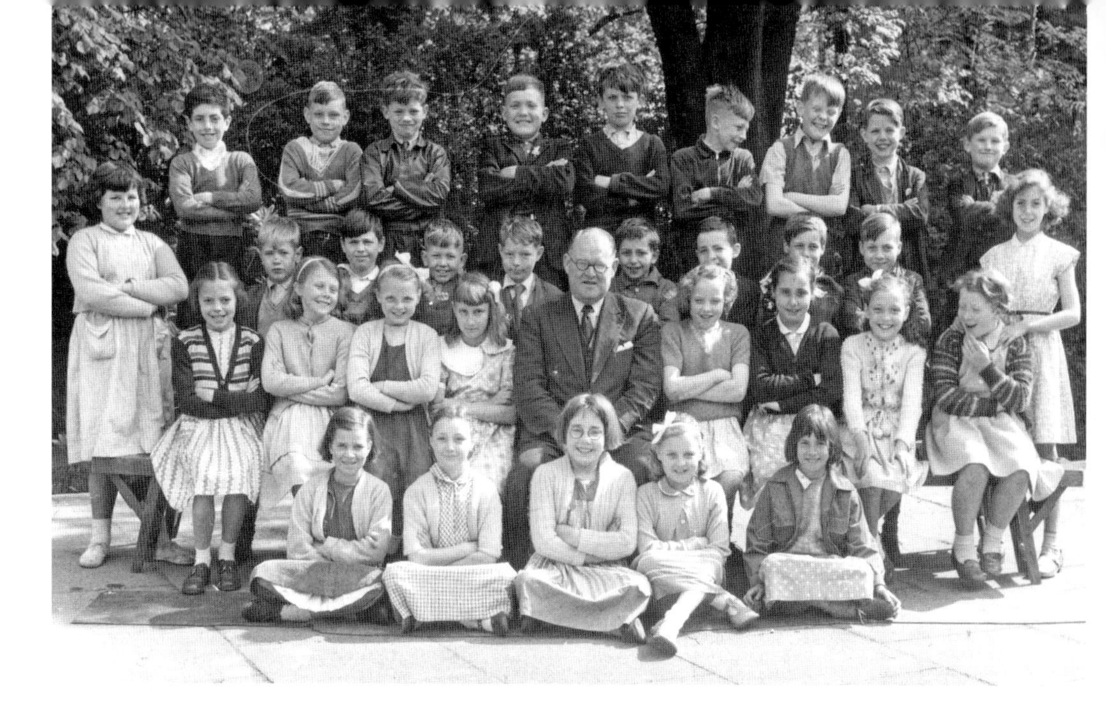

This picture shows a class of pupils from the Parochial School in around 1956. The teacher seated in the centre is Mr Moorfield; all who went to the school spoke highly of him, saying he was a real gentleman. Some still regale in the amusing memory of him falling off a ladder in front of everyone!

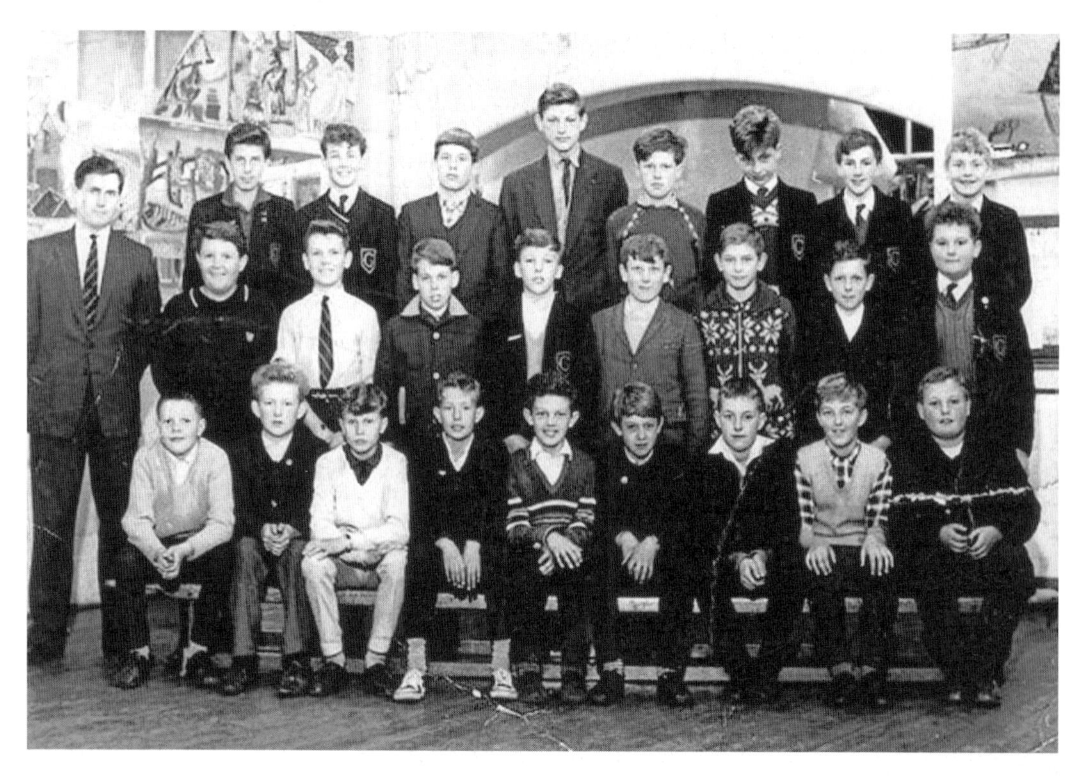

This picture shows a class from Golborne County Secondary Modern School for Boys, Talbot St Golborne, and was taken in around 1964. The teacher, on the far left-hand side, is Joe Fairhurst.

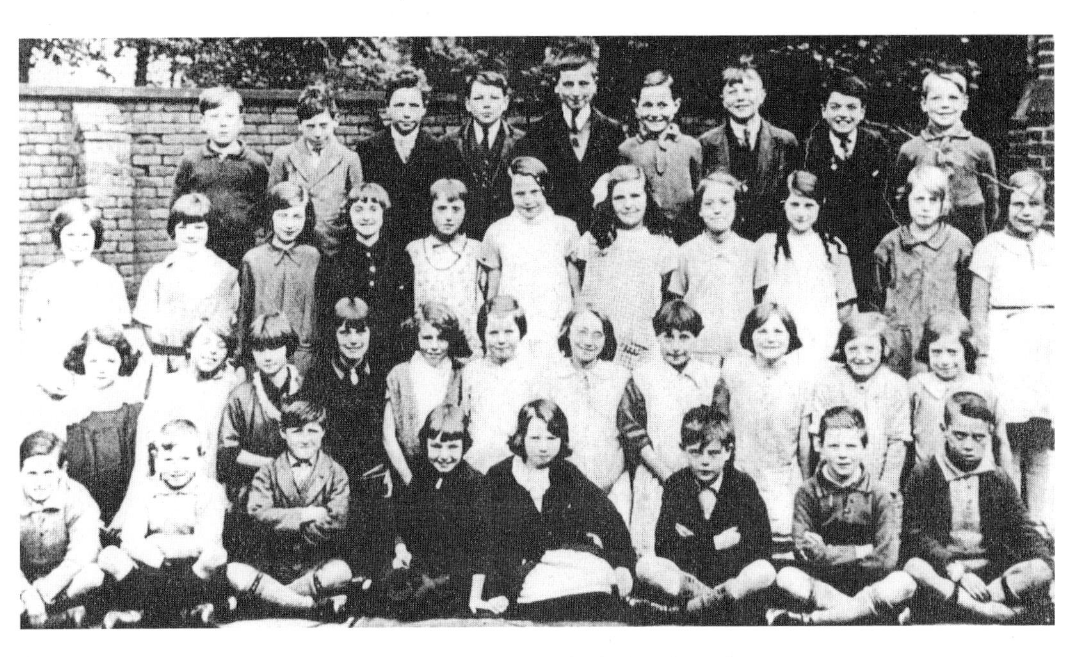

Taken in 1961, this photograph shows a group of Parochial School pupils.

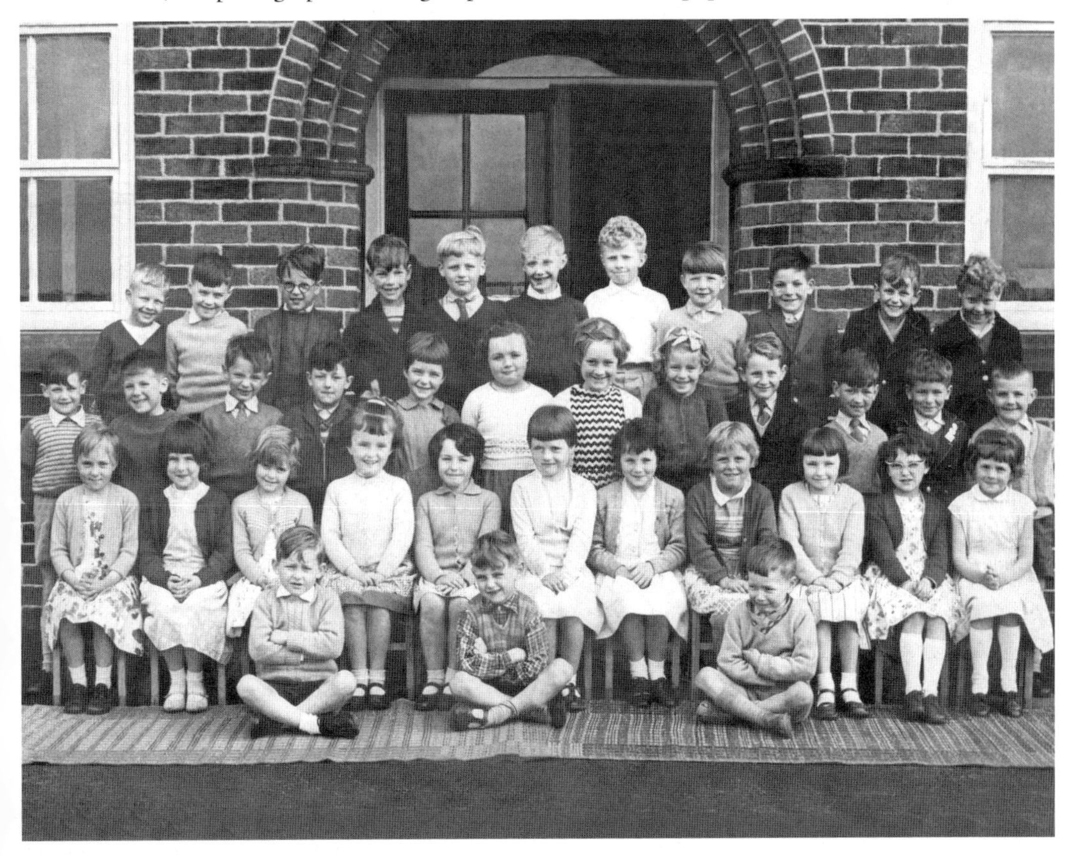

This picture shows a group of children from Golborne Council School, and was taken in the early1960s.

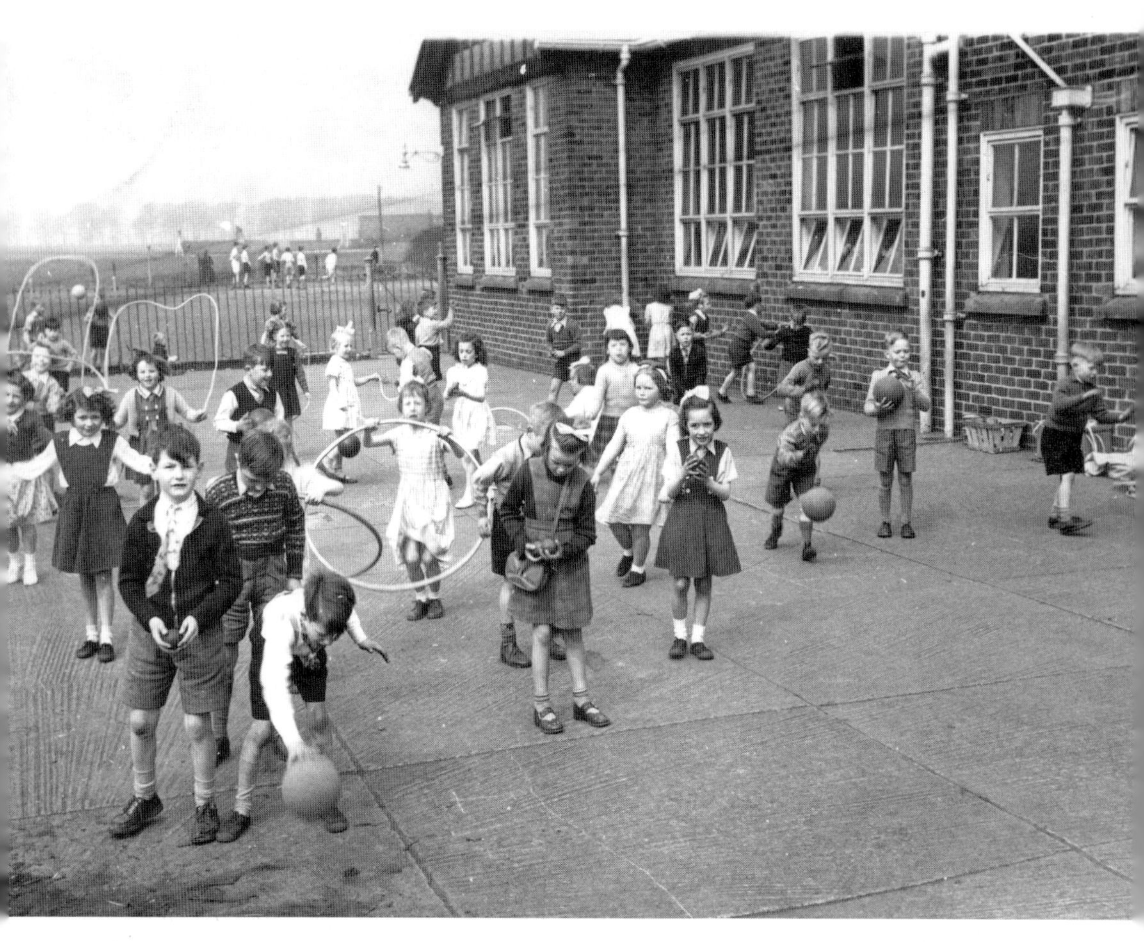

Taken in 1956, this photograph shows pupils from Golborne Council School enjoying playtime.

6

THE COLLIERY

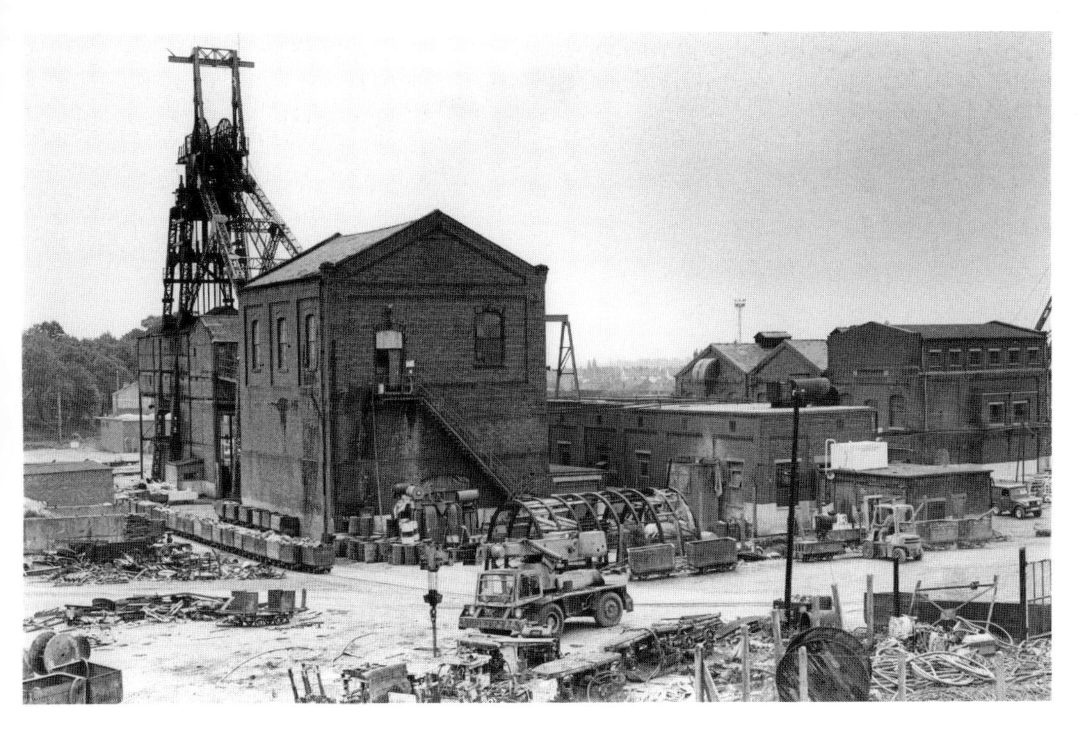

This picture captures the day-to-day workings of Golborne Colliery. The pit dates back to around 1880.

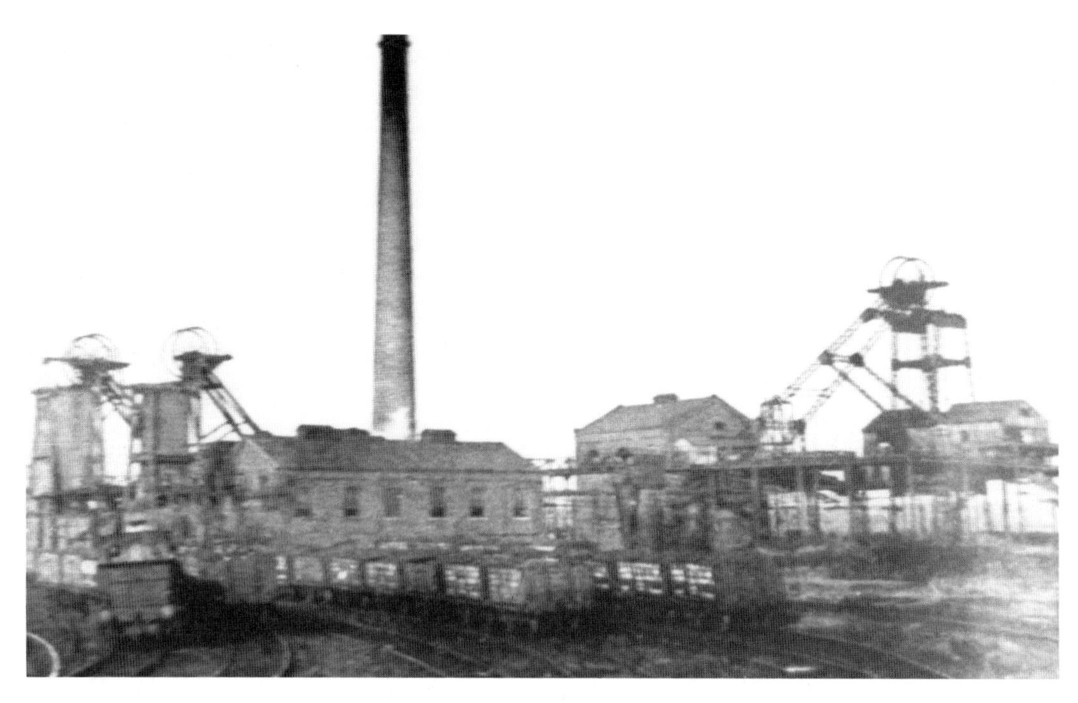

This photograph shows Golborne Colliery during the 1920s. Shafts one and two are on the left-hand side of the picture, and Shaft number three is on the right-hand side.

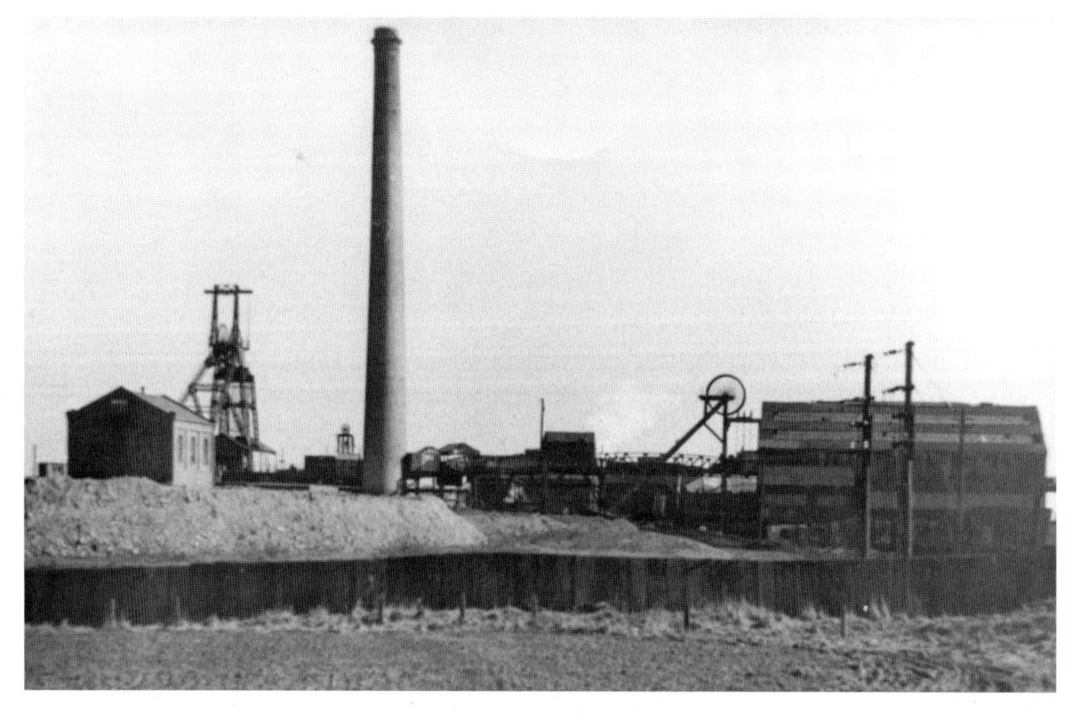

This picture shows the layout of the colliery. Three shafts were sunk and numbers two and three were deepened in 1890 to intersect the Trencherbone, Florida and Wigan series of seams. Number one shaft, which had been sunk to 136yds, was filled-in during 1967.

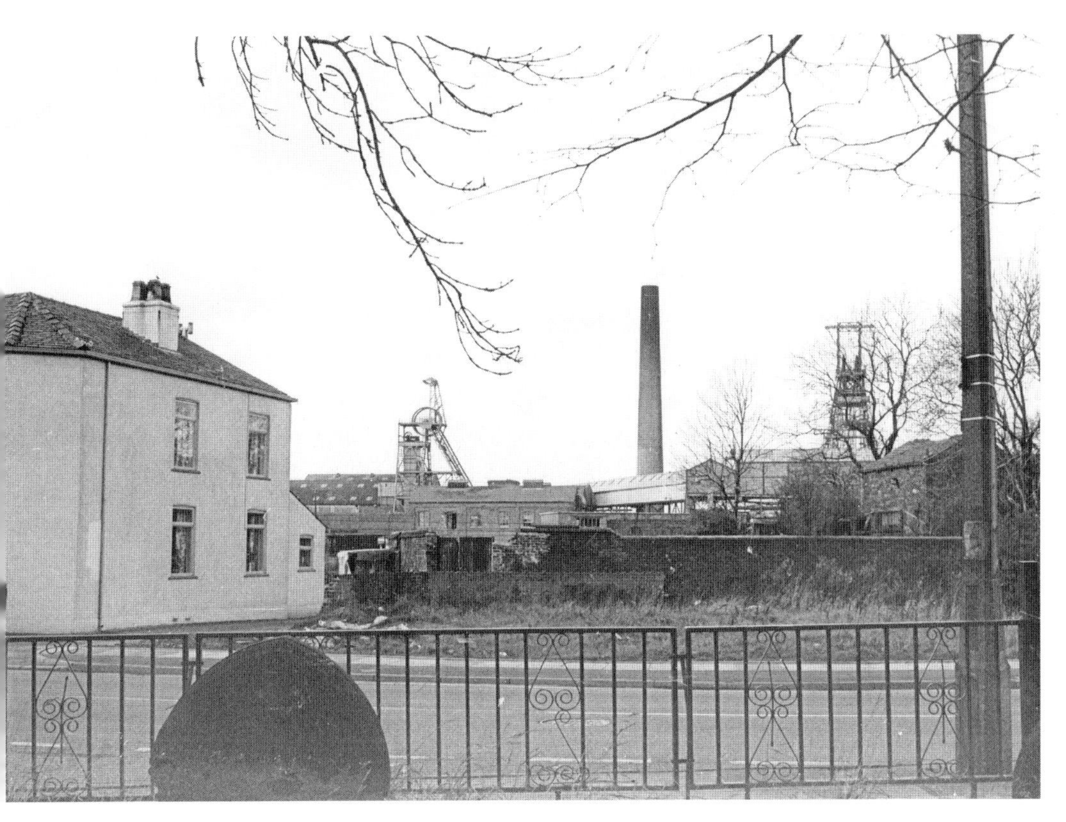

This photograph of Golborne Colliery was taken from behind the fence at St Thomas' graveyard. As you can see, it gives a sense of the scale of operations.

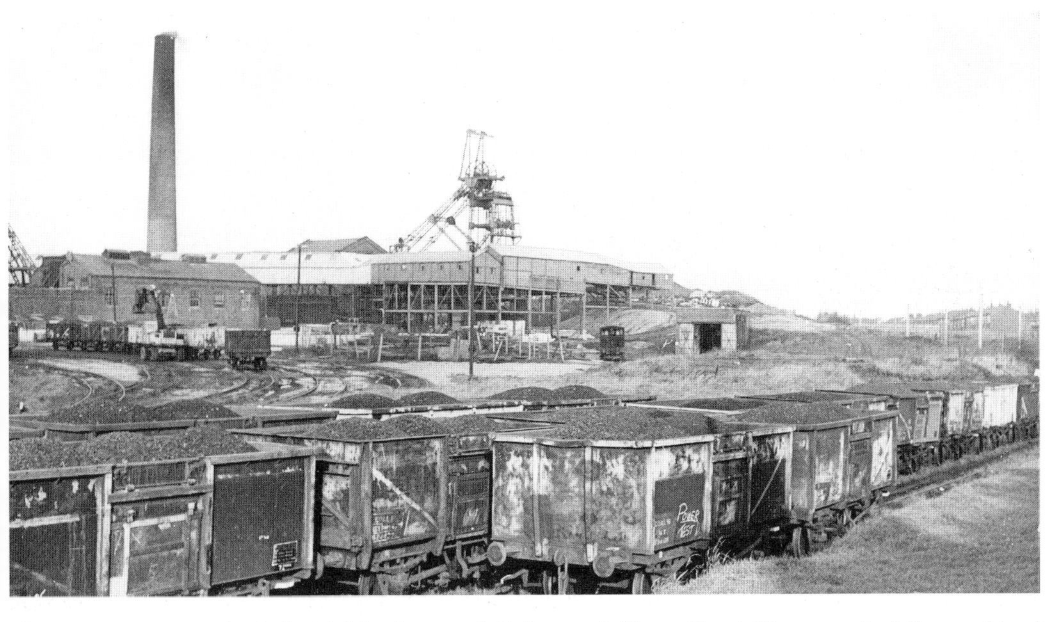

This image captures the industrial landscape of Golborne Colliery. About 75 per cent of the combined output from Golborne, Bickershaw and Parsonage Collieries went to providing power stations with fuel.

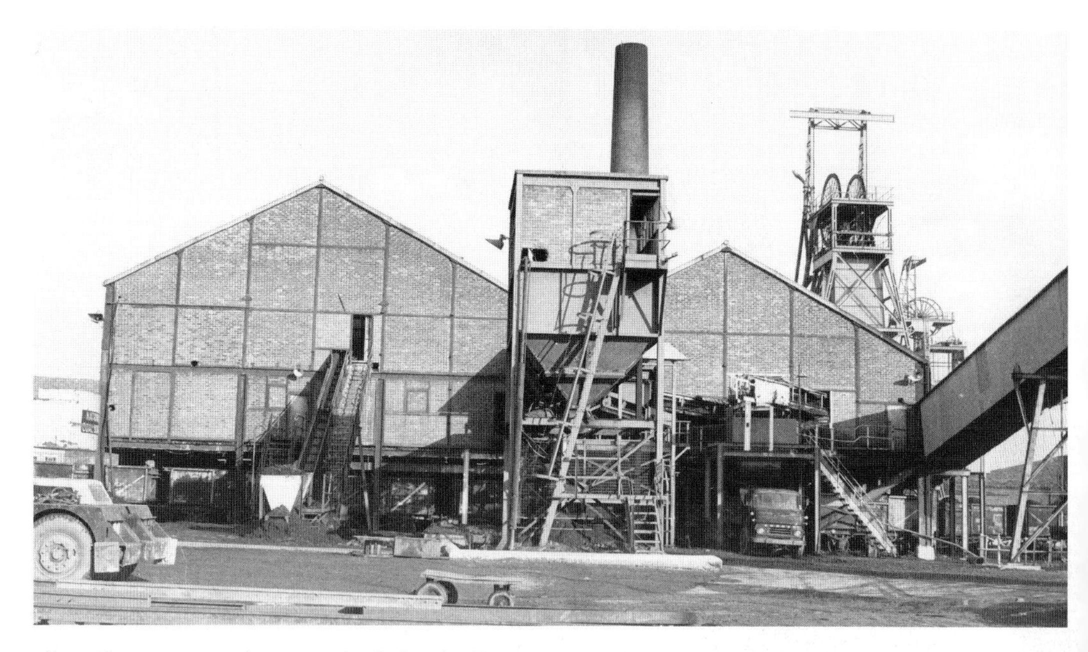

The colliery was once known as 'Kid Glove' colliery – a name believed to be derived from the high quality of the coal mined there. The year in which this photograph was taken is unknown.

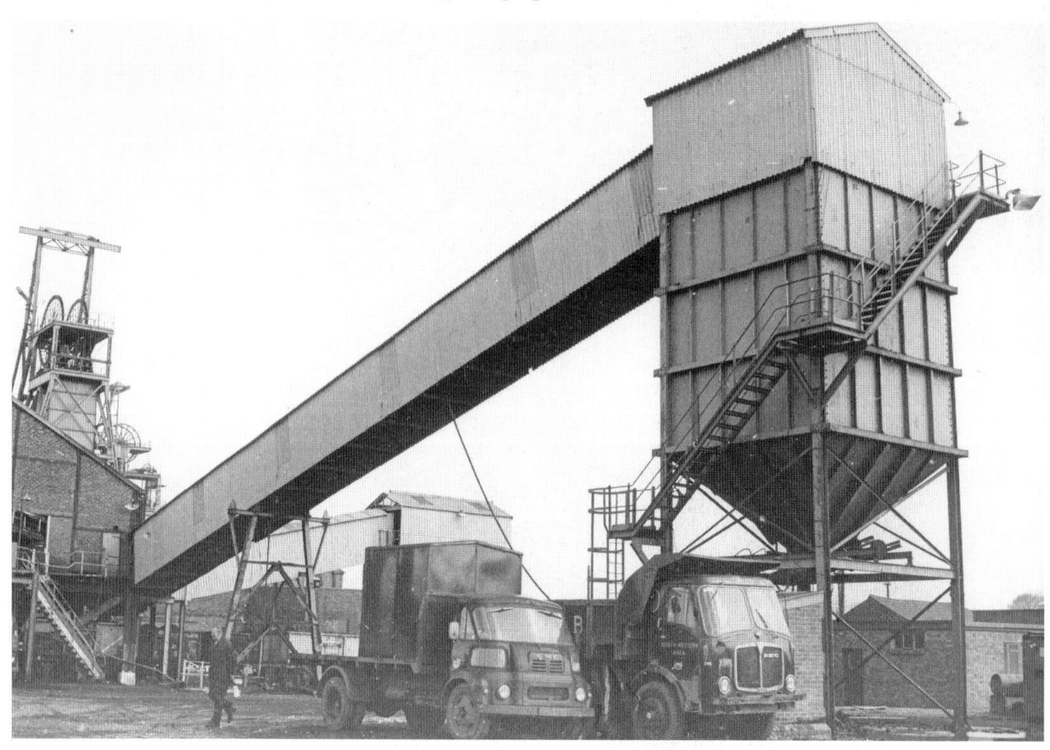

Ashton and Wigan broke all records by producing an impressive 517,675 tonnes. This productivity rate works out to 3.04 tonnes per man. This was the second successive year that records were broken in Golborne collieries. The date of this photograph is sadly unknown.

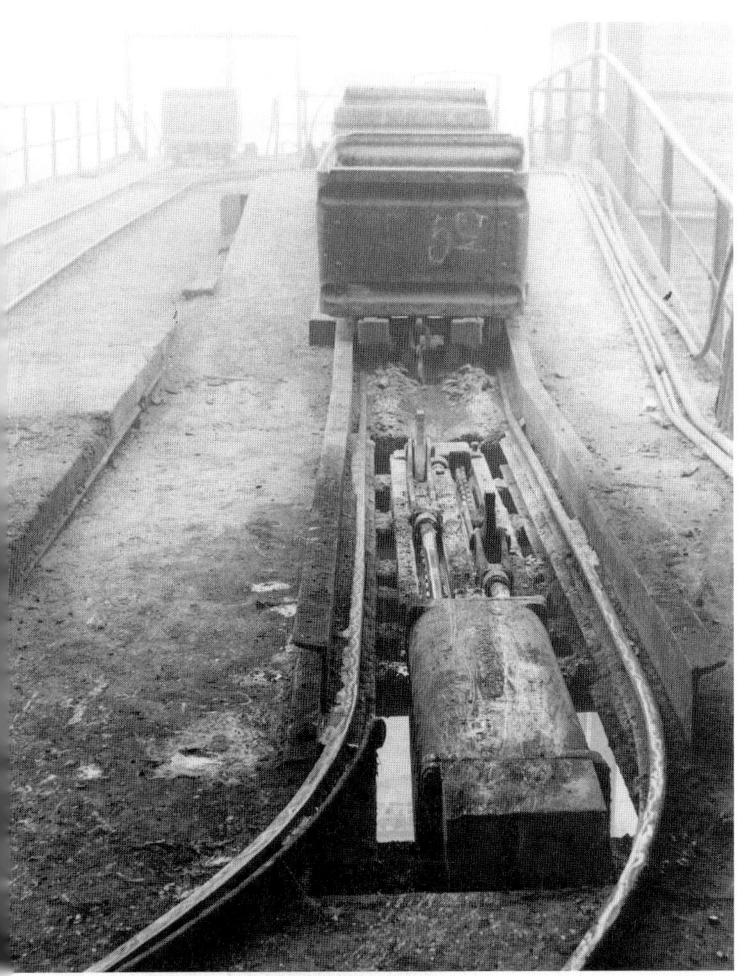

This picture shows how the coal was transported; on small train carriages along a track. The coal was mined from the Higher Florida, Plodder and the Ince 6ft seams.

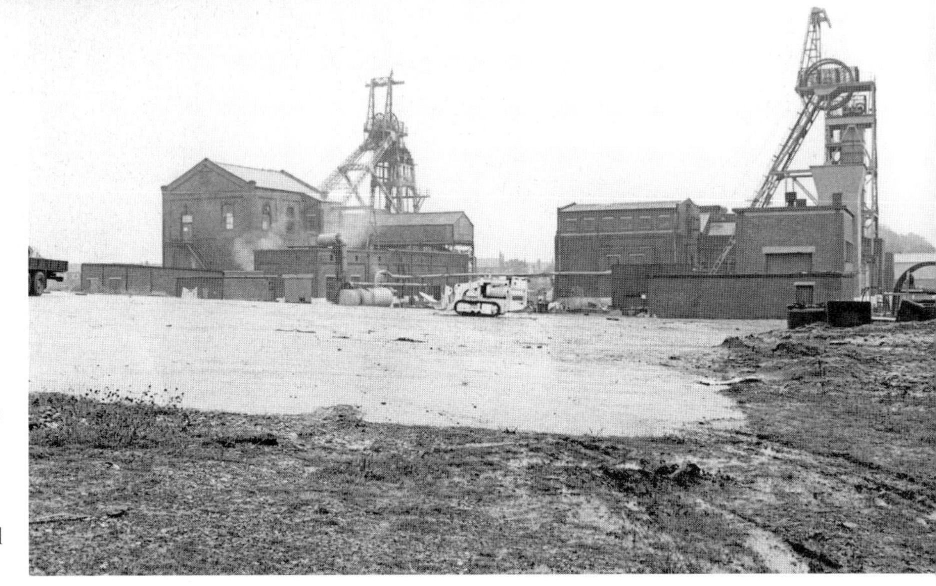

Another photograph of the colliery, showing the large scale of operations. The colliery was closed in 1989.

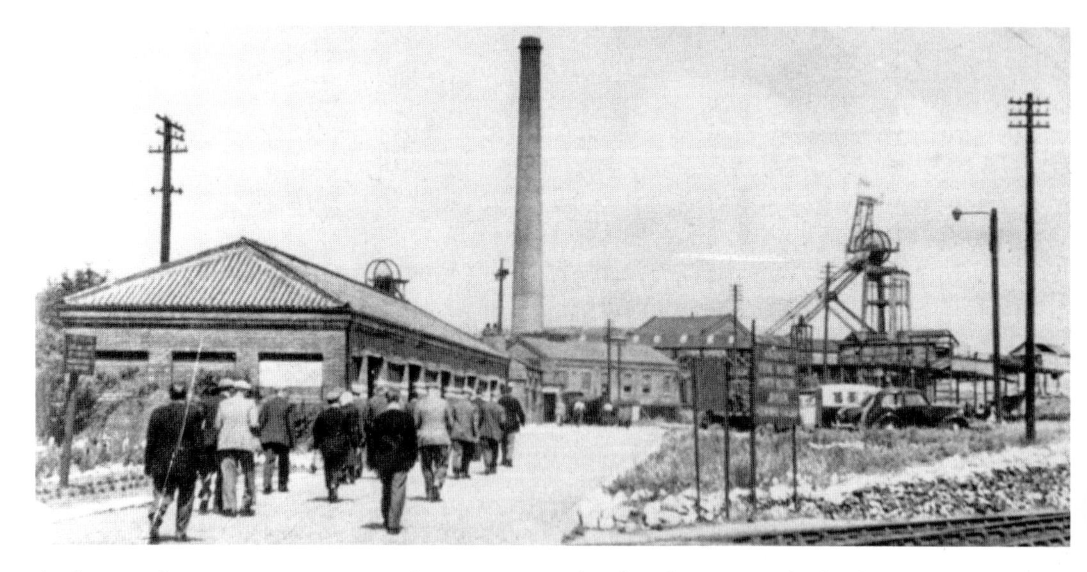

A photograph capturing miners on their way to work. The chimney in the background stood at an impressive 157.6 metres tall and was a characteristic feature of the Golborne landscape. It measures 12ft in diameter at the top and 17ft at the bottom. The walls ranged from 14in thick to 2ft 6in. During demolition, the chimney had to be taken down 'brick by brick' as opposed to a proper demolition, due to the close proximity to the other colliery buildings.

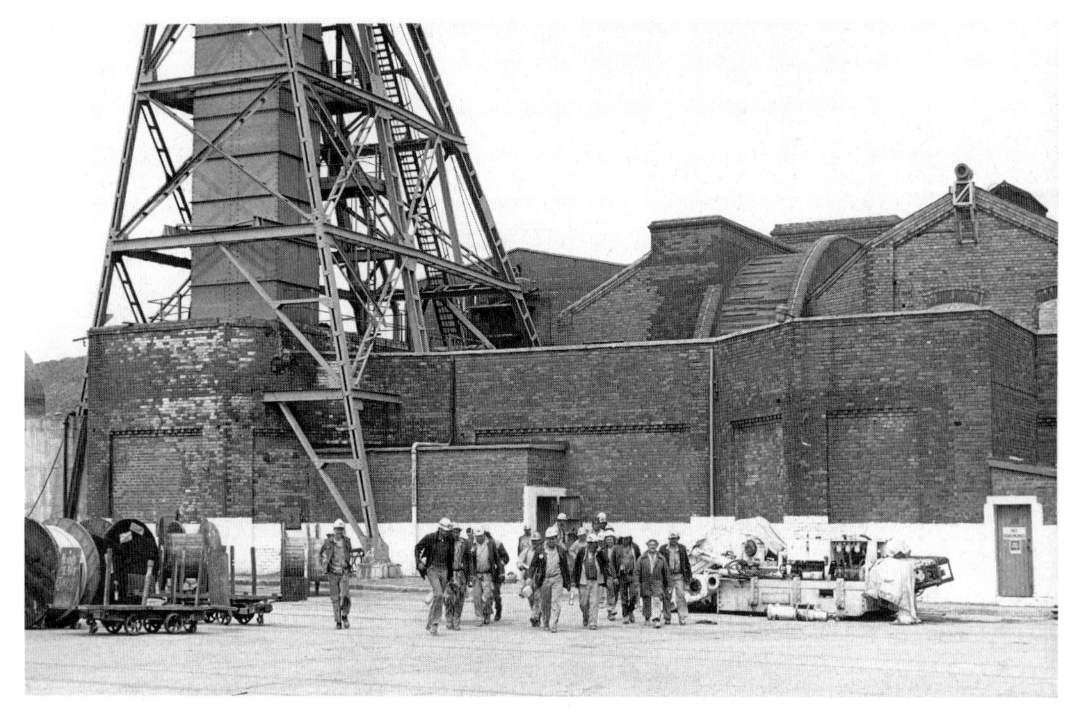

Miners finishing their shift for the day. On Sunday, 18 March 1979, an explosion in the plodder seam development occurred when eleven men were working underground on maintenance. Three men were killed in the explosion and a further seven later died in hospital. Golborne holds a remembrance service every ten years at St Thomas' Church to remember those who died in the blast.

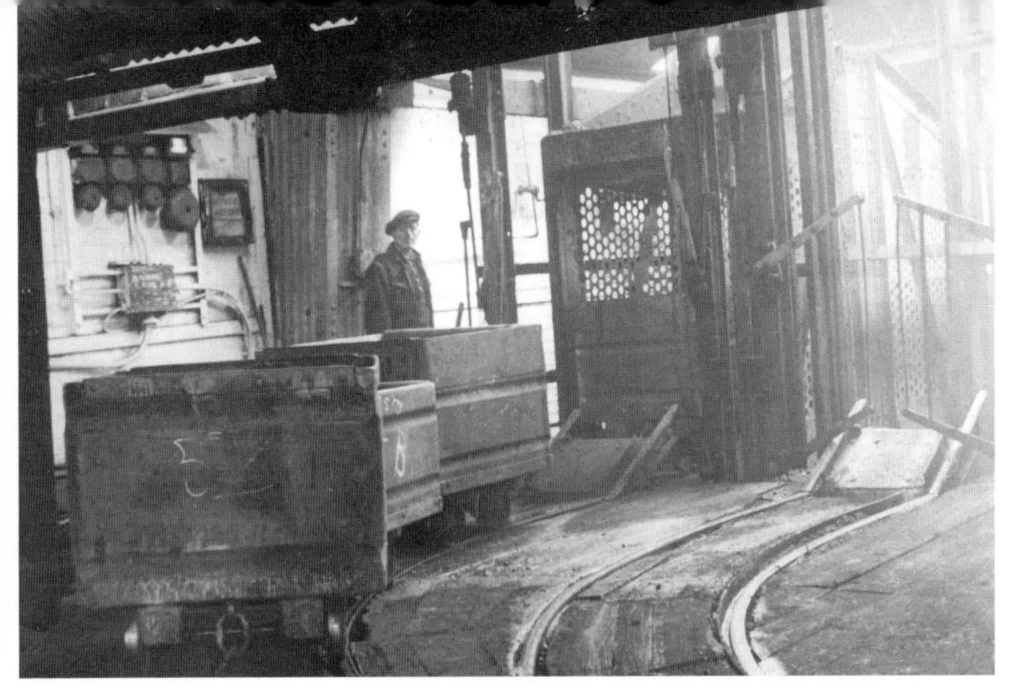

The man in this photograph is Mr Harold Prior. He is carrying out his everyday task of supervising the cage and tubs for the transportation of coal.

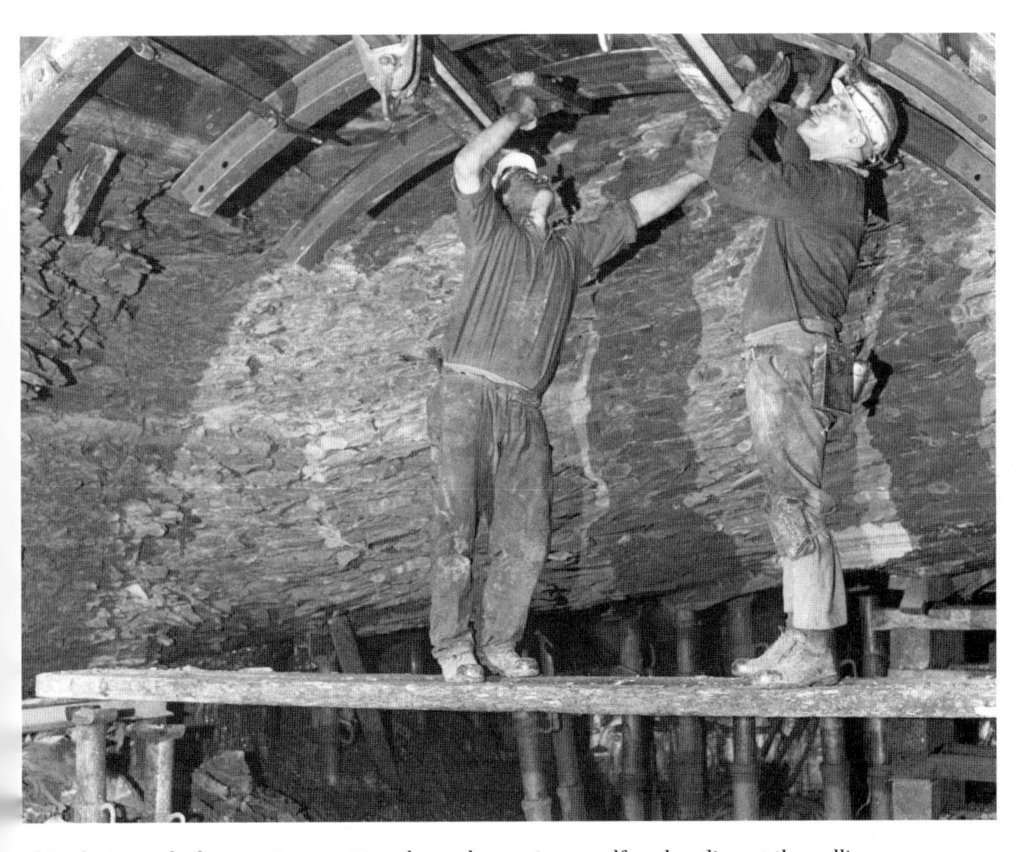

This photograph shows miners setting the archways in a coalface heading at the colliery.

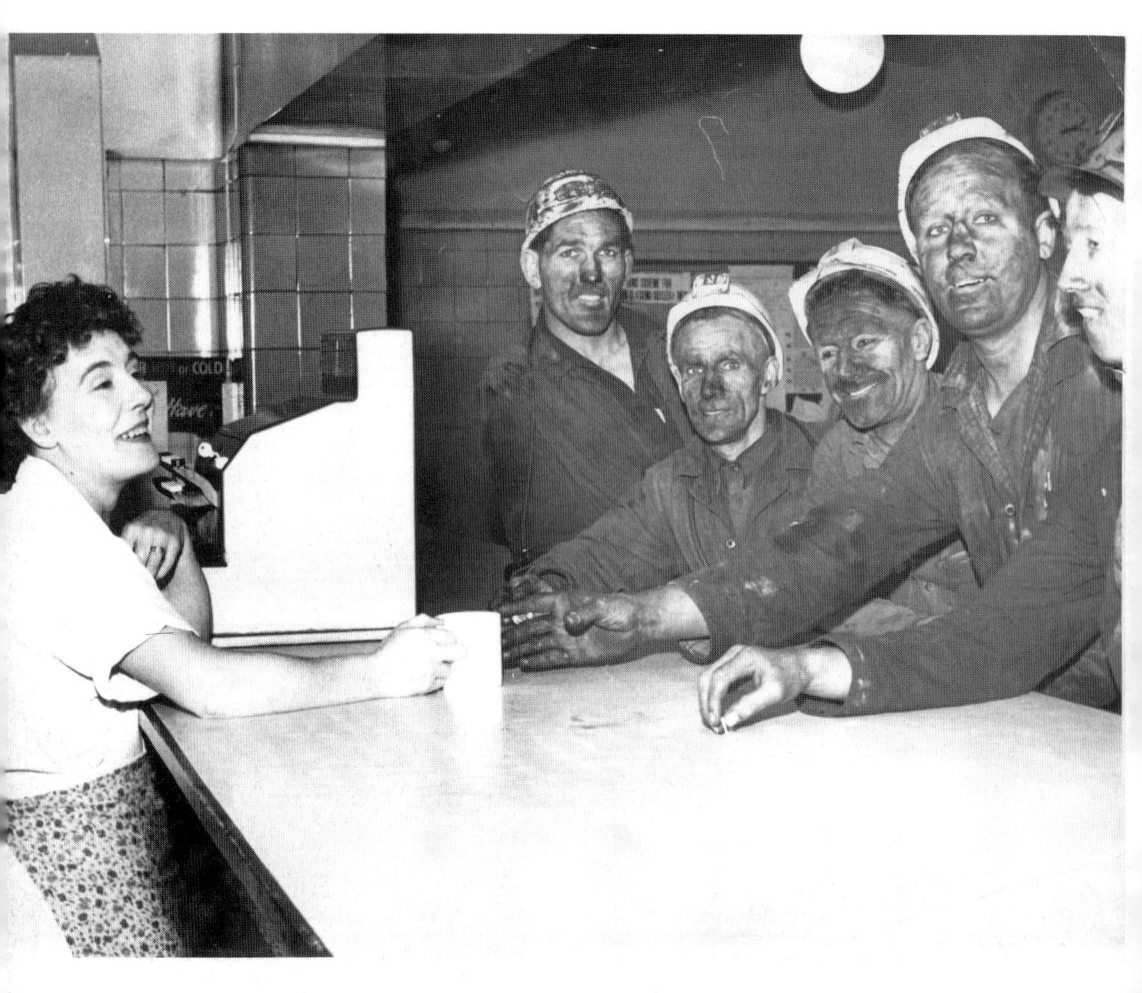

This picture shows miners queuing for a well-deserved tea break in the colliery canteen, quite a contrast between their dirty faces and that of the canteen worker!

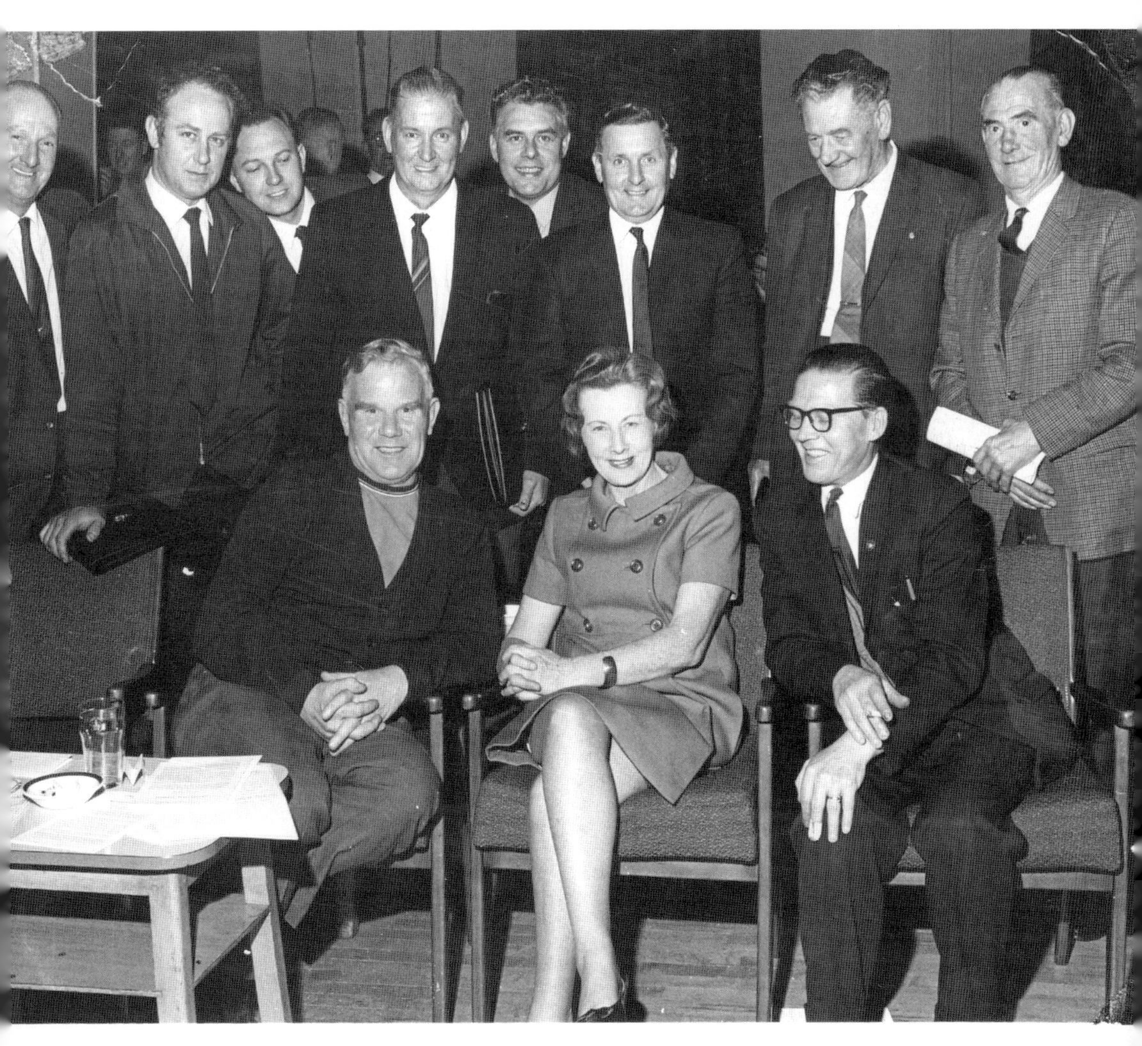

Taken in the 1970s, this picture shows Golborne miners with Labour left-winger Barbara Castle in the early 1970s.

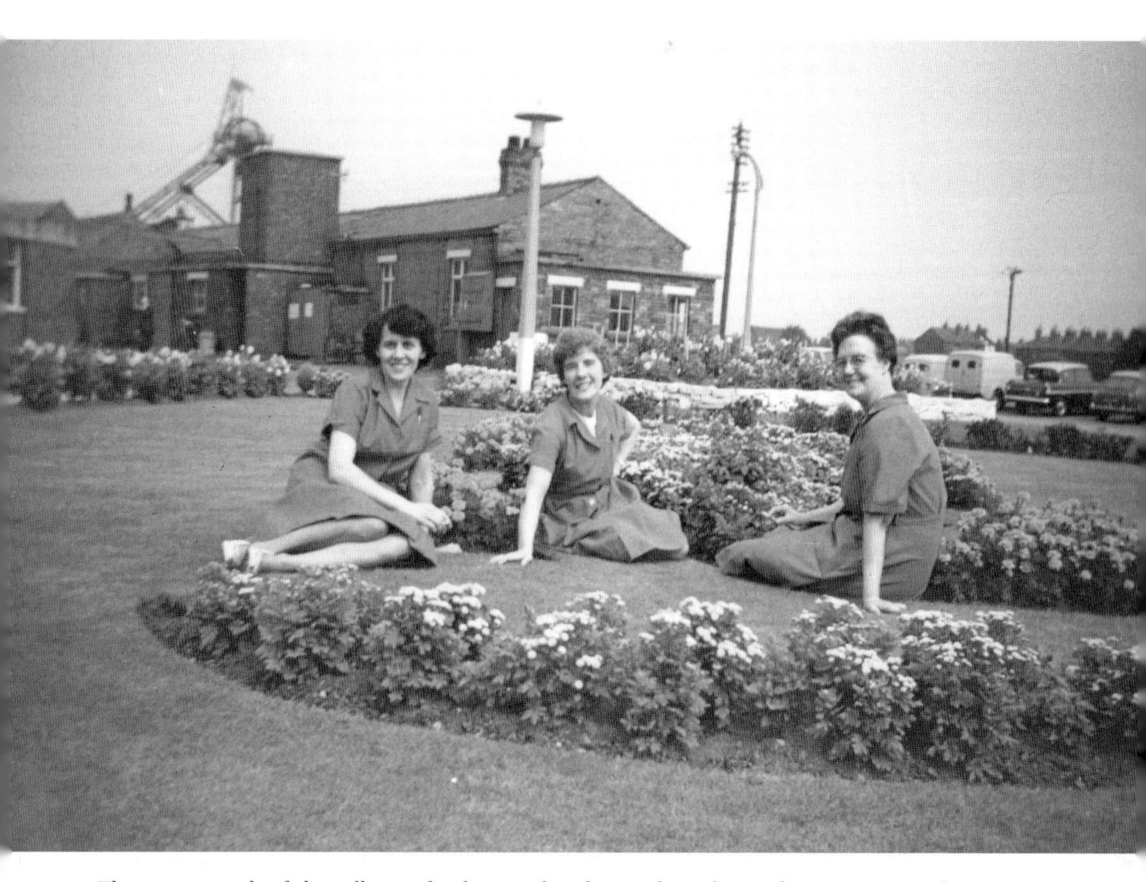

The canteen girls of the colliery take their tea break outside in the gardens on a warm day in 1960.

7

SHOPS AND OTHER BUILDINGS

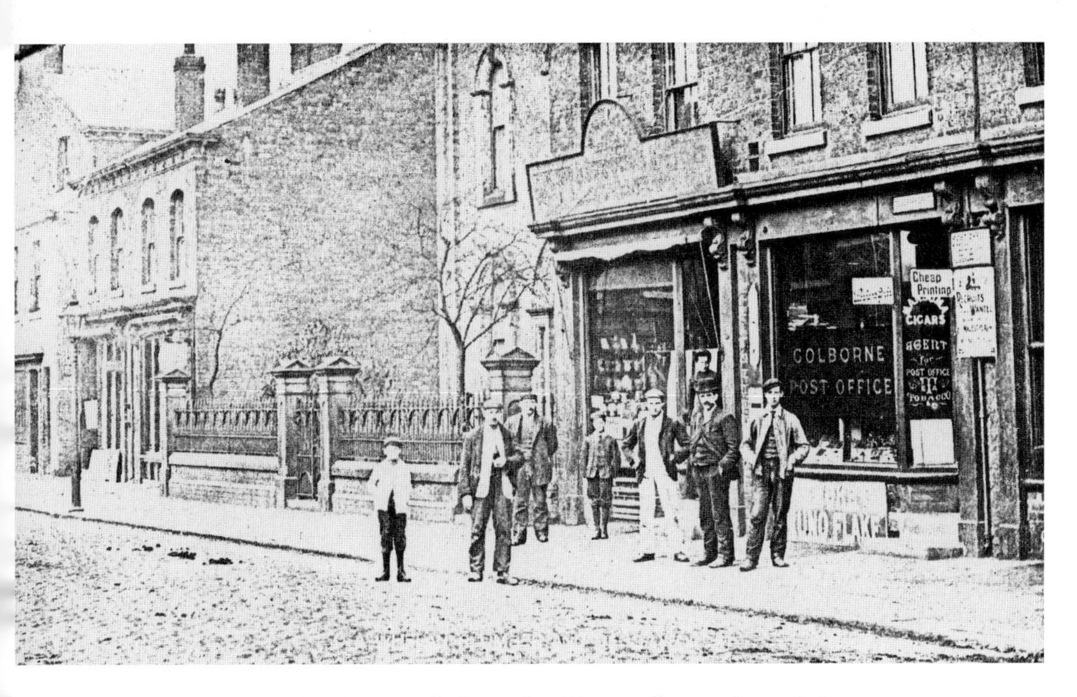

Taken in the Edwardian era, this photograph shows the old post office on the High Street.

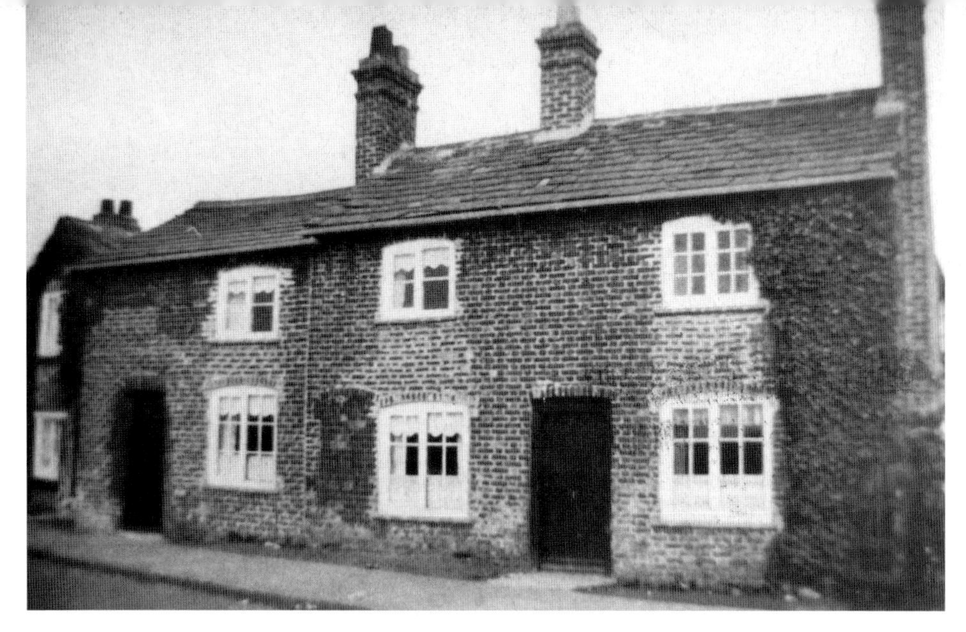

The cottages in this photograph were situated approximately 0.25 miles from Dover Lock. They were collectively known as Holtswell Brow and were demolished in 1959.

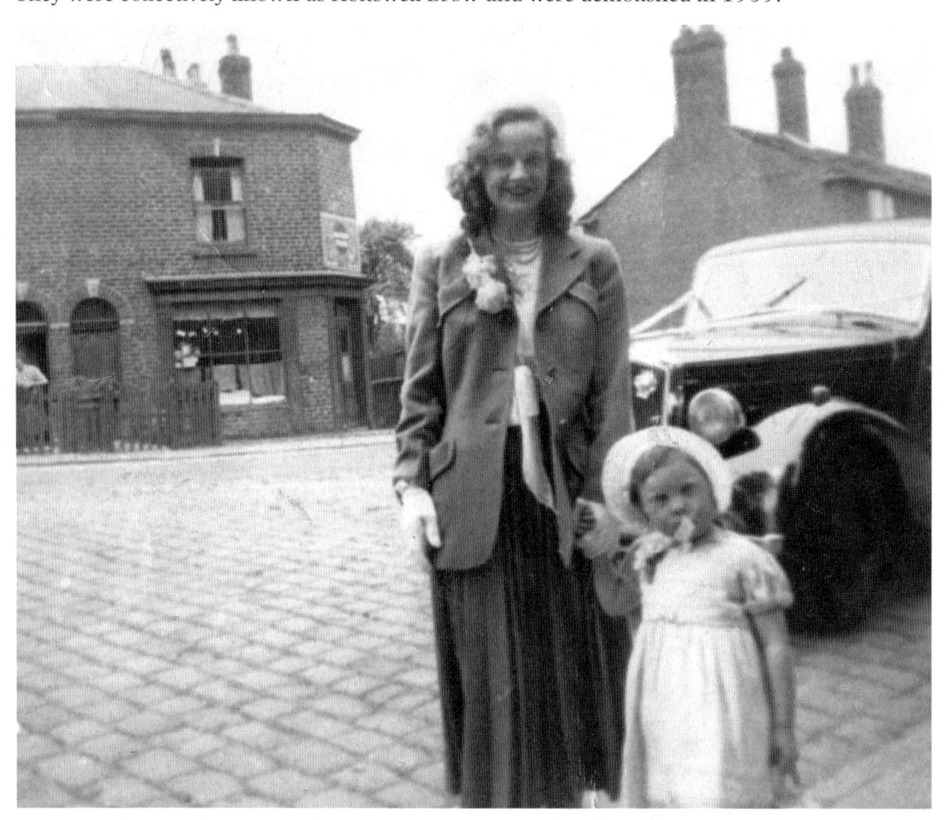

This photograph was taken outside St Thomas' Church in 1951. This is Lillian Bentham and her daughter Jeannette Baines Harrinton at sister Brenda's wedding. In the background is Ellis' shop, which sold wool, cottons and all sorts of odds and ends. Joyce and Lillian Ellis lived there. Lillian worked in the Temperance Bar in Golborne village centre for many years.

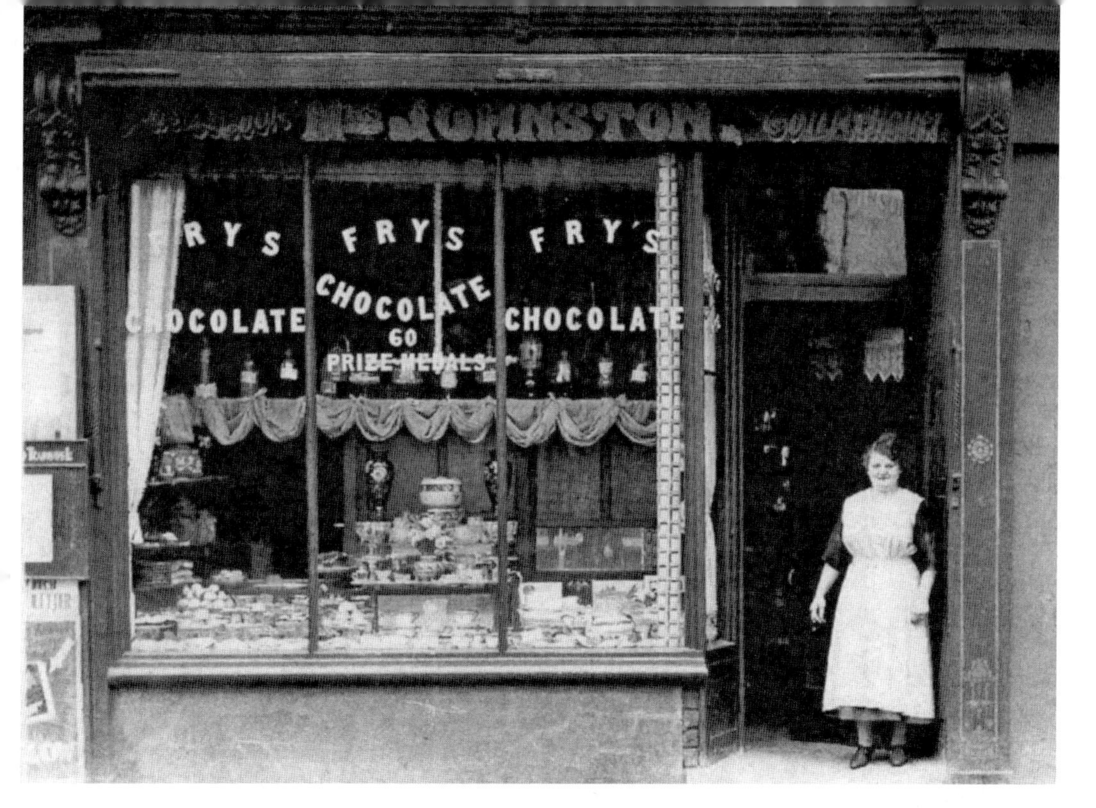

This picture shows Fanny Johnston's cake shop. It was situated where Willcock's chemist was, opposite the old police station on High Street.

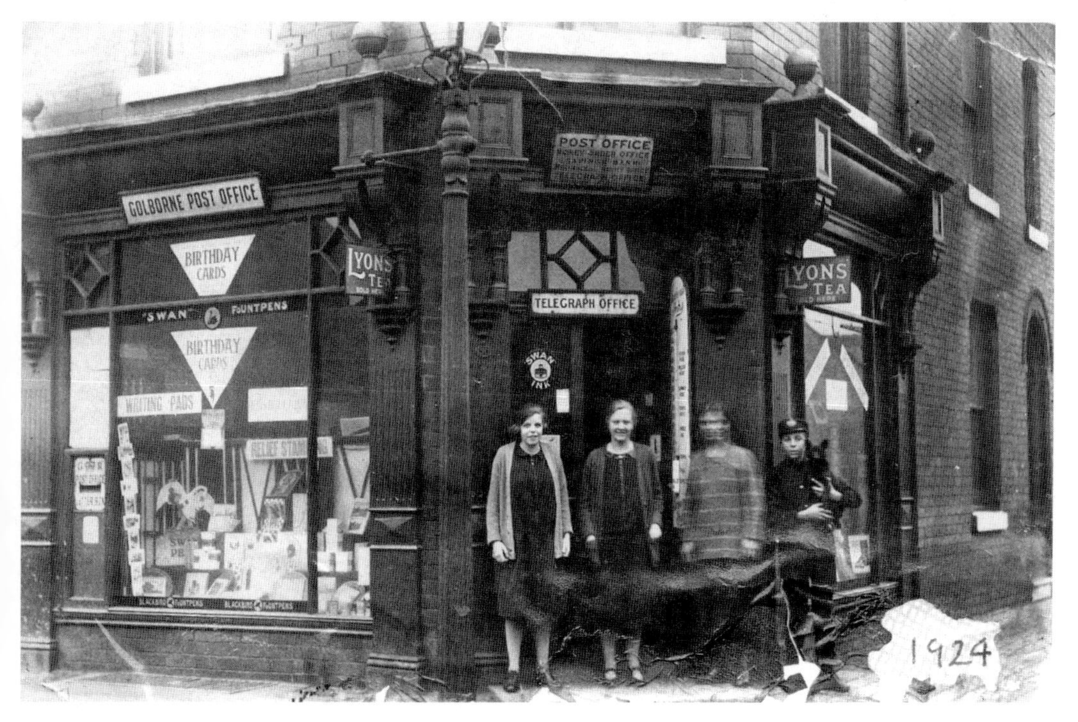

This photograph shows Golborne post office in 1924. The boy holding the dog is Ronnie Marsh. As you can see, the entrance used to be located on the corner of the building.

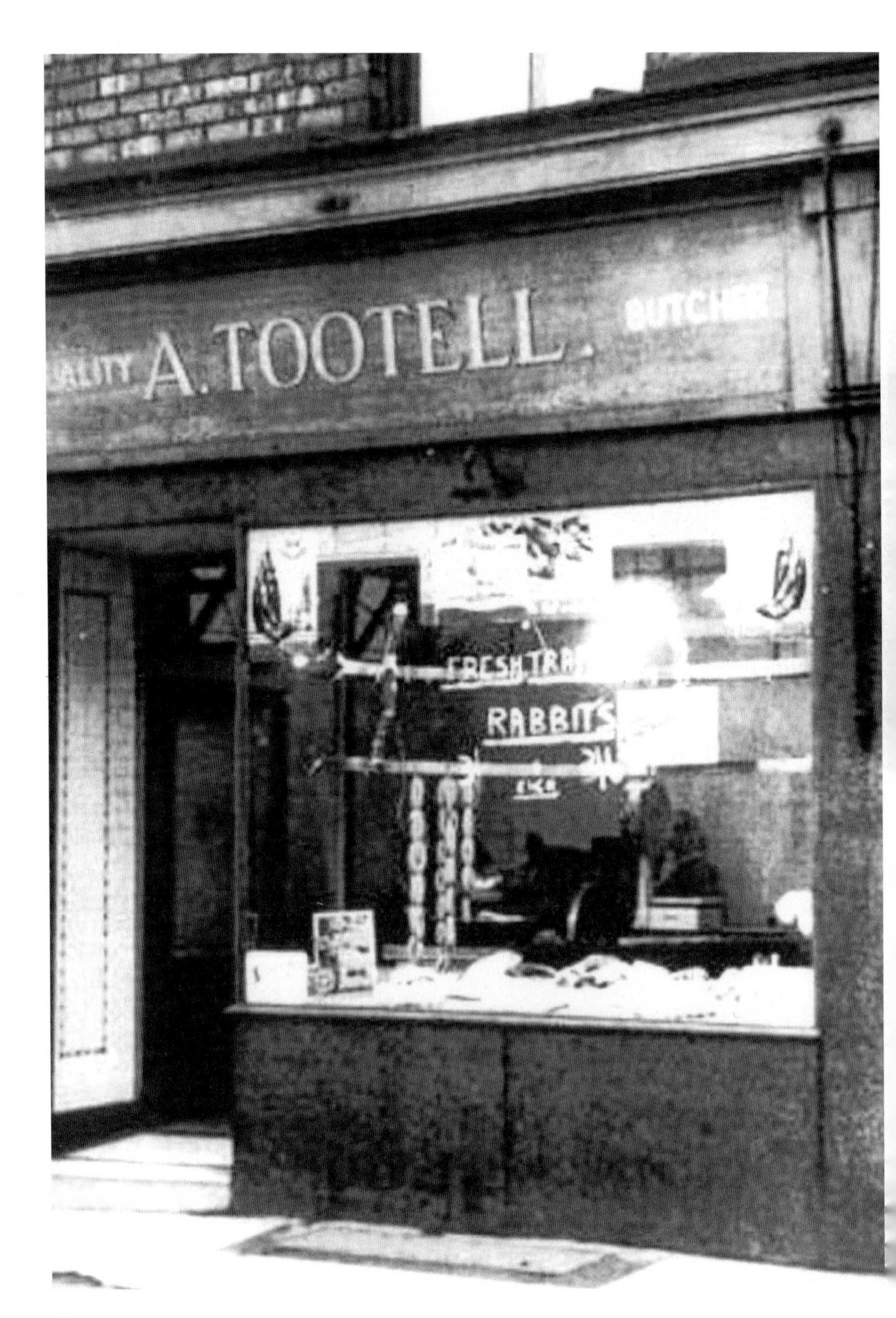
A. TOOTELL.
BUTCHER
RABBITS

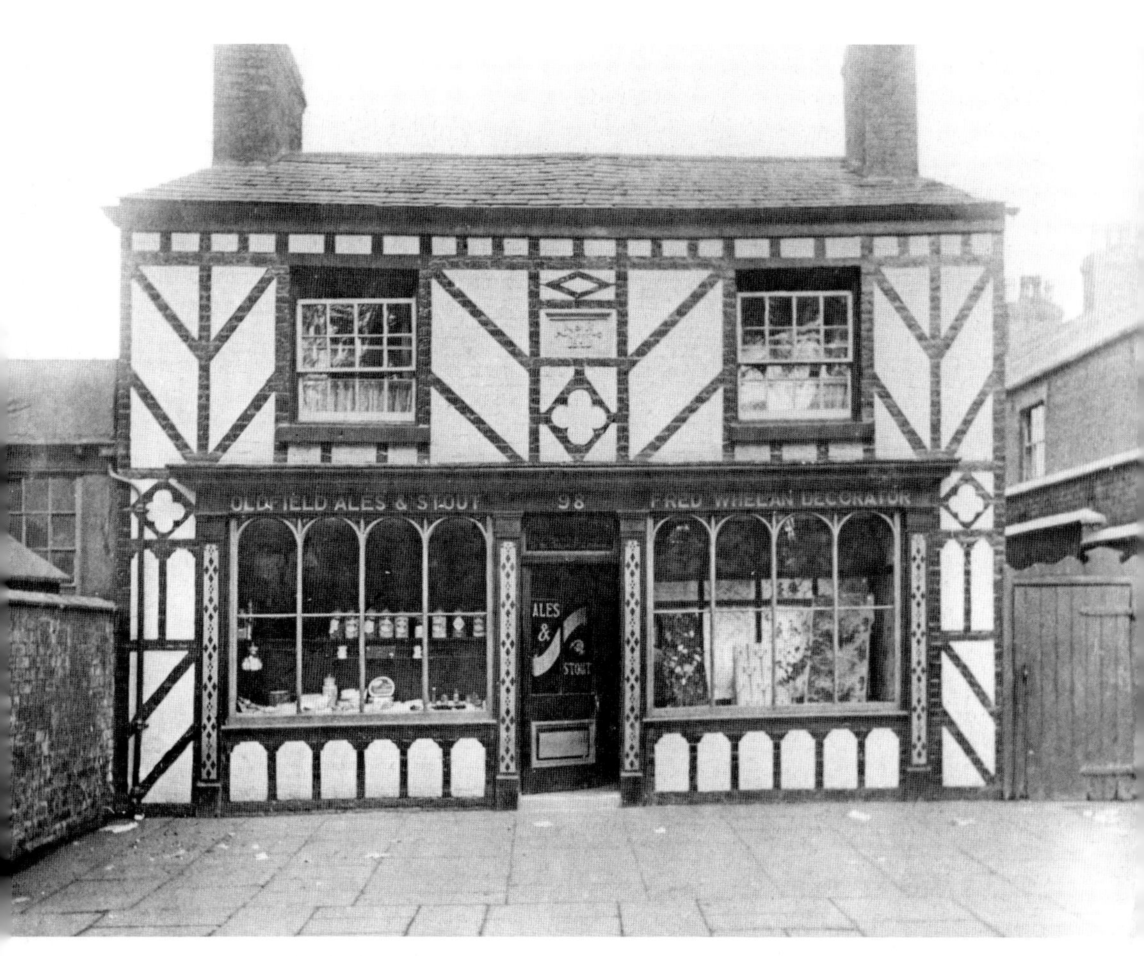

This is what the sandwich shop on Bridge Street, formally News 'n' Booze, used to look like. This shop pre-dates the much remembered owner, Ernie Bennett. This belonged to Fred Wheelan. It was a decorators and off-licence. According to Wigan 'Town and Country Rambles' book, of 1914, he sold Oldfields Ales.

Opposite: The legendary Alan Tootells' butchers shop, established in 1950. The shop, before it became a butchers, was a pawnbrokers and had the classic symbol of three golden balls hanging over the entrance.

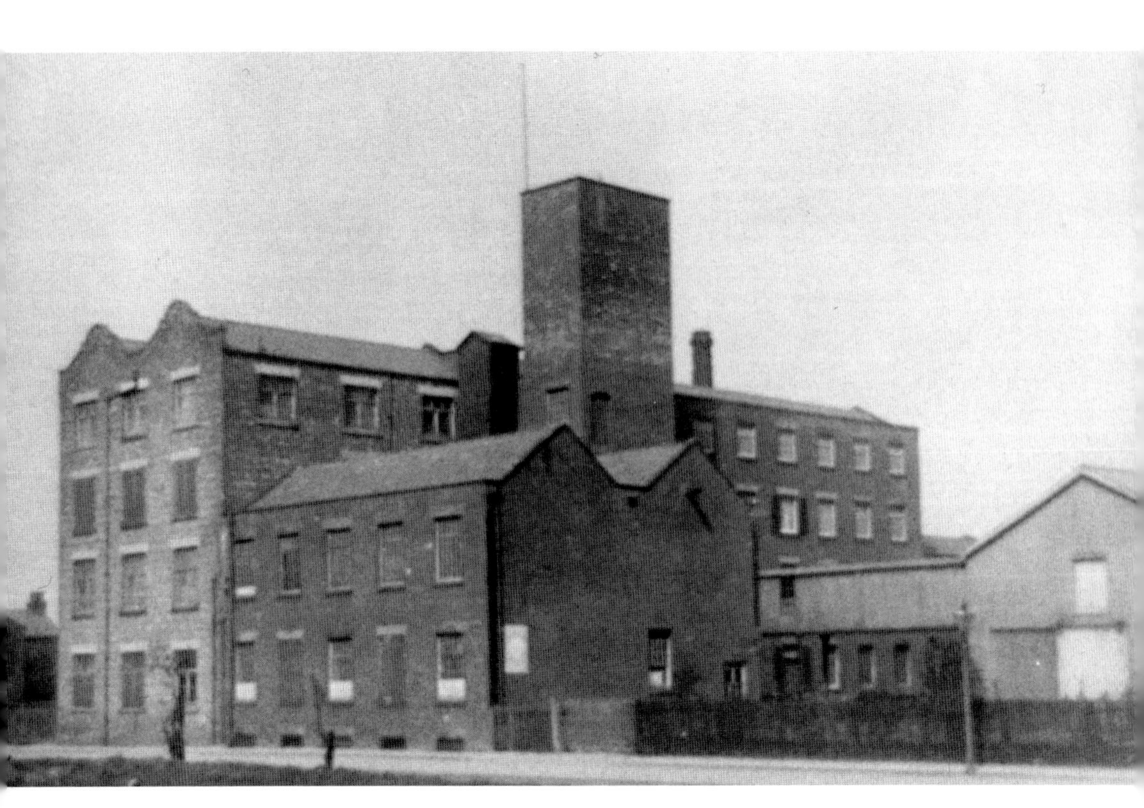

A picture of Rothwell's Chocolate Works in Harvey Lane, the makers of Welco and other chocolates. John Rothwell founded his first business, a grocery store, in 1850 in Wallage, Wigan. He then built a chocolate factory in 1887. As Mr Rothwell's empire grew he needed bigger premises, and relocated the chocolate factory to Harvey Lane in Golborne. Years later, the world-famous Walnut Whip was invented and patented in the Golborne factory, and later sold to another chocolate manufacturer.

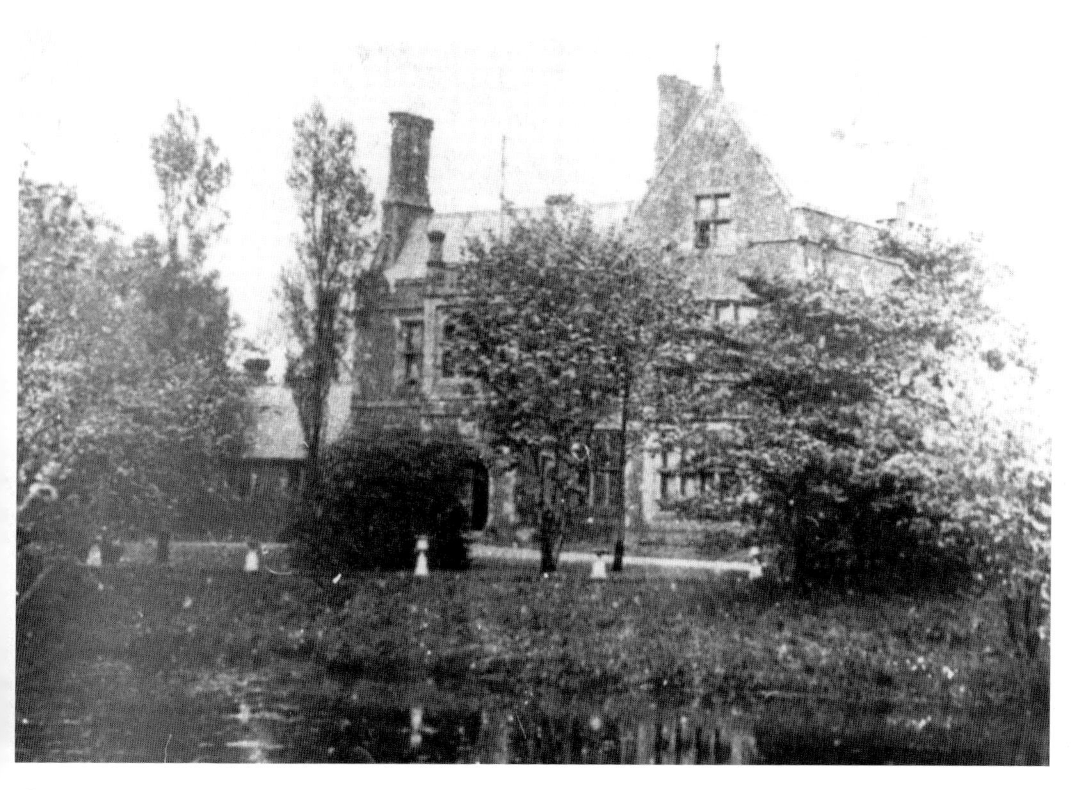

This is the only surviving photograph of Heywood Hall (or House). Built in 1851, it was originally the seat of Robert Worsley Esq. It was situated between St Thomas' Church and modern day Heywood Avenue. The Avenue was named after the house.

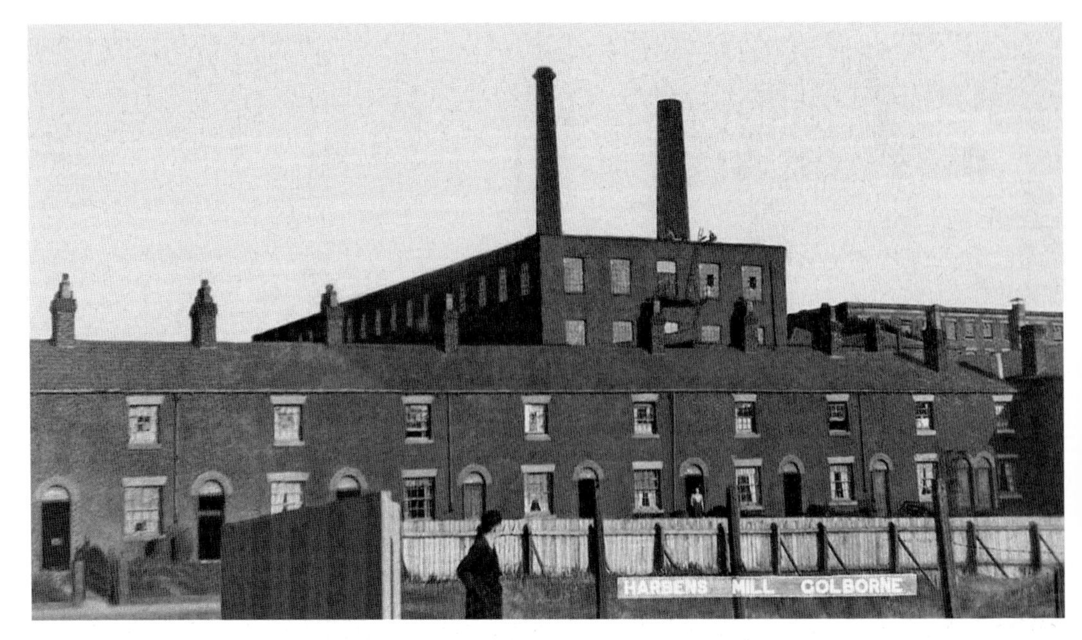

When this photograph was taken, possibly during the early1960s, this mill was run by the company Harbens. They produced artificial yarns, 97 per cent of which was crimplene. The company was bought out by Courtaulds in 1959. Through the years, the mill has been named Parkside Mills and Tattons.

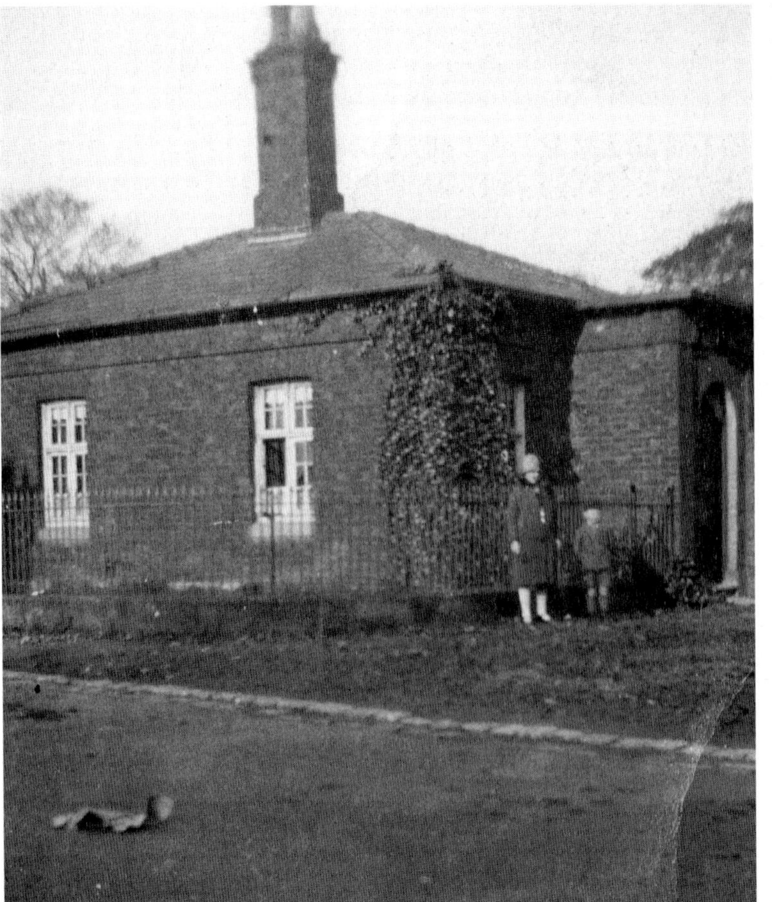

Possibly taken in the 1930s, this picture shows Holmes Lodge just off Bridge Street, facing the Queen Ann public house. Perhaps the people in this picture were residents of the lodge at the time.

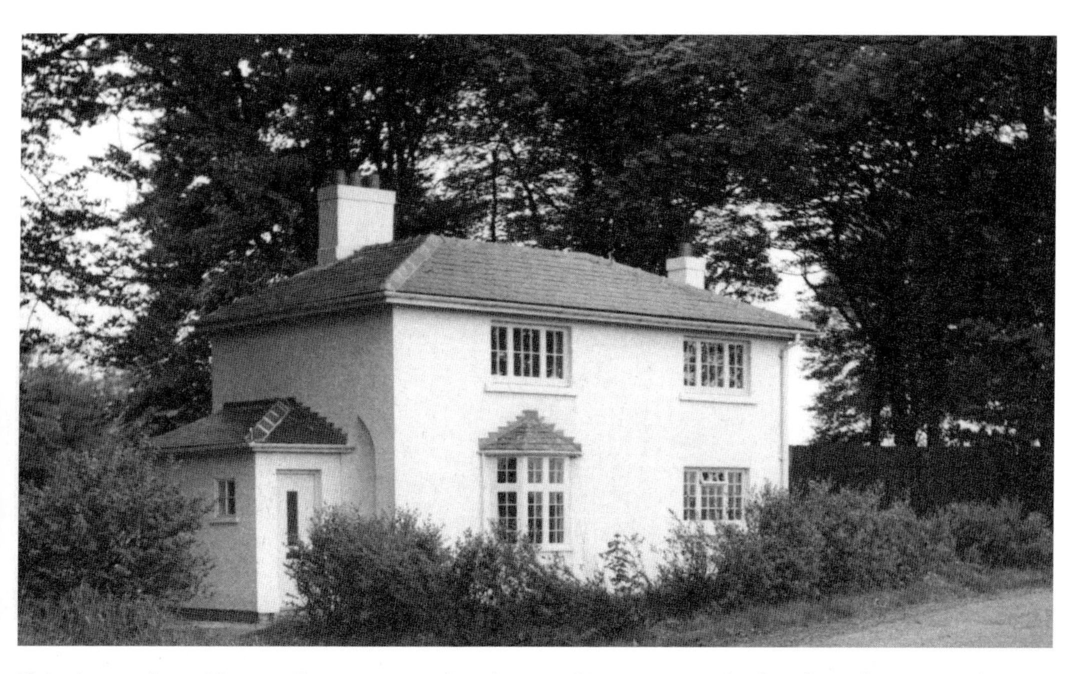

This picture shows Keepers Cottage, situated at the top of Harvey Lane, further down from Keeper's Lane. While the date of the photograph is unfortunately unknown, the building has completely changed in modern times, no longer bearing any resemblance to what it looks like in this photograph.

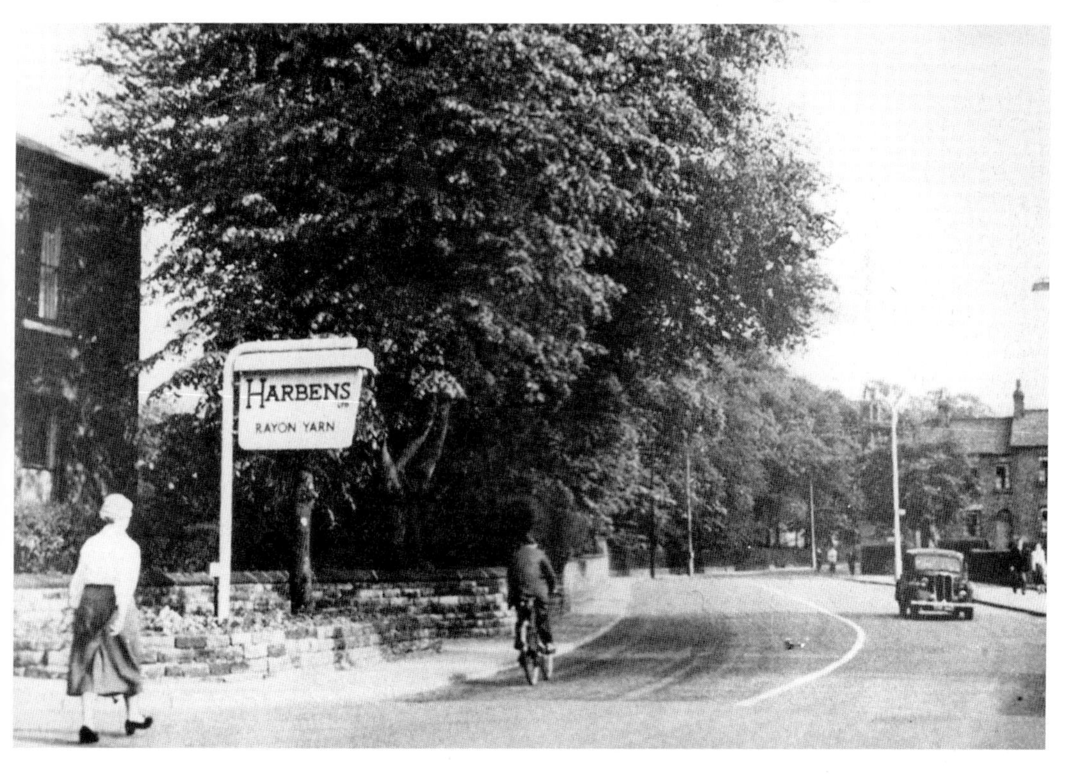

A photograph showing the entrance to Harbens Mill, manufacturers of rayon yarn, on Bridge Street.

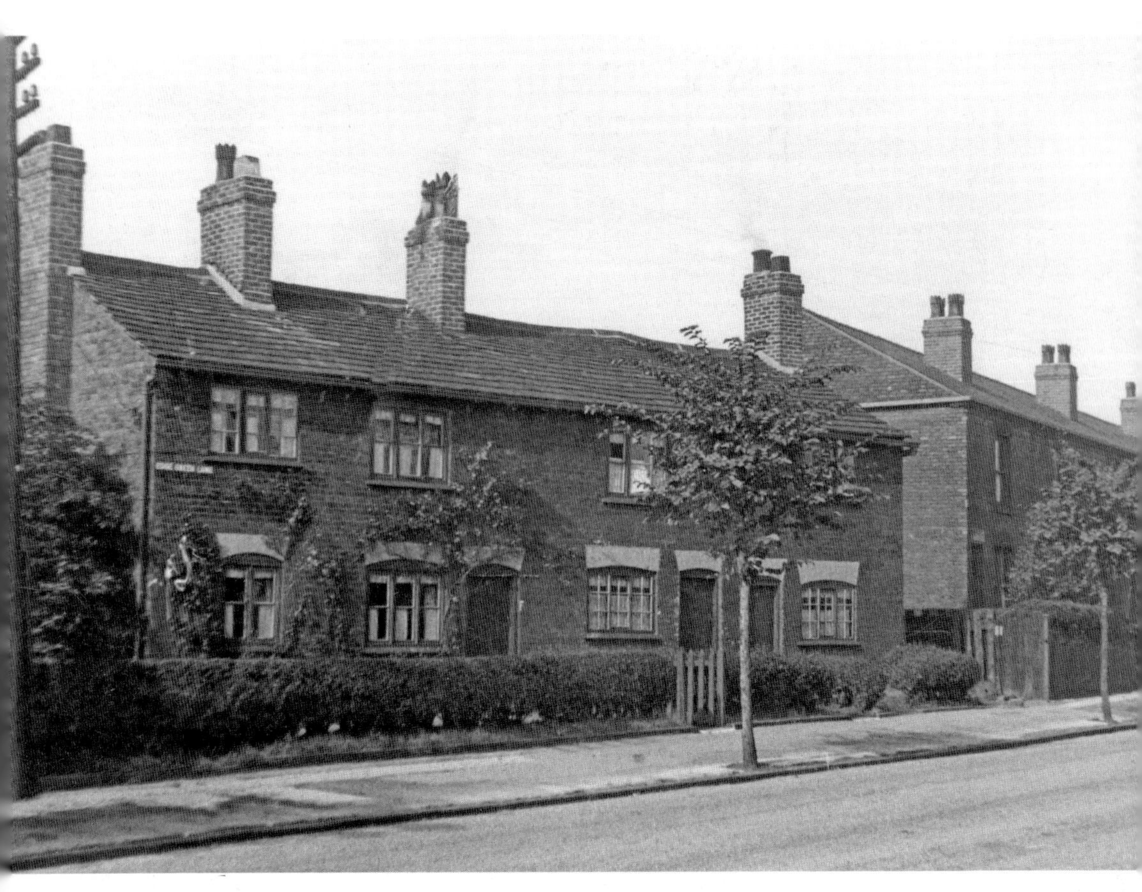

This picture shows the rather quaint-looking cottages of Edge Green Lane, numbered 2, 4 and 6. On a map of Golborne, dated 1981, these are the only houses on the lane at that time. On the map, they are called the Club Houses. They were demolished some time in the 1960s and on the site now is a semi-detached house.

8

THE RAILWAY

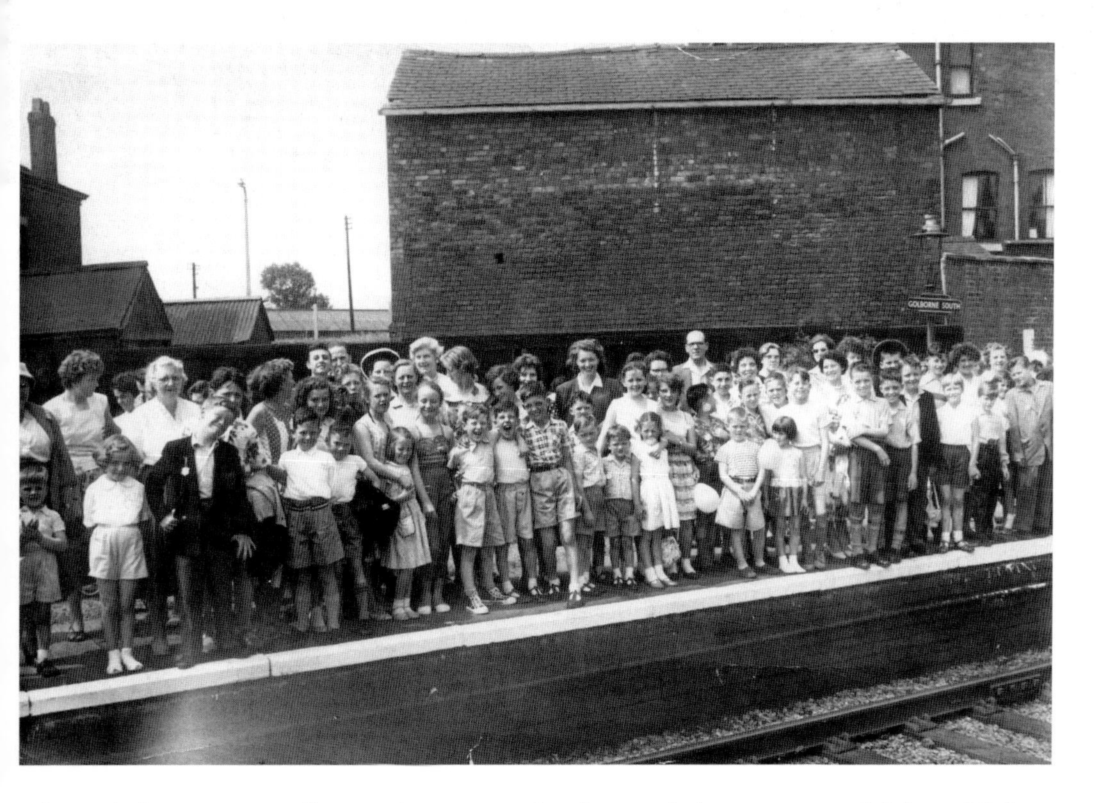

Taken in the late 1950s, at Golborne railway station, this photograph shows an outing of Golborne's Labour Club to Southport on a warm summer's day.

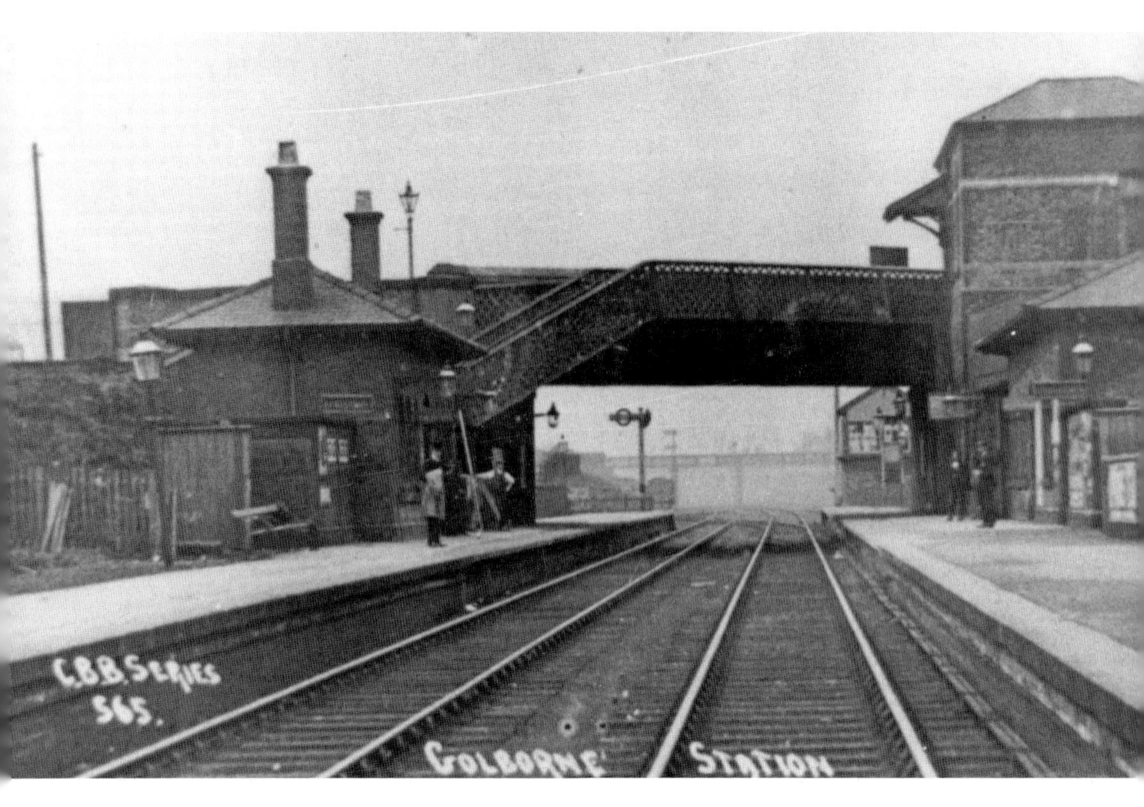

A photograph showing a classic view of Golborne station; the year is unknown.

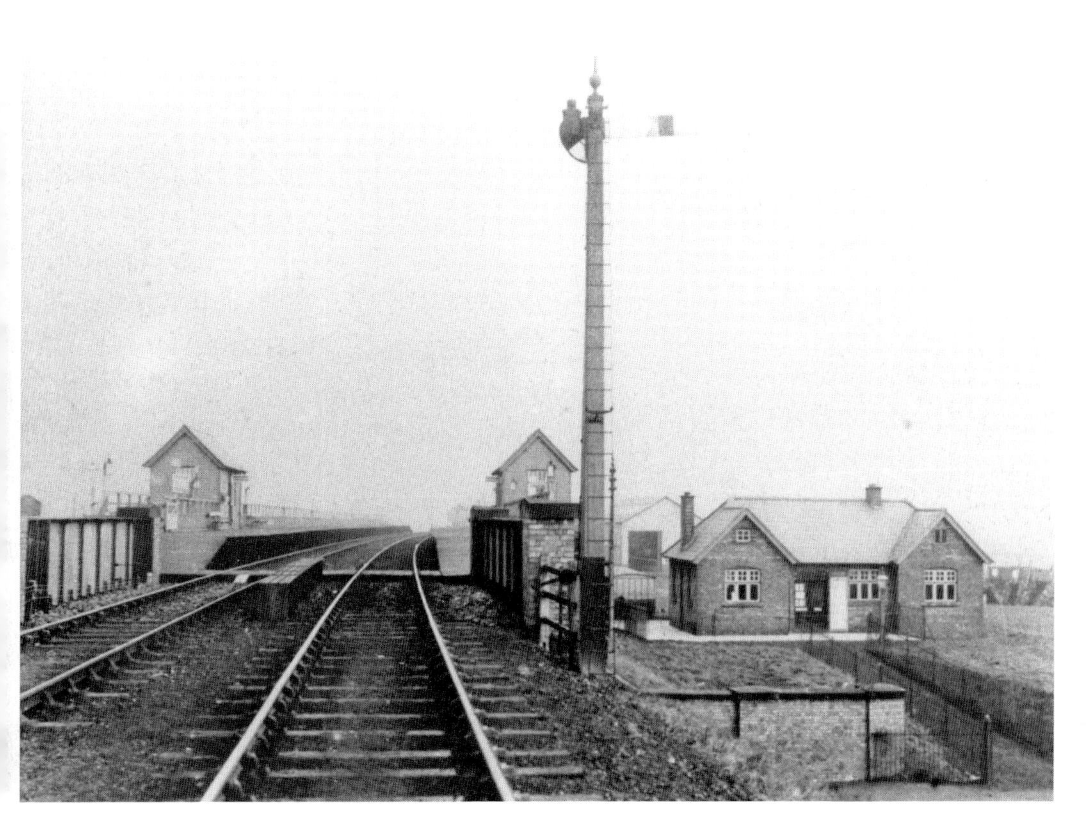

A picture of Golborne North railway station. The civil engineering company Murphy's – seen on the right of this photograph – is now on Wigan Road.

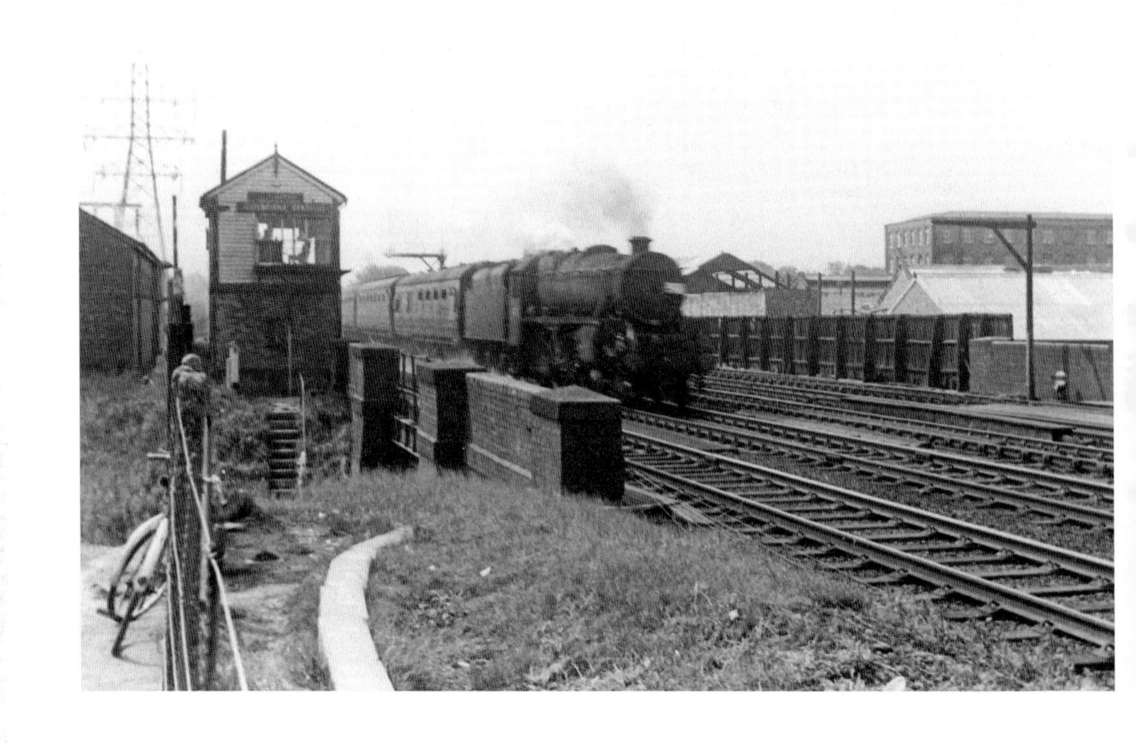

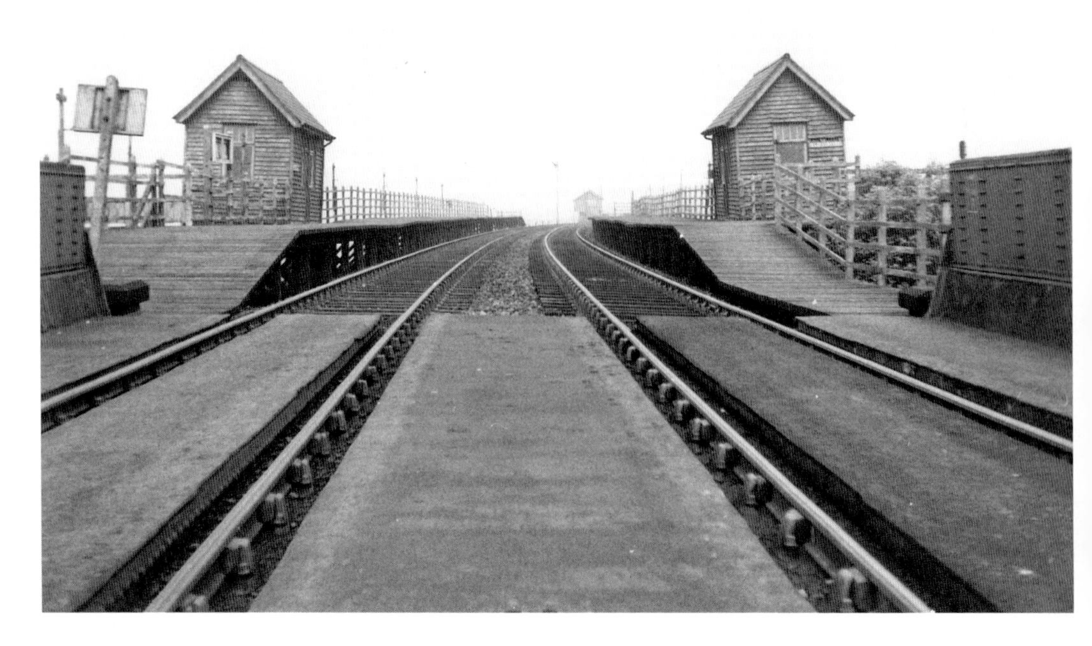

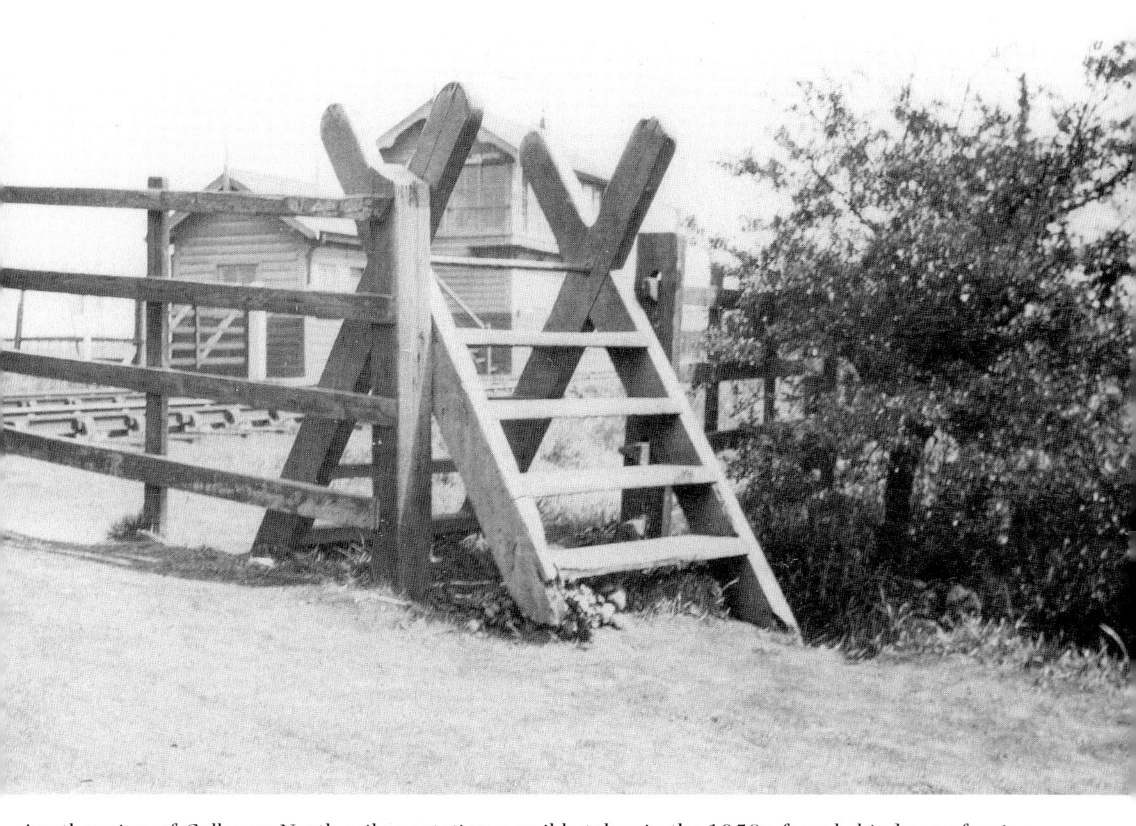

Another view of Golborne North railway station, possibly taken in the 1950s, from behind some fencing.

Opposite above: A photograph showing Golborne South railway station, with an action shot of a train.

Opposite below: An alternative shot of Golborne North railway station.

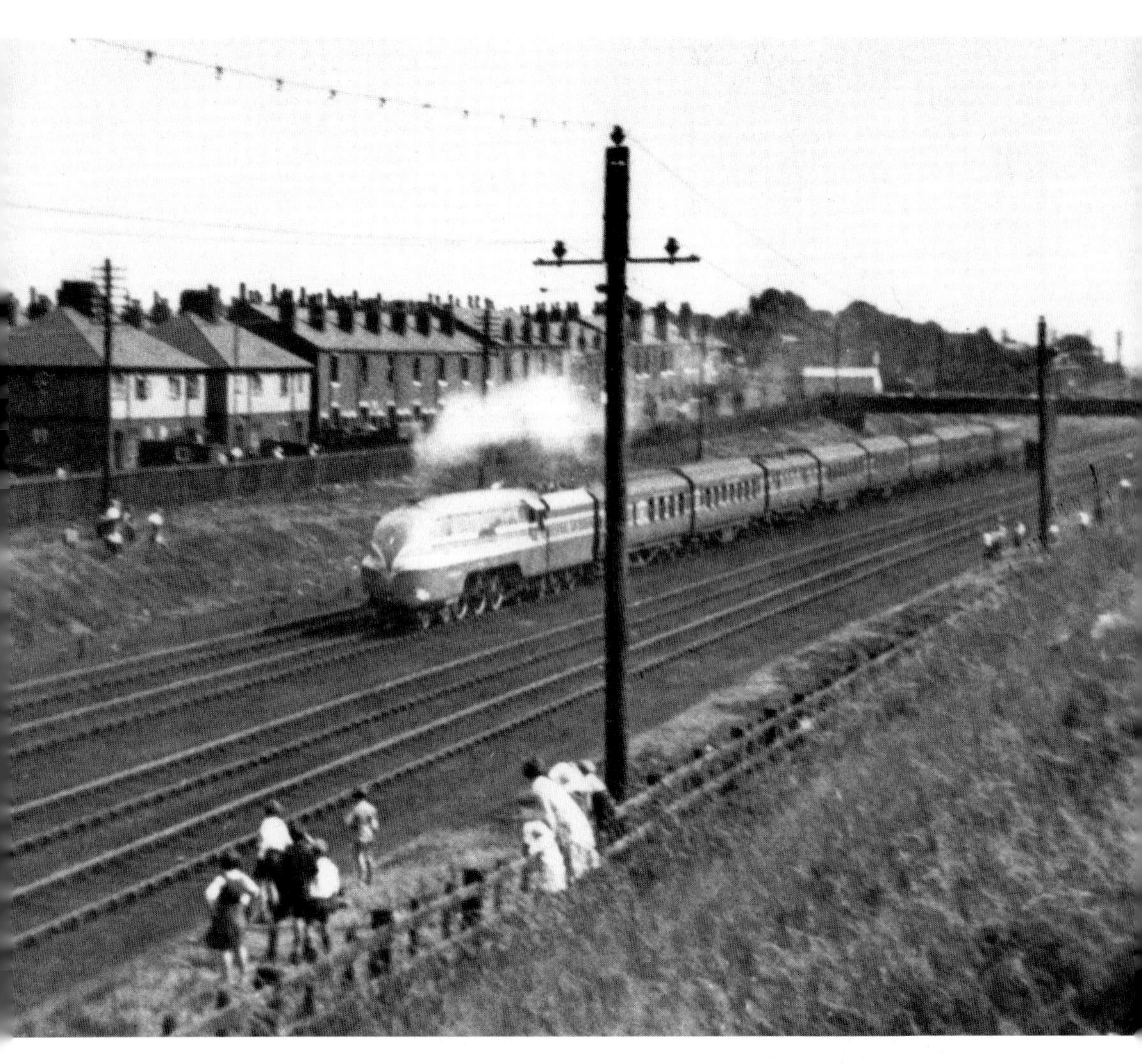

This picture was taken from the bridge at the back of May Street. This is the *Coronation Scot* passing though Golborne. The steam locomotive's route ran from London's Euston Station to Glasgow Central in a record -breaking six and a half hours. In 1937, during tests, the locomotive broke a British Railways record by reaching a maximum speed of 114mph!

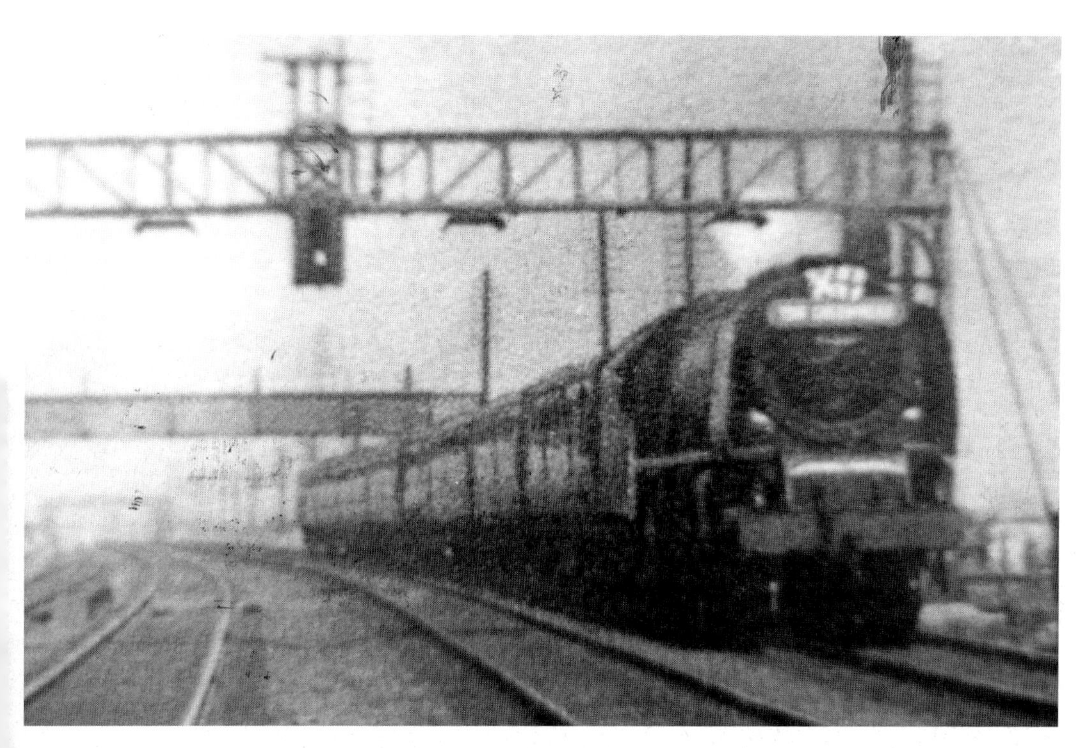

The *Caledonian* passing at speed through Golborne on the 21 June 1957.

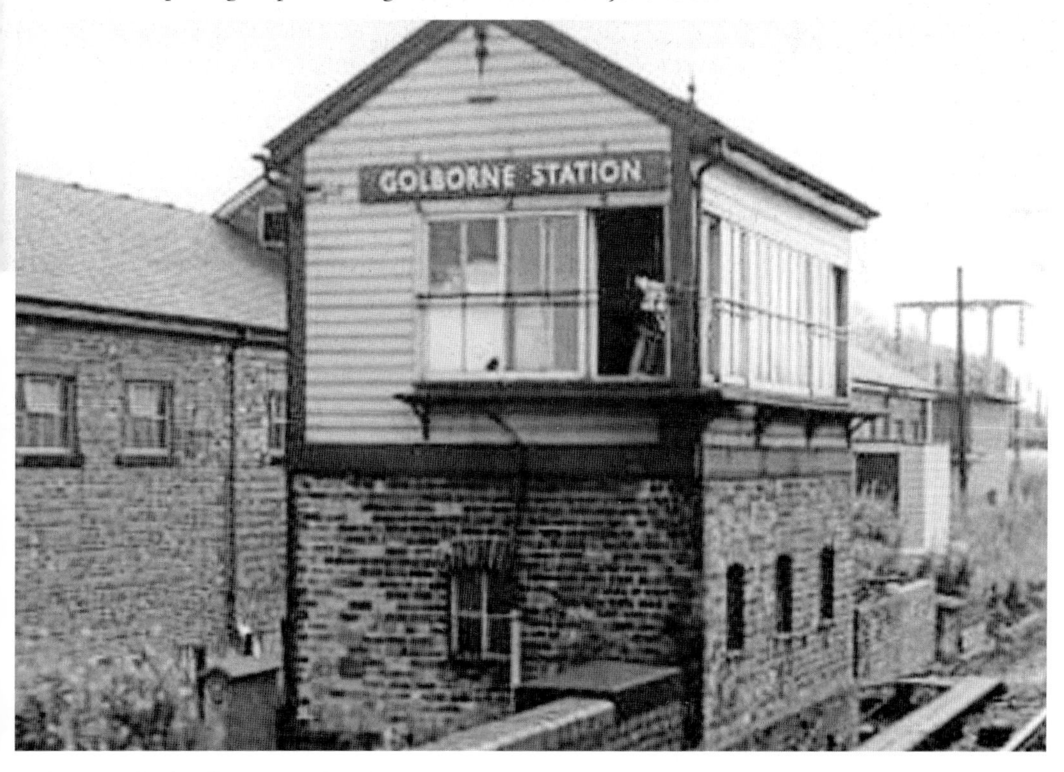

A photograph of Golborne South railway station's signal box.

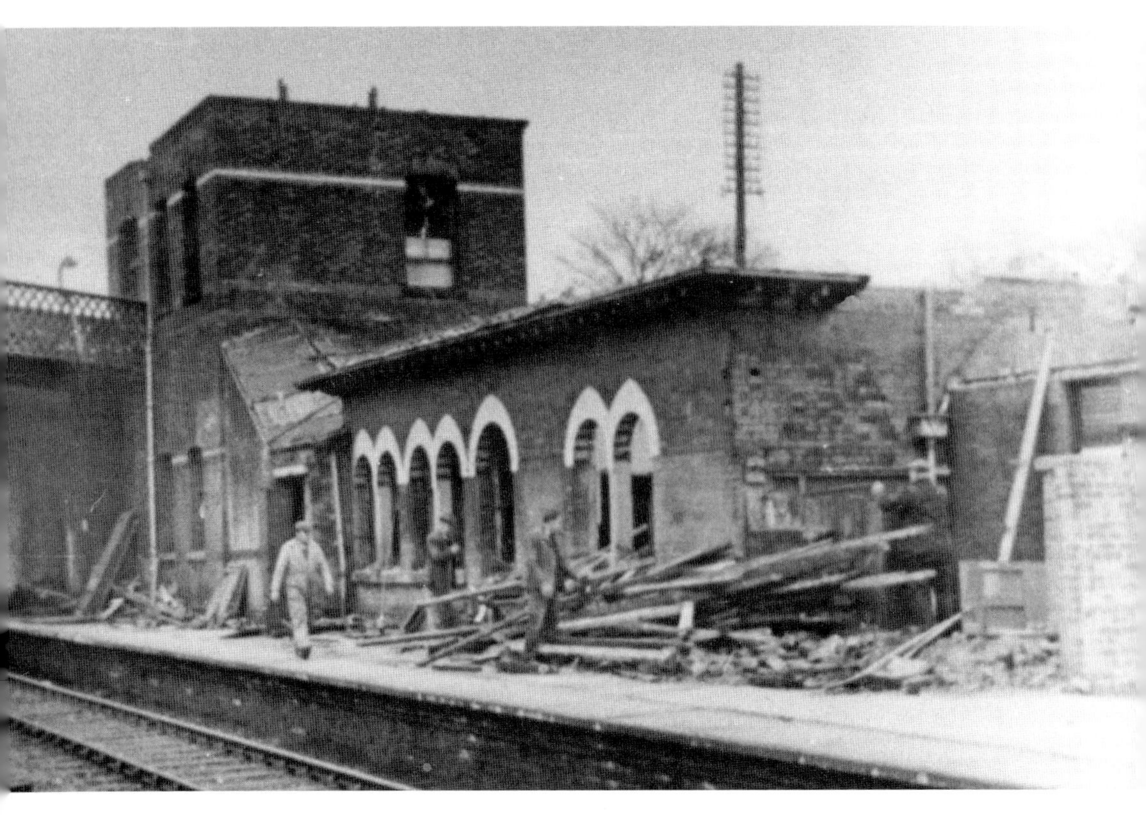

This picture captures the demolition of Golborne station in around 1959.

9

MISCELLANEOUS

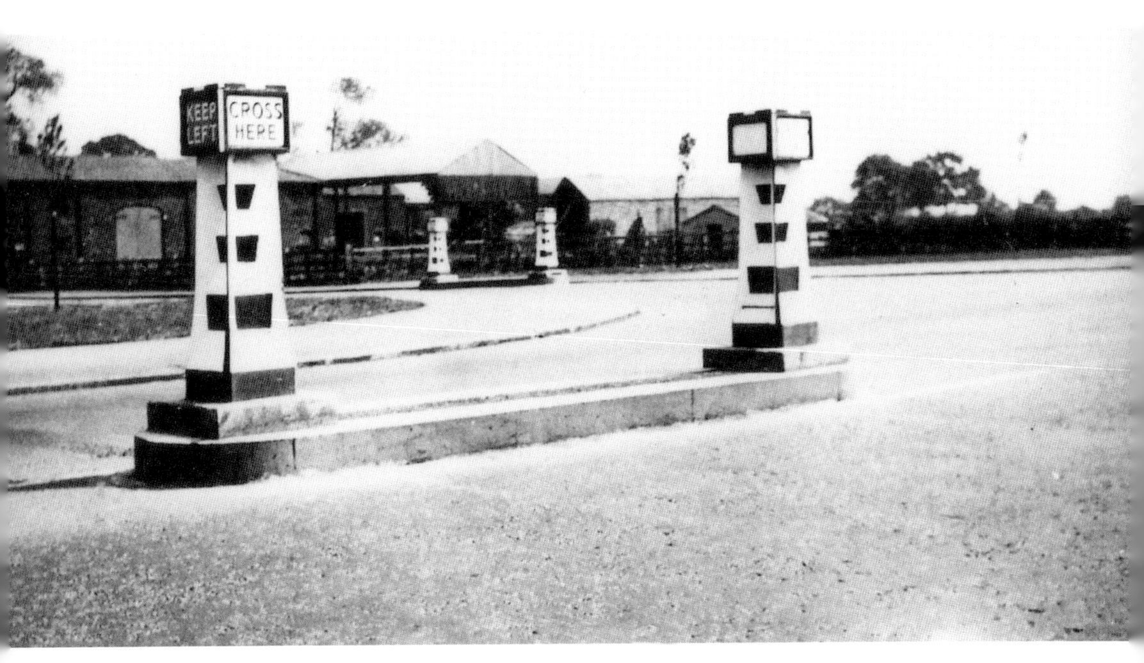

Taken in the 1950s, this photograph was taken in the place where Golborne Island is situated today. The East Lancashire Road was officially opened by King George V on 18 July 1934.

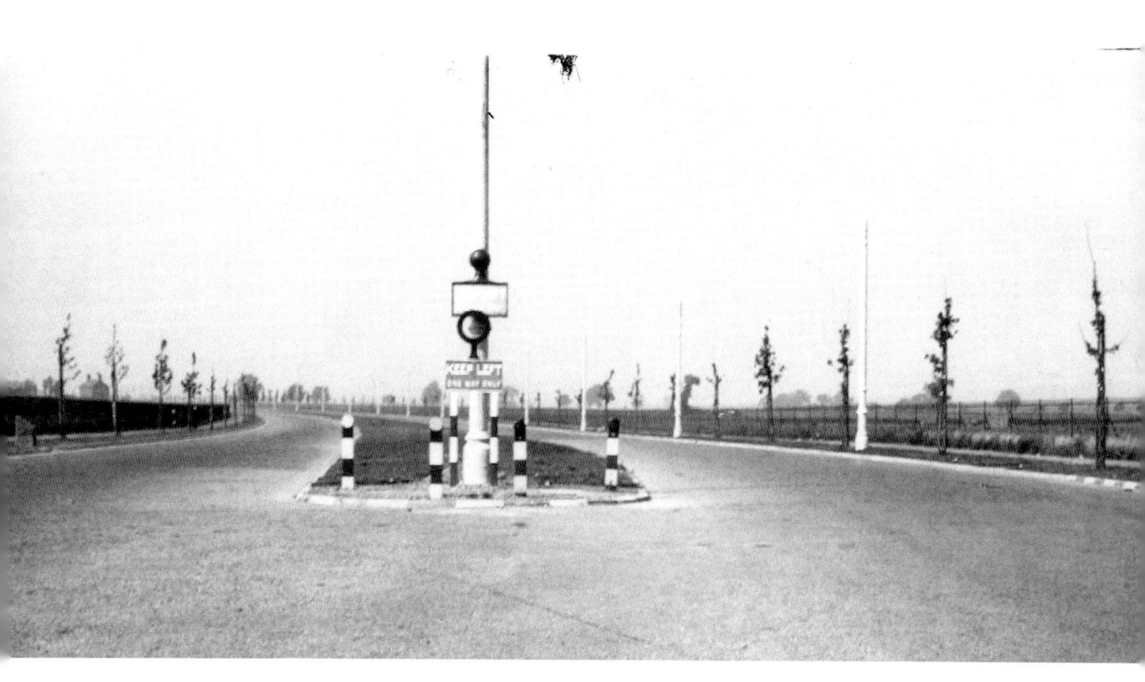

Another view of the East Lancashire Road, taken some time in the mid-to-late 1930s.

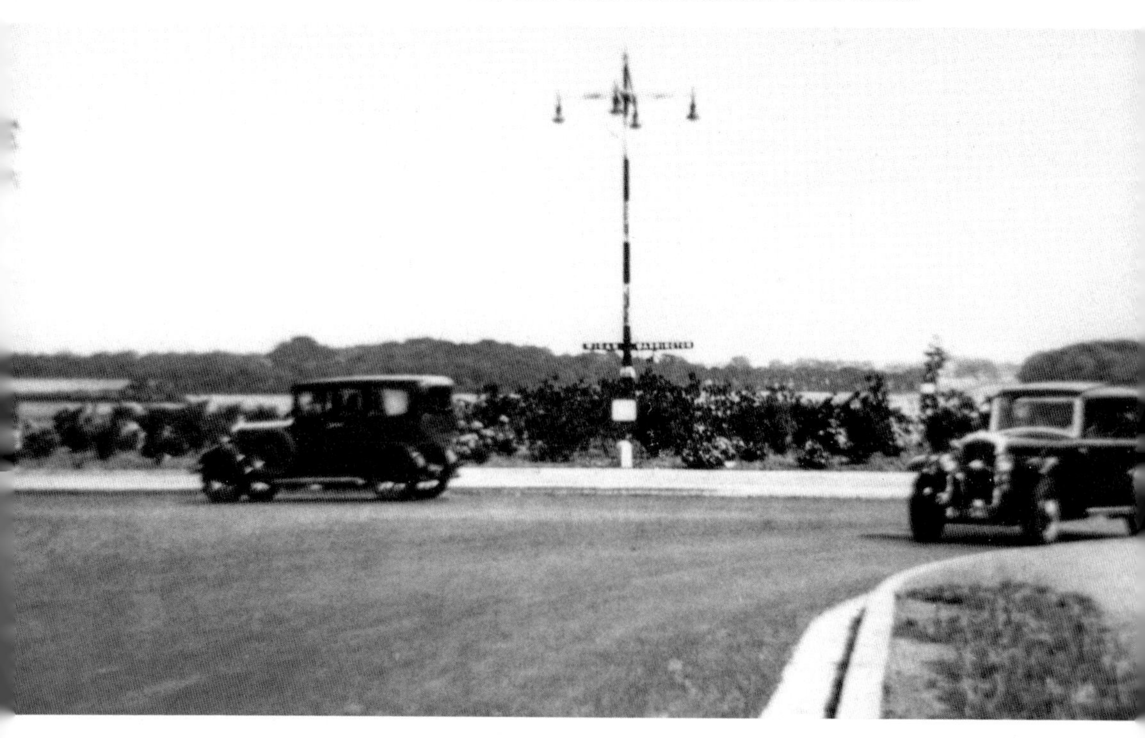

The location of this picture is something of a mystery. It could possibly be Ashton Road, looking right to Golborne Centre, towards the Red Lion public house and Abram to the left. We're also unsure of the date but the style of the cars suggests the era could well be in the late 1920s or early 1930s. An interesting photograph though!

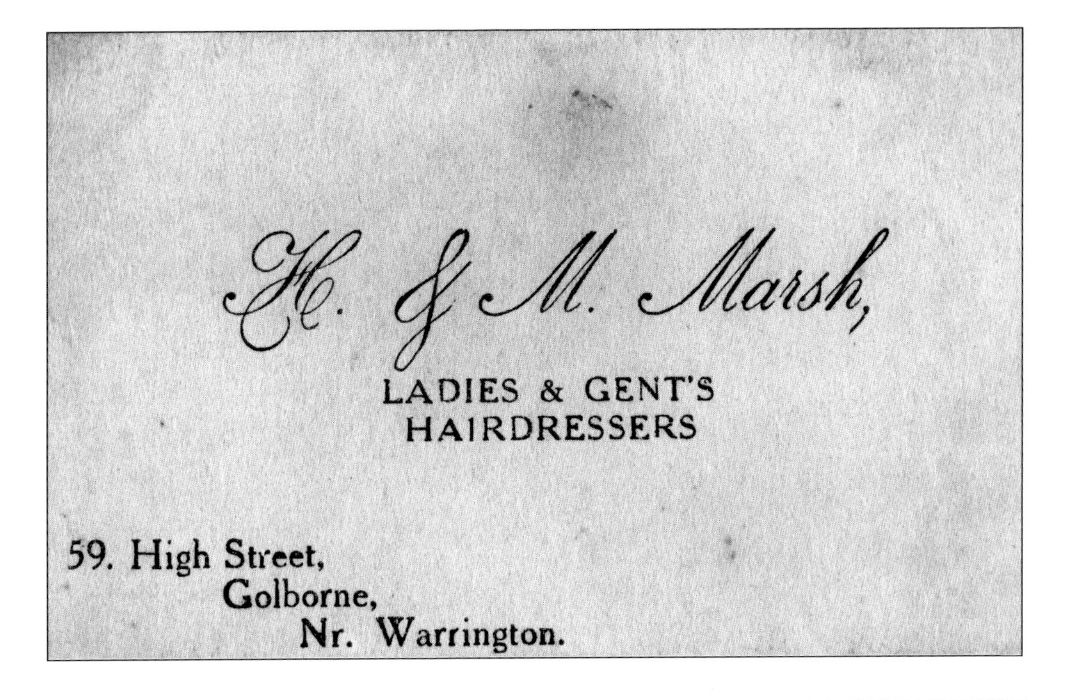

H. & M. Marsh,

LADIES & GENT'S
HAIRDRESSERS

59. High Street,
Golborne,
Nr. Warrington.

This business card is from Harold & Maud Marsh, hairdressers shop of 59 High Street. Harold bought the shop from the man whom he'd trained with as a leather boy in 1911. Harold retired in 1965.

BUCKINGHAM PALACE

The Queen and I bid you a very warm welcome home.

Through all the great trials and sufferings which you have undergone at the hands of the Japanese, you and your comrades have been constantly in our thoughts. We know from the accounts we have already received how heavy those sufferings have been. We know also that these have been endured by you with the highest courage.

We mourn with you the deaths of so many of your gallant comrades.

With all our hearts, we hope that your return from captivity will bring you and your families a full measure of happiness, which you may long enjoy together.

George R.I.

September 1945.

This is a letter from King George VI welcoming home the war heroes of the Second World War in 1945. This particular letter was sent to a Mr Jack Hayes, who suffered at the hands of the Japanese in Malaysia. Mr Hayes, from Park Avenue, and his troops were responsible for building the famous bridge over the River Kwai.

33, HIGH STREET,
GOLBORNE,
nr. WARRINGTON.

Feb 22nd 1961

M Collier Golborne

BOUGHT OF

T. STARKEY

PETROL STATION

CYCLES WIRELESS ELECTRICAL PARTS

	1 new chain fitted	7	6

Paid
T Starkey

A receipt from Tom Starkey's petrol station, 1961.

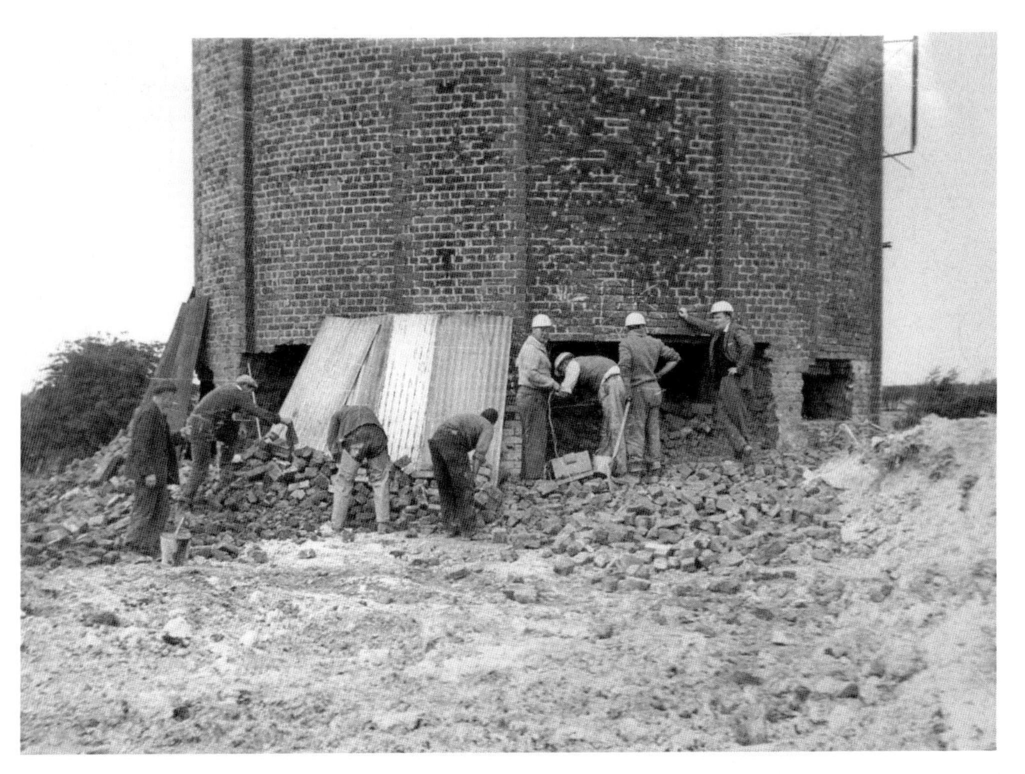

This photograph was taken at Lightshaw Water Treatment Plant at the back of Golborne High School, some time in the 1960s. It shows the preparation of the 'Water Works' tower for demolition.

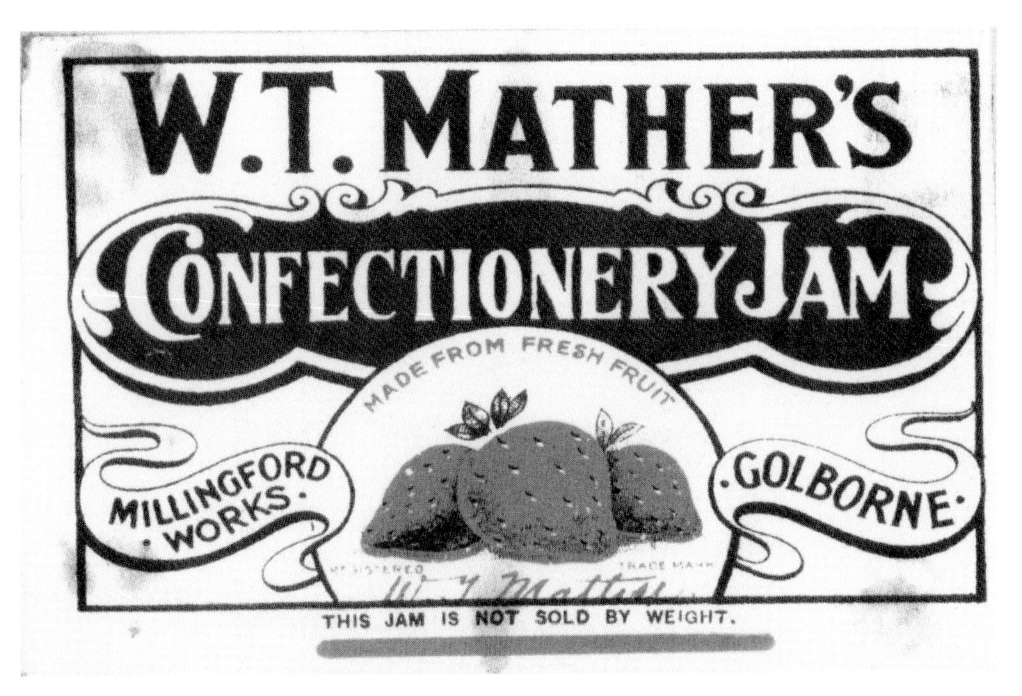

A 1920s Mathers' Jam label. The jam was manufactured at Millingford Works.

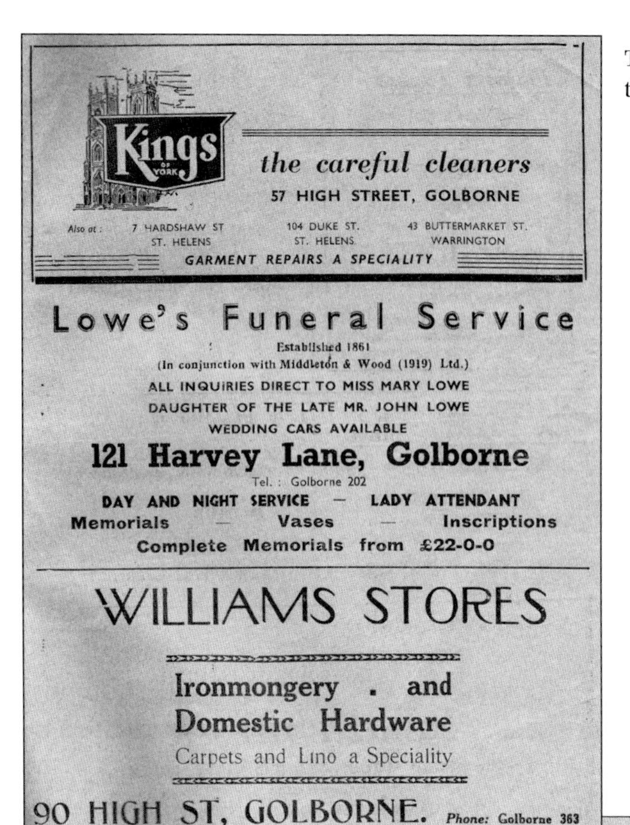

This advertisement was taken from the Parish Magazine in March 1960.

★
W. Churton
For all types of
RE-UPHOLSTERING
2 JOHN STREET
:: GOLBORNE ::
Tel.: GOL. 388

Sextons, Sons & Co. Ltd.
FURNITURE and PRAM SPECIALISTS
Agent for . . .
HOOVER CLEANERS & WASHERS
★
49/51 High Street
:: GOLBORNE ::

HILTONS
For . .
Photographic Goods
★
7 Heath Street
66 High Street
:: GOLBORNE ::

For Fresh Fish, Fruit and Vegetables
Tinned Goods Always in Stock
WREATHS CROSSES
BOUQUETS
at short notice
★
H. E. MASSEY
40 Heath Street
Golborne

This image was taken from a carnival programme in around 1951.

HOLIDAYS! HOLIDAYS!

DID YOU SAY "BREEZY BLACKPOOL?"

YOU WILL WANT A "HOME FROM HOME."

WRITE FOR APARTMENTS TO:—

MRS. WHITLOW,

(LATE OF GOLBORNE).

"GOLBORNE HOUSE,"

108, PALATINE ROAD.

PIANO. BOARD OPTIONAL.

MORT'S,

High Street, Golborne.

We Sell Only the Very Finest

QUALITY.

At the same time, we pride ourselves to sell to you as cheap as anyone in Lancashire.

Why pay 'Bus fare and go for your goods out of your own Town.

These images were both taken from Edge Green Primitive Methodist Church and constitute a remembrance souvenir from May 1928.

ARE YOU FOND OF A GOOD BOOK?

IT IS THE CHEAPEST AND BEST RECREATION . . FOR THE TIRED BODY AND MIND. . .

AN UP-TO-DATE

Circulating Library

WITH A LARGE ASSORTMENT OF MODERN FICTION. . ALL FULL LIBRARY SIZE, IS NOW OPEN AT: .

Golborne P.O.

This Library is conducted in connection with the well known ARGOSY LIBRARY. A carefully selected assortment of Modern Fiction is constantly available, and is kept up-to-date by a regular supply of fresh titles. A feature of the Library is that if any book wanted is not in stock it will be obtained from the very large stock at the Central Depot as quickly as possible, at no extra charge.

There are no vexatious rules. Casual readers can borrow a book on payment of 3d. and need not continue after returning it. Regular readers will find the subscriptions at 10/6 and 15/- per year very favourable; ensuring a constant supply of good library reading, selected with knowledge and taste. The library will be found to live up to its watchword of "Always Something New."

THERE IS NO ENTRANCE FEE.

Inspection is cordially invited and a printed list of terms can be had on application to

A. G. BEAZLEY.

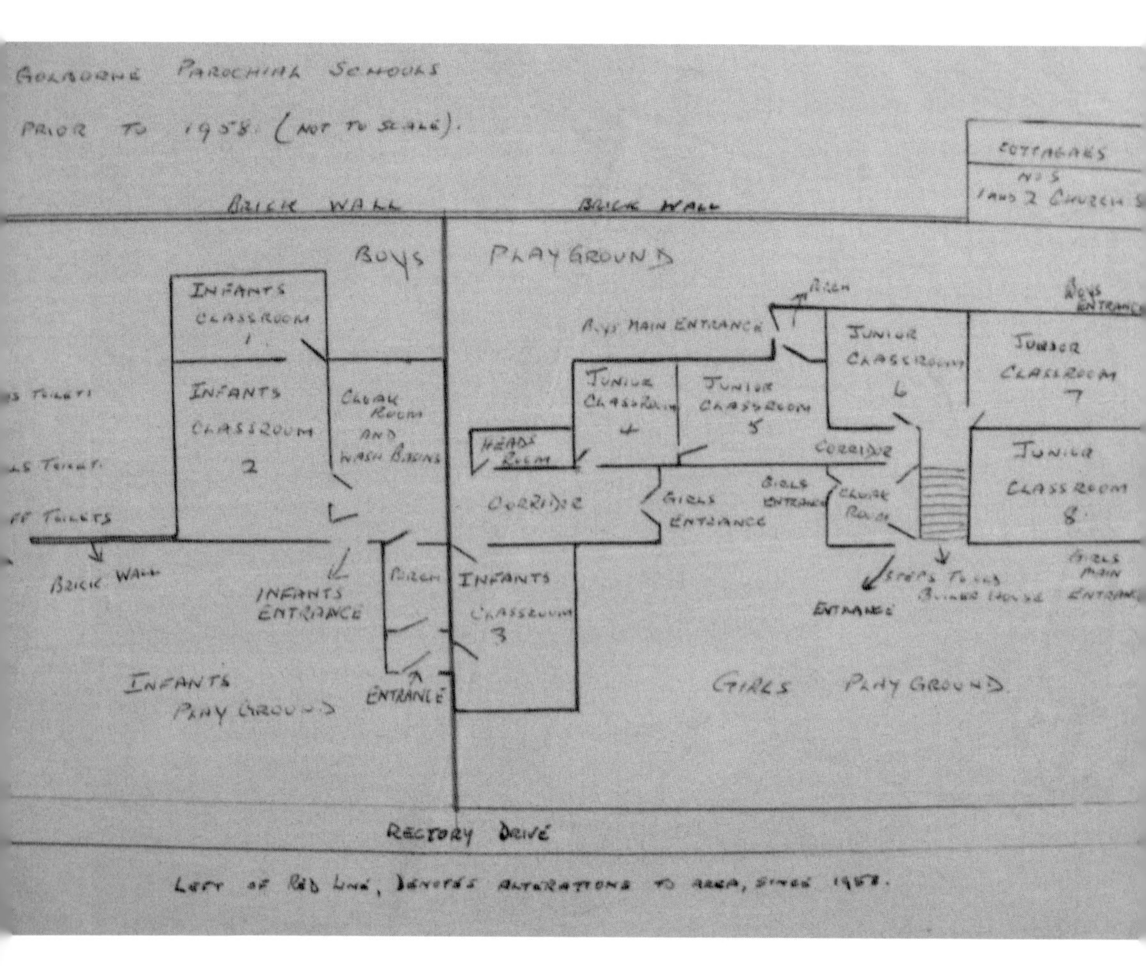

This is a diagram shows the building extension plans for Golborne Parochial School in the 1950s.

10

ADVERTISEENTS

FROM FACTORY TO FOOT.

THINK OF IT, AND SEE WHAT YOU SAVE.

THE MIDDLEMAN'S CHARGES ARE CUT OUT ENTIRELY
AND PASSED ON TO OUR CUSTOMERS.

WE TAKE A PRIDE IN THE MANUFACTURE OF OUR FOOTWEAR.

THE EXPERIENCE OF 40 YEARS SUCCESSFUL MANUFACTURING IS EMBODIED IN **EVERY** PAIR.

OUR BOOT REPAIRING DEPT. IS EQUIPPED WITH ALL THE LATEST MACHINERY.

GIVE US A TRIAL.

PIT CLOGS A SPECIALITY.

NORTHANTS BOOT Co.

BRANCHES:—

Heath Street, ... GOLBORNE.
2 Woodcock St., (Market Square) WIGAN.
58, Gerard Street, ... ASHTON.
66, Walthew Lane, ... PLATT BRIDGE.
701 Ormskirk Road, ... PEMBERTON.
5 Queen Street, ... EARLESTOWN.

Factory: NORTHAMPTON.

The advertisements in this chapter were for shops and businesses at various times in Golborne's past. Event organisers needed money to put on local events so local businesses paid to advertise in their programme. As you can see, over time the shops have changed and the telephone numbers have got longer. This and the following advertisement were taken from Edge Green Primitive Methodist Church: a remembrance souvenir from May 1928.

MAKE

J. R. CHALLENER

M.P.S.

YOUR CHEMIST

Prescriptions Carefully Dispensed

Eyesight Tested Free

Kodak Agency

THE PHARMACY, 7 HEATH ST., GOLBORNE.

EAT

Nourishes Most TAYLOR'S Pleases Most

Superior Bread.

Sold by all the Leading Shops

MADE BY

HENRY TAYLOR,

WHOLESALE AND RETAIL BAKER,

32 LOWTON ROAD, GOLBORNE

Maker of HOVIS BREAD.

The Bread we Sell, Keeps you Fit and Well.

An advertisement for J.R. Challener, chemist.

— TRY —

JOHN HOWARD,

79 HIGH STREET, GOLBORNE,

For your next BOOTS.

He is Noted for

High-Grade BOOTS & SHOES.

Latest Models. :o: Correct Fashions.

Perfection for Fit and Style.

He is now Agent for the Leading Manufacturers,

Repairs in all its Branches by Best English Leather.

Round or Shaped Rubbers when being Soled and Heeled same price.

Leather and Revets for own Repairing Cheap.

We hold the Largest Stock of Clogs in the District.—All at Rock Bottom Prices.

All Goods marked in plain figures.

No Club Checks taken thereby saving you 3/- in the £.

MORT'S

Perfect Bread

Exquisite

ASK YOUR GROCER FOR IT

An advertisement for John Howard, the shoe repair shop, and Morts' bread.

BESWICK'S STORES,

Ironmongers, etc.

90 High St., Golborne

A HOUSEHOLD NAME FOR NEARLY HALF A CENTURY

BEDDING FLOCKS RUGS
CORK LINO
ROOFING FELT

LEATHER AND NAILS for Boot Repairs

Telephone—9 Golborne

Note Address:
NEAR THE STATION

An advertisement for Beswicks' Stores, boot repairs.

A. G. BEAZLEY,

Golborne Post Office.

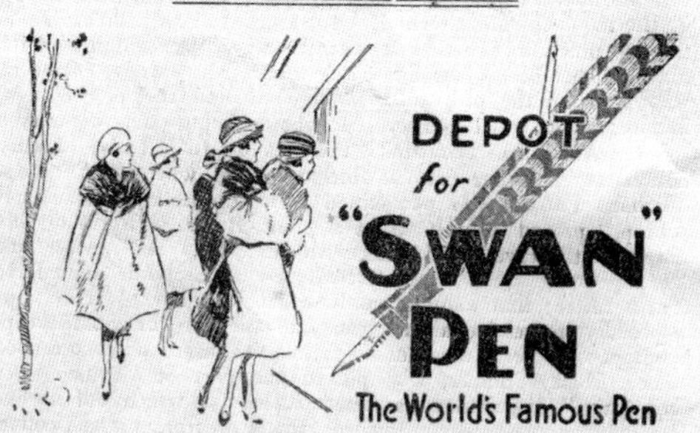

For smooth writing, unfailing reliability and lasting service, the "Swan" Pen is the best of all.

Self-filling Type from 15/-- Other "Swans" from 10/6.

ALWAYS USE "SWAN" INK.

All Office Requisites.

Envelopes a Speciality. Writing Pads—the best and most varied stock in the district.

Rubber Stamps. Embossing Presses. Printing. Relief Stamping. Bookbinding.

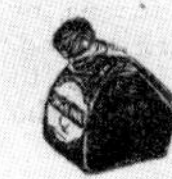

A. G. BEAZLEY,
Post Office, Golborne.

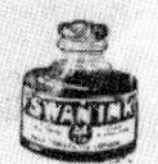

An advertisement for A.G. Beazley post office, Golborne.

FOR EVERYTHING ELECTRICAL

T. CATTERALL

High Street
GOLBORNE

R.T.R.A. Member ★ **Tel.: Golborne 361**

Approved Ministry of Works Contractor

House and Factory Electrical Installations and Maintenance

o o o

Industrial and Domestic Fluorescent Lighting Specialist

Radio Sales Service
Full Hire Purchase Facilities

o o o

Radio and Television Repair Specialist

Accredited Dealer for
FERGUSON, PHILCO, BUSH, COSSOR, G.E.C., PHILIPS K.B., ULTRA and PETO SCOTT RADIO and Television

Pimbletts

THE CONFECTIONERS

Quality is our Leading Feature

81 Heath Street
Golborne

These two advertisements were taken from a Golborne Carnival programme dated Saturday, 19 May 1951.

MEMBER RETAIL TRADE FEDERATION

REG. THOMPSON

Golborne

IS YOUR MAN FOR QUALITY FRUIT AND VEG.

★

Always on the job to give you what you want at a price that doesn't hurt you.

The man to give you a square deal.

★

MONEY ISN'T MADE OF ELASTIC

GIVE US A TRIAL AND SATISFY YOURSELF

The following advertisements were taken from The Golborne Handbook, 1960s edition.

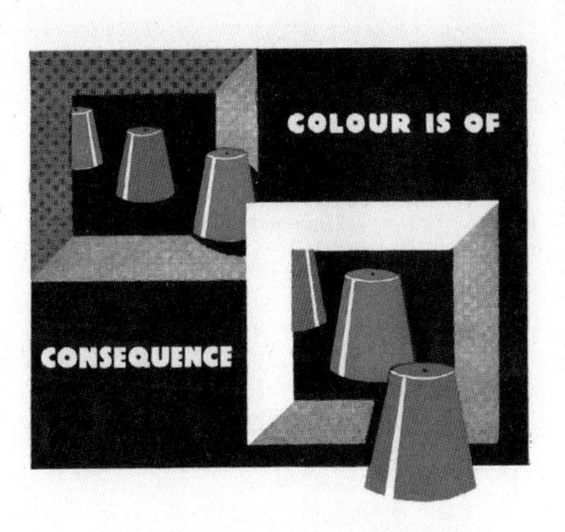

Use Neochrome — a rayon produced in colours during the spinning process. The dyestuff penetrates to the very core of the filaments, producing a solidity and fastness of shade unobtainable by other means.

NEOCHROME is fast to Light, Laundering, Perspiration, Rubbing, Dry Cleaning, Bleach and Sea Water.

Supplied as warp, weft and cone, in 60 shades in 150 den. 31 fils. and in about 24 shades each in 100 den. 24 fils., 200 den. 36 fils. and 300 den. 52 fils., and in 10 shades in 750 den. 120 fils.

HARBENS

NEOCHROME

Sales Office: PARKSIDE MILLS · GOLBORNE · LANCASHIRE

'Phone: Golborne 281. 'Grams: "Harbens Golborne, Warrington."

MANUFACTURED AT PARKSIDE MILLS GOLBORNE LANCASHIRE

PERFECT

FOR ALL

OCCASIONS

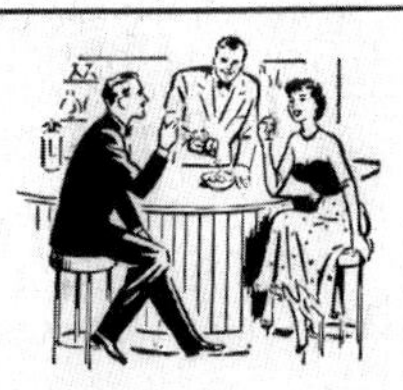

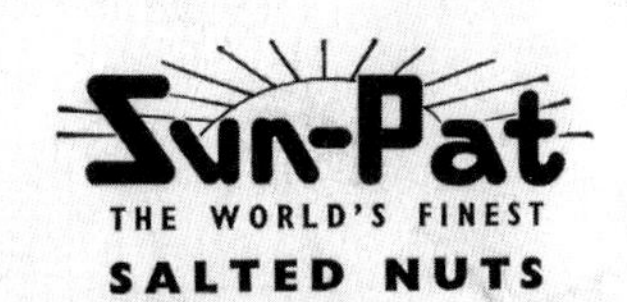

THE WORLD'S FINEST

SALTED NUTS

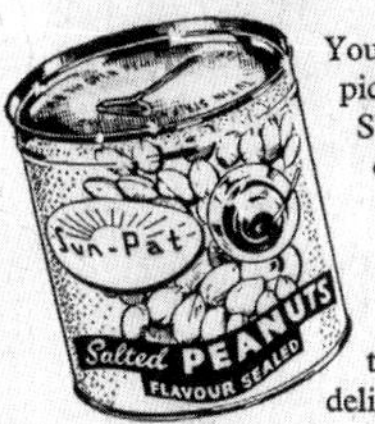

You'll love them at party time, picnic time, any time—tasty SUN-PAT Salted Nuts, full of sun-packed goodness. Crisp and crunchy, always fresh because they're packed in flavour-sealed, airtight 4 oz. and 8 oz. tins. Choose from these delicious varieties.

PEANUTS CASHEW NUTS ALMONDS HAZELS MIXED NUTS

H. S. WHITESIDE & CO. LTD · LONDON SE5

An advertisement for Sun-Pat salted nuts.

An advertisement for Peets' of Golborne, grocery shop.

PEET'S of Golborne

for

CARPETS
LINOLEUM
BEDDING
HARDWARE

ALSO

HIGH CLASS

Groceries and Provisions

GOOD SELECTION OF
ALL LEADING BRANDS

Orders delivered daily in your district

Telephone GOLBORNE 213

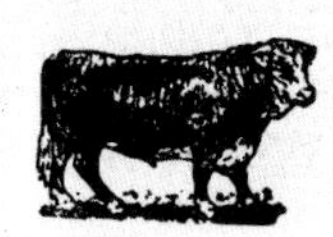

FAMILY
BUTCHER

H. PIMBLETT

28 Heath Street
GOLBORNE

QUALITY IS OUR LEADING FEATURE

For
BEST QUALITY
ENGLISH BEEF
PORK · LAMB
MEAT PIES and
COOKED MEATS,
ETC.

An advertisement for H. Pimblett, family butchers.

Telephone No. 371-2

FOULDS (GOLBORNE) LTD.

HIGH STREET, GOLBORNE

MANUFACTURERS OF

High Class Food Products

Makers of Foulds Famous :—

Pies and Pasties,
Puff Pastry,
Pork and Beef Sausage
(Skinless if required)
Puddings, Savoury Ducks,
Boiled Ham, Roast Pork,
Pressed Brisket and Brawn,
Pork, Loins, Legs, etc.,
Bacon and Beef Supplies
available

ALL PRODUCTS MADE FRESH DAILY AT MODEL FOOD FACTORY

Orders promptly attended to by road or rail to areas :—
Manchester, Liverpool, Warrington, Wigan, Earlestown, Leigh, St. Helens, Chester and Welsh Coast

Inquiries for Large or Small Orders appreciated

An advertisement for Fould's Ltd, Golborne, whose supplies were brought in from the Model Food Factory.

On Admiralty & War Office Lists

Telegrams : **Naylor Bros. Golborne**
Telephones : **Golborne 223 (4 lines)**

NAYLOR Bros.

L I M I T E D

Engineers

Golborne Ironworks, Golborne
LANCASHIRE

London Office :
Artillery House, Westminster, S.W.1
Telephone No. : Abbey 1300

Manufacturers of
COMPLETE HANDLING and STORAGE PLANTS for COAL and OTHER MATERIALS

COLLIERY EQUIPMENT

UNDERGROUND CONVEYORS

An advertisement for Naylor Bros Ltd, an engineering company.

Other titles published by The History Press

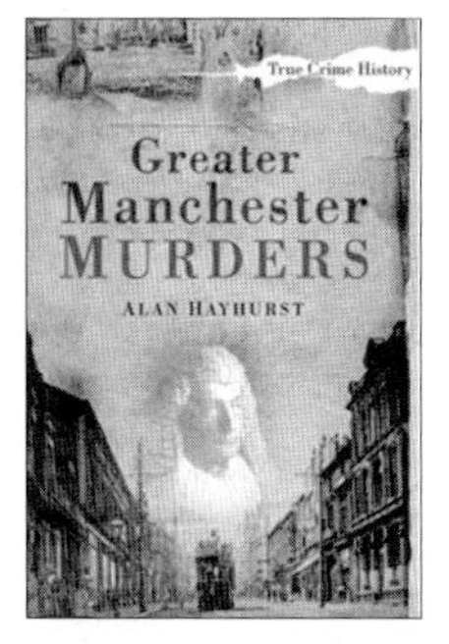

Greater Manchester Murders

ALAN HAYHURST

Contained within the pages of this book are the stories behind some of the most notorious murders in the history of Greater Manchester. They include the case of cat burglar Charlie Peace, who killed 20-year-old PC Nicolas Cock in Seymour Grove, anc only confessed after he had been sentenced to death for another murder; the sad tale of William Robert Taylor, whose young daughter was killed in a boiler explosion and whc later, desperate and in debt, murdered his landlord as well as his three remaining childre

978 0 7509 5091 6

The Golden Years of Manchester Picture Houses

Memories of the Silver Screen 1900-1970

DEREK J. SOUTHALL

This is a delightful collection of memories from the golden age of cinema in Manchest Filled with archive images, it recalls courting days and war-time air raids, the stars, the staff and all the magic of the silver screen.

978 0 7524 4981 4

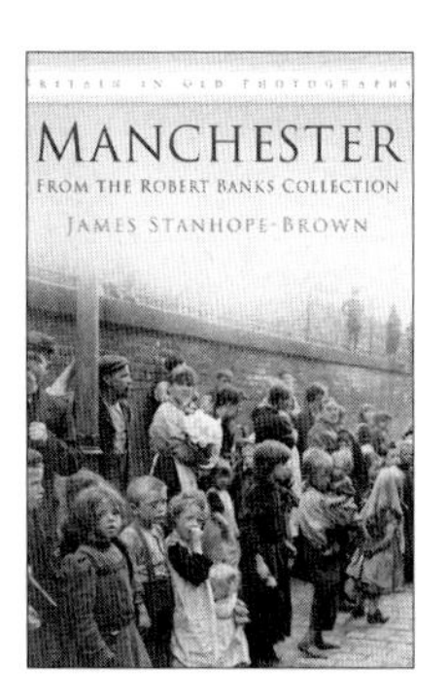

Manchester: From the Robert Banks Collection

JAMES STANHOPE-BROWN

This fascinating collection of archive photographs, taken by professional photographer Robert Banks working in Manchester during the early 1900s, offers a rare glimpse of some of the events that were taking place in the city at the time. Illustrated with over 130 snapshc – many never before published – of street scenes, buildings and the transport of yesteryear, this absorbing book captures Manchester at the turn of the last century and is an essential volume for lovers of photography and everyone with an interest in the history of the area.

978 0 7524 6013 0

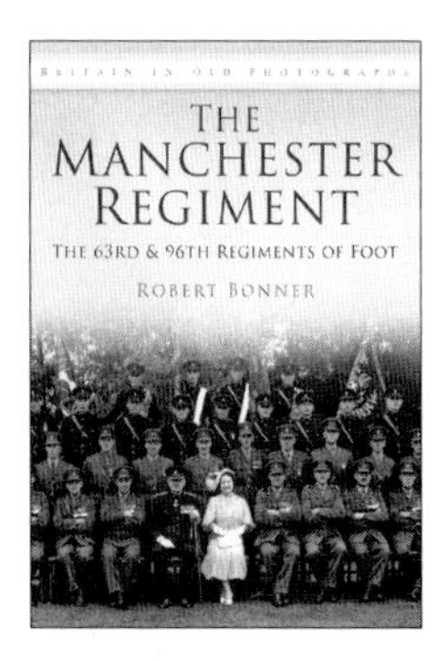

The Manchester Regiment

The 63rd & 96th Regiments of Foot

ROBERT BONNER

This illustrated regimental history contains photographs taken between the 1860s and the last da of the Manchester Regiment in 1958, when it ceased to exist as a distinct unit. During this time the regiment served in most parts of the Empire including areas as diverse as India, South Africa, Egypt, Palestine, Singapore, Malaya and, later, Germany. With 200 photographs from the regimen own archive at the Museum of the Manchester Regiment, many never before published, this volume provides a fascinating pictorial insight into the history of the Regiment.

978 0 7524 6015 4